Since World War II, many Americans have concluded that the nation-state is no longer able to ensure the peace, security, environmental safety, or economic prosperity of its citizens. Such feelings have given rise to a number of efforts to reform the nation-state system in response to global problems of nuclear armaments, escalating Cold War conflict, environmental degradation, a chaotic world economy, and frontier competition on the high seas and in outer space.

Alternatives to Anarchy examines three major supranational movements that tried to address such problems: the world government crusade of the 1940s, the Atlantic Unionist movement of the early 1950s, and the global functionalist causes of the 1970s. Each flourished during periods of perceived crisis, each offered well-reasoned arguments rooted in tough political realism, each enjoyed surprising degrees of support among normally nationalistic Americans. And each collapsed with dramatic suddenness once a sense of urgency had passed.

In this study, Wesley Wooley describes the historical contexts of postwar suprana-tionalism. He analyzes the cases advanced on its behalf and considers the reasons for the cycles of its progress and decline. While supported by diverse interests ranging from mainstream peace activists to Cold Warriors, from worried atomic scientists to confident executives of great multinational corporations, supranationalism proved to be a fragile plant. Largely dependent on a mood of crisis difficult to sustain, one-worlders needed to perpetuate delicate balances of fear and hope, emotion and reason, order and justice, authority and democracy, ideals and self-interest, while striving to create a climate for systemic reform.

Although the reformers invariably fell short of their stated goals, they helped awaken Americans to the perils of atomic weaponry, nurtured a Western European-North American Atlantic community, and popularized new approaches to global government. *Alternatives to Anarchy* is an important and instructive study of the perils and promise of their search for international cooperation.

ALTERNATIVES TO ANARCHY

ALTERNATIVES TO ANARCHY

American Supranationalism since World War II

WESLEY T. WOOLEY

INDIANA UNIVERSITY PRESS
Bloomington and Indianapolis

Portions of Chapter One, "Learning to Fear the Bomb," have previously appeared in Jeannette Maas and Robert Stewart, eds., *Toward a World of Peace: People Create Alternatives* (Suva, Fiji: University of the South Pacific, 1986).

Grateful acknowledgement is made to Harcourt Brace Jovanovich, Inc. for permission to reprint a selection from Carl Sandburg's *The People, Yes*, 1936, copyright renewed by Carl Sandburg in 1964.

Manufactured in the United States of America

Library of Congress Cataloging-in-Publication Data

Wooley, Wesley T., 1942–
Alternatives to anarchy.

Bibliography: p.
Includes index.
1. United States—Foreign relations—1945–
I. Title. II. Title: Supranationalism since World
War II.
E744.W63   1988   327.73   87-45393
ISBN 0-253-30506-3

1 2 3 4 5   92 91 90 89 88

For both Janes

CONTENTS

onvinced that the traditional system of nation-states was not competently addressing the world's most serious common problems. President Harry Truman, important cabinet officers such as Robert Patterson, William Clayton, and John Foster Dulles, corporate spokesmen like George Ball and the presidents of Dow Chemical and IBM, labor leaders inspired by Walter Reuther and David Dubinsky, respected jurists such as William O. Douglas, Owen Roberts, and Grenville Clark, scores of major journalists and academics, including political realists Hans Morgenthau and George Kennan, and even troubled young California actors like Ronald Reagan—all advocated fundamental reform of the dysfunctional international order.

This book considers all three major types of postwar American supranationalism—the world government crusade, Atlantic unionism, and global functionalism. The historical context for each movement is described, its ideas explained, and its political fortunes analyzed. The study then attempts to answer the most significant question regarding supranationalism in general: why, despite broad acceptance of their basic arguments, especially during periods of deepest fear about the probable effects of international anarchy, reformers have repeatedly failed to achieve their major objectives. Supranationalists have tangentially influenced events from control of atomic energy in the 1940s to a new Law of the Sea Treaty in the late 1970s, yet the state system remains essentially unaltered. Regardless of cogent accounts of the nation-state's growing obsolescence, governments have not been interested in systemic change.

For reformers who have believed that nothing less than human survival is at stake, that official opposition, or complacency, has seemed tragic. For other interested Americans faced with contradictory descriptions of global problems, uncertain predictions of future crisis, and unpalatable political choices, the prevailing attitude has been anxious ambivalence. Commonly, the traditional system of world order has been perceived as breaking down, but there has been concurrent fear of proposals that would diminish the realities and illusions of national sovereignty. Paradoxically, Americans have been the world's most enthusiastic supranationalists while generally remaining one of the most nationalistic of peoples. Explaining that contradiction enables one to understand the triumphs and defeats of one of the most ambitious reform movements in recent times.

A project of this size requires the assistance of many people. I would like to thank Canada Council and Project '87 (established by the American Historical Association and the American Political Science Association) for their financial support, and the University of Victoria for granting a timely leave. I much appreciated the competent service provided by the librarians and archivists at the University of Chicago, the Chicago Historical Society, Indiana University, Rice University, the University of Pittsburgh, the University of Michigan, Princeton University, and the Library of Congress. Tessa Wooley helped prepare the bibliography, and June Belton translated

PREFACE

Since the end of World War II, many Americans have questioned th
of the anarchic nation-state system. In a world in which atomic arm
made major conflict suicidally dangerous, it was hardly clear how n
governments could safely defend their security and independence.
Soviet-American rivalry intensified in the early postwar period, wc
cold warriors wondered how the West could endure as a loosely organ
coalition of competing nations unable to pool resources or coordi.
political and military policies. And, more recently, in an increasingly in
dependent world, reformers have insisted that sovereign states are inca}
ble of sufficient cooperation to protect the environment, administer a
integrated global economy, or regulate frontier competition on the hig
seas and in outer space. Effective supranational management has seemed
vital to human welfare, perhaps even to the survival of life on earth.

Proposals to transcend the state system have been common ever since
Hiroshima awakened Americans to their unprecedented vulnerability.
These plans for world government, Western democratic union, or functional integration have differed in many respects, but they have also had
much in common. Supranationalists have presented their case with impressive intellectual competence and, when assisted by a sense of crisis,
have been surprisingly popular. Generally avoiding weightless emo-
tionalism, they have consistently relied on reason as much as on fear and
have anchored their prescriptive idealism in hard analysis of the customary
behavior of men and nations. Moreover, one-worlders have seldom neglected American national interests or been hesitant to suggest that reformed global institutions be patterned after American experience. Indeed,
the paradoxical nationalism of supranationalism has been one of its major
sources of appeal.

Well-reasoned, rational, committed to political realism, subtly nationalistic, and sometimes substantially supported by elitist and general
public opinion, supranationalists have been poorly understood by American diplomatic historians. Mistakenly perceived as an idealistic component
of the mainstream peace movement and easily overlooked because of their
marginal influence on critical cold war diplomacy, global reformers have
seldom been the subject of detailed historical examination, a peculiar neglect given the significance of their concerns and the persuasiveness of
their critical analysis. Since 1945 numerous thoughtful Americans became

my very rough drafts into finely typed manuscript. Finally, special thanks to my wife, Jane, who provided valuable encouragement, and to my son, Jeff, who has already suggested several ways of overspending anticipated royalties.

Victoria, British Columbia   WESLEY T. WOOLEY
March 1987

Part One

One-Worlders: The World Government Movement, 1945–1951

I.

LEARNING TO FEAR THE BOMB

> If atomic war comes, your whole country
> will be a target. In one flaming instant, your
> city and thousands of people in it, will
> disappear as puffs of vapor.
>
> —*Look*, March 5, 1946

On August 14, 1945, at 7:00 P.M., eastern war time, President Harry Truman announced the official surrender of the Japanese Empire. After nearly four years of awful world war that had claimed the lives of over four hundred thousand American soldiers, the United States could celebrate a victorious peace. Responding to thousands of well-wishers at the White House gate, the jubilant president declared a special national holiday, and parties and street demonstrations followed all through the night to the accompaniment of church chimes, bands, car horns, and air raid sirens. One New Yorker described the scene as "ten New Year's Eves rolled into one" as five inches of scraps and ticker tape floated down on the garment and financial districts and as the largest crowd in the city's history gathered in Times Square. In Chicago, citizens with no sense of history ignited huge bonfires, and in San Francisco, sailors on leave went on a rampage. Statues were defaced, streetcars overturned, and shop windows on Market Street broken and looted. All the previously restrained emotion of a war-weary people seemed to be released in a single moment.[1]

Yet almost immediately the joy of victory was dampened by sober reflection about the way the war had finally been won. During the previous week, two atomic bombs had been dropped on Japan, terrifying new weapons that had killed 100,000 Japanese with dramatic suddenness and efficiency. "All thoughts and things were split," *Time* reported. "The sudden achievement of victory was a mercy, but mercy born of a ruthless force beyond anything in human chronicle. The rational mind had won the most Promethean of its conquests over nature." It had split the atom and "had put into the hands of common man the fire and force of the sun itself."[2]

Soon, detailed accounts from Japan documented the awesome power of atomic weapons. Pictures of Hiroshima and Nagasaki were published, as were drawings and charts showing the extent of the destruction. Visiting scientists such as Philip Morrison returned home to tell congressmen and

the general public about the devastation caused by various phases of an
atomic explosion—a ball of fire one-third mile in radius heating the air to
four million degrees, a great expansion of air creating a shock wave of five
hundred to one thousand miles per hour, hurricane winds, and extensive
radiation. Radiation, he testified, "affects the blood-forming tissues in the
bone marrow, and the whole function of the blood is impaired. The blood
does not coagulate, but oozes in many spots through the unbroken skin,
and internally seeps into the cavities of the body."[3]

Scientific descriptions of the bomb's effects were invariably chilling, but
especially moving were accounts that penetrated beneath the faceless statistics of Hiroshima to consider the fates of particular individuals victimized
by the heat, the blast, the radiation, and the civil chaos all caused by a
single atomic weapon. Novelist John Hersey's long article for the *New Yorker*
personalized, and hence made more understandable, the suffering experienced by tens of thousands:

> There had been no breeze earlier in the morning when Dr. Fujii walked to the
> railway station to see his friend off, but now brisk winds were blowing every
> which way; here on the bridge the wind was easterly. New fires were leaping
> up, and they spread quickly, and in a very short time terrible blasts of hot air
> and showers of cinders made it impossible to stand on the bridge any more.
> [From under the bridge] Dr. Fujii saw a nurse hanging in the timbers of his
> hospital by her legs, and then another painfully pinned across the breast. He
> thought he heard the voice of his niece for a moment, but he could not find
> her; he never saw her again. . . .
>
> Just before dark, Mr. Tanimoto came across a twenty-year-old girl, Mrs.
> Kamai, the Tanimoto's nextdoor neighbor. She was crouching on the ground
> with the body of her infant daughter in her arms. The baby had evidently
> been dead all day. Mrs. Kamai jumped up when she saw Mr. Tanimoto and
> said, "Would you please try to locate my husband?"
>
> Mr. Tanimoto knew that her husband had been inducted into the Army
> just the day before and had reported to the Chugoku Regional Army Head-
> quarters—near the ancient castle in the middle of town. [Mr. Tanimoto]
> knew he hadn't a chance of finding Mrs. Kamai's husband, even if he
> searched, but he wanted to humor her. "I'll try," he said.
>
> "You've got to find him," she said. "He loved our baby so much. I want
> him to see her once more."

This special issue of the *New Yorker* sold out quickly and, reprinted, was a
Book-of-the-Month Club selection and a nationwide best seller. It was even
read in its entirety on the ABC radio network.[4]

The story of Hiroshima descended on an American people already filled
with anxiety about the nation's future in international politics. In part, that
anxiety derived from historical experience, an awareness that, like World
War I, World War II was unlikely to be the war to end all wars. As early as
V-E Day, in May 1945, 36 percent of the American public expected the
United States to fight another war within twenty-five years. That percent-

age rose to forty-four by September and sixty-eight by the following March.[5]

By that time, of course, fundamental cynicism about the probability of permanent peace was reinforced by a maturing cold war with the Soviet Union. In February 1943 George Gallup found that 46 percent of Americans polled believed that Russia could be trusted after the war (61 percent of those who had an opinion on the subject). In March 1945, during the euphoria of Yalta, 55 percent had faith in Russo-American cooperation, but soon such confidence began to erode. By mid-1946, 58 percent were convinced that the Soviet Union sought world domination.[6]

Americans thus emerged from World War II with a more highly developed sense of political realism than in the past. They tended to assume the inevitability of international conflict and quickly jettisoned their unquestioning faith in their major wartime ally. They were aware that neo-isolationism was risky, and they were not convinced that the United Nations could assure an enduring peace. Among many knowledgeable Americans, therefore, the news of Hiroshima was especially alarming.[7]

Not merely fear of another war was present here but also a keen awareness of the atomic bomb's implications for America's security and her status in international politics. For example, not all nations were equally vulnerable to an atomic attack. A small island nation like Britain was most in danger: a dozen well-placed bombs could destroy her economy and social organization. A large, essentially rural nation such as China with primitive industries was theoretically best able to survive an atomic war. As a highly urbanized, industrial society, the United States was closer to Britain than to China on the scale of vulnerability; thus, Americans had a special interest in seeing that an atomic war did not occur. Furthermore, like the Colt revolver on the Western frontier, the atomic bomb was the great equalizer—even relatively weak nations could become suddenly powerful by developing the latest military technology. David Lawrence, editor of *United States News*, observed that all nations were now of potentially equal strength, and *Time* similarly lamented that America's postwar predominance of power would be only temporary. Small and medium powers would soon achieve parity.[8]

Even America's assumed adherence to Wilsonian morality was a handicap in the new atomic age. As many scientists argued, a considerable, perhaps decisive, advantage in an atomic war would go to the nation firing the first salvo. As a democratic, unmilitaristic, essentially peaceful nation, the United States would likely lose any first-strike advantage to a more secretive, totalitarian aggressor. Here was the frightening prospect of an atomic Pearl Harbor.[9]

But were most Americans deeply frightened by atomic weapons, frightened enough to act on their fears? In the fall of 1945 a public opinion survey revealed that 83 percent of Americans perceived a "real danger" of the world's urban population being annihilated in another war. Yet only 38 percent saw much danger of atomic weapons being used against the United

States within the next twenty-five years, and 64 percent believed that the bomb made major war *less* likely.[10]

Even many early comments from government officials were disturbing to people who thought that Hiroshima had revolutionized military and political affairs. President Truman spoke of monopolizing the "secrets" of atomic bomb production, as did General Leslie R. Groves, the military director of the Manhattan Project. Senator Tom Connally, chairman of the Senate Foreign Relations Committee, predicted the development of an effective defense against atomic weapons and remained confident that civilization could survive an atomic war. Also, the Truman administration's May-Johnson Bill for domestic supervision of atomic development made absolutely no provision for international control of atomic energy.[11]

Among journalists, politicians, and the general public shortly after V-J Day, there was thus a peculiar compound of anxiety and complacency that did not auger well for meeting the political challenge of Hiroshima. Reformers concluded that Americans were not fearful enough and that since fear was the beginning of wisdom, it had to be encouraged and nurtured as an essential motivator of political action. Fear was once associated with the ignorant, uneducated, and credulous, but now it was the ignorant and credulous who complacently believed that there was nothing to fear "if only we keep our plutonium dry."[12]

Such concerns among those informed enough to be alarmed led to a campaign during late 1945 and early 1946 to frighten the American people. Writing for *Collier's* in January 1946, Harold Urey, a Nobel Prize-winning chemist who had contributed much to nuclear energy research, told his readers: "I write this to frighten you. I'm a frightened man myself. All the scientists are frightened—frightened for their lives—and frightened for *your* life." Radio commentator Raymond Swing observed that "fear is part of our stock equipment as human beings. Under its pressure, we take measures to protect ourselves. I am sure that the desire to be safe is much stronger than the desire to be good. . . ." And religious writer Winthrop Hudson concluded in *Christian Century*: "Fear can be a tremendously powerful unifying force in society. What Pearl Harbor did for America, the atomic bomb can do for the world if mankind becomes aware of the peril. It is not a question of scaring people to death. It is a question of scaring them that they may live."[13]

The flow of frightening news items was continuous during the early postwar period. In late 1945 scientist J. Robert Oppenheimer testified that a one-night atomic raid on American cities could destroy forty million inhabitants. The American Institute of Architects petitioned Congress urging that all cities of more than two hundred thousand population be broken up and reorganized into independent units connected by tunnels, and Congresswoman Clare Boothe Luce suggested the construction of vast air raid shelters and underground factories. In early 1946 columnists Joseph and Stewart Alsop in a *Saturday Evening Post* article entitled "Your Flesh Should Creep," reported on the implications of a recent study prepared by the

Army General Staff: only three atomic bombs would be needed to "flatten" Washington, ten to extinguish New York City. A smuggled bomb exploded in Washington's Union Station would blast the marble of the Capitol into powder finer than flour.[14]

Coordinating this campaign of fear were the same people who had made Hiroshima possible, the atomic scientists. These men were in the best position to realize the significance of their new discoveries—they knew that the atomic bomb was not just another weapon, and they were well aware that the Hiroshima and Nagasaki bombs were only the first generation of deadly new methods of mass destruction. The scientists were among the first to perceive that military technology had made a qualitative, not merely quantitative, developmental leap, a reality that had profound implications for international politics. Could the nation-state any longer offer much security to its citizens? What did warfare accomplish if both victor and vanquished suffered enormous loss of life and property? Might not civilization itself be imperiled?

The atomic scientists felt especially obligated to raise such questions because they had contributed so much to creating the problem. The scientists had rationalized their work on such a terrible weapon by arguing that the Germans might have invented the bomb and harnessed it to the purposes of the Third Reich. Also, it was comforting to agree with President Truman that the atomic bomb had helped end the war, thus saving hundreds of thousands of lives, Japanese as well as American. Yet use of the bomb after the defeat of Germany, combined with a growing awareness that the Japanese had been close to surrender prior to Hiroshima, made scientists uneasy. So too did the dropping of a second bomb on Japan at Nagasaki. Many scientists had reluctantly concluded that a demonstration of the bomb on some remote test site would have been an ineffective substitute for its actual use on a Japanese city, and some, including Oppenheimer, even argued that Hiroshima provided a necessary, dramatic lesson to mankind regarding the destructiveness of atomic weapons. But the second bomb seemed pointless, a needless taking of human life that indicated how difficult it was for wartime political leaders to resist using any weapon available to them.[15]

So guilt flourished. Protesting what he called the "Massacre of Nagasaki," Massachusetts Institute of Technology scientist Norbert Wiener felt aghast, "as though a man in a confused dream"; an Oak Ridge chemist complained that he had lost hope and felt "a terrible guilt"; and Albert Einstein compared his fellow physicists to Alfred Nobel, who, after inventing TNT, devoted much of his time and money to the promotion of peace. "Today," Einstein observed, "the physicists who participated in producing the most formidable weapon of all time are harassed by a similar feeling of responsibility."[16]

This sense of guilt can be exaggerated. Chicago scientist Harold Urey, a major participant in early postwar political activities, told a reporter that scientists could not prevent war by refusing scientific work. Atomic energy was there in nature, and scientists had merely discovered it. He denied that many scientists felt, or ought to have felt, guilty about laboring on the atomic bomb. As Einstein suggested, a sense of "responsibility" is the best description of the atomic scientists' state of mind. They had produced the bomb, knew its power and some of its political implications, and could not understand how anyone could fail to realize that there had been a fundamental change in human circumstances when men had invented such suicidal weapons.[17]

Scientists working on the Manhattan Project, particularly those at the Metallurgical Laboratory at the University of Chicago, had been meeting informally since late 1944 to consider the probable power of the new bomb, the political effects of its use, and the peacetime applications of atomic energy. Those meetings were irregularly held and sometimes had to find ingenious means of circumventing tight military security regulations, but the Chicago group was able to produce the Franck Report which warned the Secretary of War about the repercussions of dropping the atomic bomb. After the successful test of the bomb in New Mexico, its employment against Japan, and the federal government's release of the Smyth Report on atomic energy in late August, groups of scientists all over the nation met and exchanged information about the future of atomic energy. By early October, there were especially active formal organizations established at Chicago, Los Alamos, and Oak Ridge, Tennessee.[18]

While scientists were generally alarmed by the public's initial ignorance about atomic energy, they were galvanized into political action by a more concrete issue, the government's plans for postwar control of atomic research and development. The May-Johnson Bill, suddenly introduced by the administration and given only one day of hearings in the House, could have imposed military control of atomic energy and severely limited freedom of research. Scientists mobilized a powerful attack on the measure and on the complacency they believed lay behind it. With the president's blessing, the military seemed already to be preparing for World War III.[19]

Among the mobilized scientists were some of the stars of the Manhattan Project—Einstein, who had originally proposed the idea to Franklin Roosevelt; Leo Szilard, who, with Enrico Fermi, created the first nuclear chain reaction at the University of Chicago; Edward Teller, one of the leading project scientists at Los Alamos; and Oppenheimer, the man who supervised the actual making of the first atomic bomb. Along with hundreds of junior colleagues, these were the brilliant theoreticians and technicians who had competed successfully with their German counterparts to produce the weapon that won the war and who had unlocked the secrets of a new source of power likely to revolutionize human society. When Einstein, Szilard, Teller, and Oppenheimer spoke, Americans took notice; aware of this, the scientists were convinced that they could communicate their vitally important message.

That message was clear and uncomplicated and had the virtually unanimous support of scientists who knew and thought about the problems of atomic weaponry. Essentially, they argued that atomic bombs could be made relatively cheaply and that they would become increasingly destructive. There was no effective military defense against such weapons, and none could be expected. Indeed, atomic bombs did not even need to be delivered in the normal manner—they could simply be smuggled in and placed near their intended targets. Furthermore, there were no secrets of the atomic bomb that could be long monopolized. Relevant scientific knowledge was generally known throughout the world's scientific community, and other great powers could expect to develop a working bomb within three to five years. If war then occurred among those powers, the new weapons would inevitably be used, at enormous cost to modern civilization. Therefore, international control of atomic weapons was imperative, and ultimately war itself had to be eliminated as a means of resolving international disputes.[20]

By November 1945, the atomic scientists had organized themselves for educational and political action. Various local groups, such as the Association of Los Alamos Scientists, the Atomic Scientists of Chicago, and the Association of Oak Ridge Engineers and Scientists, coalesced into the Federation of Atomic Scientists with a national office in Washington. Soon thereafter the National Committee on Atomic Information was formed, supported by over sixty national, civic, labor, religious, professional, and educational organizations. And in May 1946 an Emergency Committee of Atomic Scientists, with Einstein as president, was established to raise money for the movement. Meanwhile, in December 1945, the Chicago group launched the *Bulletin of the Atomic Scientists*, a well-edited journal that printed news from local organizations as well as general articles relating to the problems and promise of atomic energy.

From October 1945 to late 1946 the atomic scientists and their interested colleagues participated in a political effort unprecedented in the history of American science. Many scientists slighted or abandoned their research in order to organize national meetings on atomic energy, to arrange seminars and informal dinners for senators and congressmen, to testify before congressional committees, to write articles for the popular press, and to deliver speeches to anyone who would listen. Even the prestigious Edward Teller was typically willing to spend a long day in May in Shaker Heights, Ohio, addressing a conference organized by the pastor of a local church.[21]

Publications were produced as well. The Chicago scientists prepared a pamphlet, *The Atomic Bomb*, intended mainly for members of Congress. Linguist S. I. Hayakawa was enlisted to write *One Minute War*, and many scientists pooled their talents to produce *One World or None—A Report to the Public on the Full Meaning of the Atomic Bomb*. Introduced by Arthur Compton, Nobel laureate and former director of the Chicago Metallurgical Laboratory, this book contained articles by Neils Bohr, Oppenheimer, Hans Bethe, Einstein, and journalist Walter Lippmann. Over one hundred thousand copies were sold.[22]

The scientists offered advice to MGM on the making of a popular motion picture about the invention of the atomic bomb. The film, *Beginning or the End* (a title reputedly suggested by President Truman), was hardly a masterpiece. While it successfully chronicled the development of the atomic bomb from the University of Chicago chain reaction to Hiroshima, Hollywood could not resist melodrama: foreign scientists were given exaggerated accents; the chain reaction, in truth a quiet event, was pictured as a riot of humming equipment, blinking lights, and ear-splitting explosions; and a stale love story of a dedicated scientist who neglected his lovely wife was added. Nonetheless, the film, especially in its re-creation of the great power of the atomic bomb, helped the scientists to deliver their message.[23]

The message continued to be simple—the bomb was a revolutionary weapon; there were no atomic secrets; other nations would have the bomb soon; there was no likely defense against atomic attack; and civilization itself was in danger unless nations could agree on international control of atomic energy. Avoiding complicated and potentially controversial political questions such as the desirability of world government, the scientists repeated their basic propositions, convinced that they were clearing the way for international control of a force that, if left alone, might extinguish life on earth. Fear remained their primary weapon and the nurturing of fear their intermediate goal. The *New Yorker* reported that "in the course of their educational campaign, the scientists have found that only one tactic is dependable—the preaching of doom." Chicago scientist, Albert Cohn, said it even more succinctly: "We turned ourselves into twenty-five Jeremiahs."[24]

One of the best examples of the scientists' campaign of fear was an article that the Washington office of the Federation of American Scientists prepared for the March 5, 1946, issue of *Look*, entitled "Your Last Chance." Within a dozen pages of dramatically presented pictures and text, the scientists hammered at their essential thesis. "Never again, so long as war is possible, will your home and hearthside be safe from direct attack. You have a last chance to save your civilization. . . ." On the first page of the article was a large mushroom cloud and, nearby, a drawing of a despairing woman standing in the ruins of her bombed-out house. The caption warned that "in one night forty cities could be wrecked, forty million Americans killed." A terrible catastrophe—and something that might well happen in the middle of the night!

Even the continued *possibility* of atomic war, the article insisted, would produce terrible consequences: "Your life will be unbearable in a world where the atomic bomb may fall at any hour." Concern about sabotage would lead to frequent search and surveillance, harsh treatment of suspects, and gun battles between spies and counterspies. The need to be constantly alert would require a huge defense establishment, armed guards on American frontiers, tight restrictions on research, and unceasing vigilance even from the nation's frightened children. Lack of any defense against the atomic bomb would encourage wild rumors, panic, and a mass exodus from urban areas. The possible anonymity of an atomic attack—the inability to identify the nation responsible—would produce xenophobia within the United States, the creation of concentration camps for foreigners, and riots targeted at various ethnic groups. Finally, the disadvantages of democratic government in facing secret, efficient, aggressive totalitarian regimes would force Americans themselves to accept dictatorship.

The consequences of all this for the daily life and livelihood of individual Americans were enormous. Insurance agents were told that they would "have a hard time selling life insurance to a prospect who knows that his family is likely to be wiped out in an atomic war"; teachers were asked if they wanted children to grow up in an atmosphere of chronic fear; and real estate salesmen were warned about the impact of population dispersal on property values. Indeed, dispersal would have many unfortunate results—the inefficient decentralization of economic activity, the creation of underground sweatshops, and an acute housing shortage. Jobless Americans, their urban property rendered worthless, would be wandering about the countryside "disputing title to caves."

There were three realistic choices, the *Look* article argued. One was to prepare for atomic warfare, a course that might deter conflict for a while, but at considerable cost in military expenditures, civil defense requirements, and diminished political liberty. America would become a police state with a "giant Gestapo." A second choice would be to conquer the world while the United States retained a monopoly of atomic weapons, but this course also implied gigantic military expenses, the erosion of freedom at home and abroad, and a heavy loss of American lives. The third choice, the one advocated by the scientists, was to achieve international control of atomic energy and an end to war itself. A difficult task, the article conceded, but not impossible if, as Oppenheimer observed, "it is recognized that this, for us, in our time, is the fundamental problem of human society, that it is a precondition not only for civilized life or for freedom, but for the attainment of any living aspirations."[25]

After nearly a year of this sort of speaking and writing, what did the scientists accomplish? At the governmental level, their press releases, informal lobbying, and congressional testimony had considerable effect. President Truman's public statements indicated increased awareness of the dangers of atomic energy and the need for international control. The power of the atom, he told Congress, was "too revolutionary to consider within the framework of old ideas." In Congress, the May-Johnson Bill was sidetracked, and revised legislation for the domestic control of atomic energy was approved in 1946. The new bill, which provided for greater freedom of research and diffusion of scientific information and which accommodated itself to the possibility of international regulation, was far more acceptable to the scientists. Meanwhile, the administration gained British, Canadian, and Soviet agreement to consider international control of atomic energy by a special United Nations commission. By June 1946, Bernard Baruch presented an American control plan to the United Nations, an event greeted by scientists with cautious optimism.[26]

The scientists could also be pleased by the cooperation they had won from the nations' editors and commentators. Most major magazines and newspapers had approvingly communicated the scientists' message, and some publicists had enlisted in the crusade, including radio commentator, Raymond Swing; *Newsweek* columnist, Ernest K. Lindley; and *Saturday Review* editor, Norman Cousins. From such individuals, if not from the scientists themselves, interested Americans became fully aware of the atomic bomb's implications.

As for the public generally, the results of the scientists' long campaign were mixed. Extensive polling was done in June and August 1946 by the Social Science Research Council's Committee on the Social Aspects of Atomic Energy, an effort funded by Cornell University, the Carnegie Corporation, and the Rockefeller Foundation. Discovering that 98 percent of the American people knew of the atomic bomb and its destructiveness, the pollsters concluded that "the impact of the bomb on the minds of the American people has had few parallels in our history." Yet further probing demonstrated that the scientists had not been entirely successful in their educational efforts. Among Americans expressing an opinion on the issue, nearly all believed that "the secret of the bomb" could not be monopolized for long and that other countries would be able to make the weapon within ten years. Yet, ironically, the scientists' own case regarding the revolutionary significance of their atomic research encouraged Americans to assume that science could somehow provide a large measure of future security. Two-thirds of those who had an opinion thought that defenses against the bomb could be developed before other countries learned how to make it. The scientists could take comfort that there was an increase in negative responses on this question from 18 percent to 24 percent between June and August and that negative responses rose considerably in relation to respondents' levels of information about world affairs. Nevertheless, many Americans would not abandon their immense faith in science and technology. Somehow, American ingenuity and American resources would allow the United States to "always keep ahead" by inventing an effective system of national defense.

Relatedly, public awareness of the horrors of atomic warfare nurtured hopes that the new weapons would never be used. Here again, menacing technology offered its own salvation. Intuitively grasping the logic of mutual deterrence, many Americans reasoned that no nation would use an atomic bomb against a similarly armed opponent. Indeed, atomic proliferation could contribute to peace: as the threat of retaliation became universal, all might be safe. In the short-term, no nation would dare attack the United States, but it was not obvious that the end of the American monopoly would bring inevitable doom. If war itself became suicidal, who would dare provoke it?

Even more discouraging from the scientists' perspective was the reluctance of the general public to remain deeply fearful about atomic weapons. Few denied that the bomb constituted a danger, but only 25 percent of the respondents admitted to being more than slightly worried. Deep, abiding fear is a difficult emotion for people to sustain. From listening to a radio program or reading an article, an individual might be momentarily frightened and might later admit to a vague, generalized concern. But life demands attention to everyday routine, and in the absence of an immediate crisis, most people will not long allow fear to dominate their thoughts. "I don't think I devote much time to worrying about it [atomic energy]," offered a man questioned in the Social Science Research Council poll. "The building business is too complicated now for me to worry about the bomb. It's too remote."[27]

While most Americans did learn to fear the bomb in the abstract, its threat did not preoccupy them and needed to be constantly reinforced. One of the scientists noticed this in the midst of his political efforts: "It doesn't matter who it is. You have to go way back to the beginning every time and explain what a menace atomic energy is. You have to shake them by the shoulders." This state of affairs did not bode well for a mass political movement based essentially on fear to achieve international control of atomic weapons or to eliminate war as an instrument of national policy. Einstein seemed to realize this by the spring of 1947 when he told his associates that they should not devote so much time and attention trying to reach the masses. "We are scientists," he said, and we should "not use razor blades for chopping wood."[28]

But by the time scientists themselves generally returned to their own daily routines they could point to considerable achievement. They had taught Americans that the atomic bomb was a revolutionary weapon and that their nation's atomic monopoly could not last. They had facilitated the efforts of reformers to harness fear, however vaguely it was felt, to political action. While public complacency remained a problem, memories of Hiroshima were still fresh, and many people, especially thoughtful, well-informed people, were concerned enough to seek ways of escaping their predicament.

What was needed now was a sense of direction. Fear by itself is unproductive. Indeed, it can be counterproductive if it breeds only resignation, cynicism, paranoia, and greater preparations for war. Fear of annihilation had to be wedded to the hope that political action could save men from their own scientific advance. The scientists had awakened millions to the dangers of atomic energy; now, political programs were necessary to achieve the security for Americans that V-J Day had failed to provide.

II.

REALISM, REASON, AND RESOLUTION
THE CASE FOR WORLD GOVERNMENT

The argument of the advocates of the world state is unanswerable. There can be no permanent international peace without a state coextensive with the confines of the political world.

—Hans J. Morgenthau, *Politics among Nations*, 1948

We must remember that if the animal part of human nature is our foe, the thinking part is our friend. We do not have to wait a million years to use our reason. We can and must use it now—or human society will disappear in a new and terrible dark age of mankind—perhaps forever.

—Albert Einstein, CBS Radio Broadcast, May 28, 1946

There comes to mind a scene from one of the old "silent" films. An outcast, lost somewhere in a mountainous forest, stands on the edge of a canyon. Behind him rages a forest fire, drawing ever closer. In front of him is a sheer drop of several hundred feet. But the gap across this canyon to the other side is only ten feet wide. Ten feet! He has never jumped ten feet before. He has no way of knowing that he can jump it now. He has no choice but to try.

—Norman Cousins, *Modern Man Is Obsolete*, 1945

By the time the atomic scientists had concluded that political programs were essential to assure lasting peace, the case for world government had been eloquently made in a series of widely read books. World War II had inspired many Americans to consider means of preventing future conflicts, a difficult objective made urgent by the discovery of atomic energy. Dozens of proposals emerged from this concentrated and inspired effort, proposals ranging from support for a new League of Nations to unembarrassed demands for an imposed *Pax Americana*, but the idea that most excited the imagination of interested Americans during the mid-1940s was world government. Logically, it was difficult to resist, even though emotionally it challenged powerful nationalistic sentiment.

The most important book advocating world government was published in June 1945, shortly after the defeat of Germany but just prior to both the San Francisco conference (which established the United Nations) and the dropping of the first atomic bomb on Japan. By fall, the book was a best seller warmly endorsed by Albert Einstein and recommended in an open letter to the *New York Times* signed by a group of prominent Americans led by former Supreme Court Justice Owen Roberts. By the spring of 1946, the book had gone through several reprintings, had been condensed in two issues of *Reader's Digest*, and was scheduled to be released in soft cover and in Braille. Emery Reves's *The Anatomy of Peace* became the major testament of the world government movement.[1]

The son of a local lumber merchant, Reves was born in the small village of Bacsfoldvar in southern Hungary in 1904. After local schooling he received his secondary education in Budapest and then attended universities in Germany, France, and Switzerland. In 1926, at the age of twenty-two, he was awarded the degree of Doctor of Political Economy by the University of Zurich. For several years thereafter he tried to establish himself as a political journalist, a failed effort despite his considerable intelligence, energy, and self-confidence. Then, in 1930, he founded the Cooperation Press Service, a company that distributed to newspapers throughout the world the views of major western statesmen concerning international affairs. For a decade he attended all major international conferences, became acquainted with many European diplomats, and eventually served as literary agent for such important leaders as Clement Attlee, Winston Churchill, Léon Blum, Anthony Eden, Edouard Herriot, Paul Reynaud, and Count Carlo Sforza.

Such work in the storm-tossed 1930s was not without its perils. Having used his news service to oppose Nazism, Reves was forced to flee Berlin in April 1933 only a few hours before the S.S. raided his company's office; and in later years he had to make similarly hasty departures from Vienna and Paris as Nazi troops entered those cities. In 1940, after escaping from Bordeaux to England in a cargo ship, he became a naturalized British citizen; a year later, he shifted his publishing headquarters to New York City.[2]

After financing several memoirs and histories written by German and Italian nationals hostile to fascism, he wrote his own book about the future of democracy. Generally, he argued for a tougher, more realistic liberalism that recognized that in both domestic and international society freedom had to be balanced with sufficient authority to prevent the strong from tyrannizing the weak. Paradoxically, in international politics the maximization of national self-determination was more likely to lead to war than to peace, and since autonomy was in any case illusory in an increasingly interdependent world, he suggested that democratic forces, particularly in Europe, champion a form of supranationalism that could effectively promote their common political and economic interests. His book, *A Democratic Manifesto*, gradually won critical acclaim and captured an audience for his more ambitious study several years later.[3]

That study, entitled *The Anatomy of Peace*, developed the basic argument that the world had changed so much since the eighteenth century that the nation-state system had become obsolete. All governments, he observed, viewed conditions and events as if their countries were at the center of the universe. In such a geocentric world, governments perceived economic, social, and political issues to be essentially national problems that could be solved within the nation by law and government or internationally through diplomacy. However, scientific and technological developments accompanying the industrial revolution produced an integrated international economy of mass production and consumption and nurtured an enormous population growth that filled the world's empty spaces and brought peoples into closer contact with each other. As a result, problems of food, employment, currency stability, and even war and peace could no longer be solved on a national basis. Our political and social conceptions are Ptolemaic, he wrote, while the integrated industrial world in which we live is Copernican.[4]

In Reves's judgment, both capitalism and socialism had failed, due in part to excessive nationalism. He believed that prosperous capitalist economies required free trade, open access to raw materials, and widespread division of labour. These requirements collided, however, with the demands imposed by the nation-state system for increased national planning to enhance economic self-sufficiency and to prepare for war, demands that took a severe toll in economic freedom and productivity. Similarly, socialism was forced by fears of foreign intervention to concentrate on strengthening the power of the state even to the extent of creating a totalitarian dictatorship. Neither capitalism nor socialism, Reves concluded, could successfully develop under the constant threat of war, and maintaining industrial growth within the anarchic nation-state system required the destruction of democracy and individual liberty. Fascism simply made a virtue of necessity.[5]

According to Reves, the nation-state was not always such a pernicious institution. When the Roman Empire collapsed and the Catholic church proved too weak to replace it, feudalism evolved to provide badly needed local order and security. However, as populations grew and local peoples, or their lords, came into increasing contact with each other, conflicts multiplied to the point where national governments were required to impose order on the chaos. In the eighteenth century sovereignty within those governments was in many instances theoretically transferred from kings to the people still organized into nation-states, a system that offered considerable security and freedom.

This advantageous situation ended as industrialization, territorial expansion, and population growth threw nations competitively together. Again there was chaos, and freedoms had to be sacrificed to ultimately futile efforts to guarantee national security. Wars were inevitable, since conflict always results from nonintegrated political units of equal sovereignty coming into contact, and warfare became more destructive as science perfected the instruments of death.[6]

"By now," Reves claimed, "people must realize that human beings are exceptionally perverted and ferocious creatures capable of murdering, torturing, persecuting, and exploiting each other more ruthlessly than any other species in the world." These dark forces of human nature, harnessed to nationalistic purposes, could only be held in check by rules imposed by a higher authority. The fundamental problem of peace was the problem of sovereignty.[7]

Thus two lines of argument converged to make the case for world government. Due to economic interdependence and industrialism's need for a borderless world, the nation-state could not assure prosperity; and due to the basic aggressiveness of men armed with modern weapons and organized into closely competing political units, the nation-state could not provide security. In short, nation-states were no longer fulfilling the purposes for which they were created.

The solution to that problem was not for people to surrender their sovereignty, but rather to delegate it to various levels of government, including a new world state that could regulate human relations in their international context. In Reves's opinion:

> Logical thinking and historical empiricism agree that there *is* a way to prevent wars between the nations once and for all. But . . . they also reveal that there is *one* way and one way alone to achieve this end—the integration of the scattered conflicting national sovereignties into one unified, higher sovereignty, capable of creating a legal order within which all peoples may enjoy equal security, equal obligations and equal rights under law.[8]

Reves insisted that less fundamental reforms of international behavior and institutions could not assure peace. Religious or ethical admonitions create only "a thin crust of civilization" and thus fall far short of making man a responsible member of civilized society. International treaties are static instruments that vainly attempt to freeze the status quo in a constantly changing world. The principle of self-determination of peoples perpetuates international anarchy, while balances of power preserve peace only during those brief periods when power is neither in balance nor grossly unbalanced. And collective security depends upon an unachievable unanimity among the major powers in permanent defense of mutually acceptable political relationships. None of these remedies addresses the basic problems of nationalism, the ancient tribal loyalties and the collective anxieties over status that inexorably lead to conflict.[9]

Anticipating various objections to a powerful world government and doubts regarding its feasibility, Reves reminded his readers that, even without a world state, nations had little remaining autonomy, that national governments were themselves becoming superstates and that most countries were already confronted with armed forces larger than their own. As for the argument that political differences and cultural diversity made the attainment of world government impossible, Reves countered that of course people are different and pursue different interests—that is what makes government necessary. But such differences did not place common government beyond reach. Successful countries like Switzerland and Canada were culturally diverse, and all the world's peoples had a clear, compelling common interest in preventing another war. Surely "national fetishes, prejudices and superstitions" could be destroyed by "the explosive power of common sense and rational thinking."[10]

Reves was vague regarding the precise nature of his proposed world government. While suggesting a federal arrangement with a democratic world state, he avoided specifics in insisting that the first need was agreement on overall principles or standards. To disarm potential criticism, he did suggest that representation in a world legislature be based not on population alone but on national power, industrial potential, and level of education. But nothing else was clarified.[11]

And how would world government be achieved? Much would depend on reasoned argument, spreading the "Word" to as many people as possible. All those willing to listen needed to learn that democracy, industrialism, and nationalism could not effectively coexist and that war among the major powers would certainly result from their predetermined efforts to maximize their own security. Perhaps enough men of influence would then, regardless of opinion polls, seek to lead their respective nations toward a new supranational order. There was simply no choice. "After a disastrous half a century of antirationalism guided by mysticism, transcendental emotions and so-called intuition," Reves concluded, "we must return to the lost road of rationalism, if we want to prevent complete destruction of our civilization."[12]

In most respects, *The Anatomy of Peace* was a typical world government tract for the mid-1940s. While few other writers developed their arguments as extensively as did Emery Reves, they shared his taste for classical realism, his opinion that the nation-state was obsolete, his insistence that only a world state could prevent war, his confidence in reasoned argument leading to fundamental institutional reform, and his vagueness about the nature of world government and what was required to achieve it beyond simple political determination. It may seem peculiar to describe advocates of world government as realists, since they were so universally condemned by their critics as idealistic dreamers, but in fact most of the supranationalists' arguments regarding the necessity of world government were clearly within the mainstream of classical realism. Nearly all of these reformers held a dark view of human nature and assumed the inevitability of political conflict. Like individuals, nations competed for power and influence, and within the anarchic nation-state system, any country's failure to defend vigorously its own security would leave it at the mercy of those who did. Wars, therefore, were not primarily the product of evil men or of particular social systems or ideologies but rather were endemic to the political system. Peace could be sustained only by subordinating that system to a new, higher level of political organization.

The 1940s were conducive to an almost faddish pessimism about human nature and about mankind's potential for social progress. Earlier faiths in education, in liberal or socialist reform, and in social scientific engineering all wilted in the primitive heat of Stalinism, Nazism, and Italian fascism. Who could believe in human perfectibility after the outbreak of a second great world war in twenty-five years, and who could assume the basic goodness of man after Buchenwald and Hiroshima? Americans who thought about such questions after World War II sampled existential philosophies that denied the essential meaningfulness of life or turned to the theological neo-orthodoxy of Reinhold Niebuhr who described man as tragically suspended between his spiritual aspirations and his preoccupation with immediate and mundane self-interests.

In the field of international politics, realism reappeared as one of the main currents of American diplomatic thought. Writers such as Walter Lippmann, Frederick Schuman, and Hans Morgenthau argued that America's traditional idealism, vigorously championed by major statesmen since Jefferson's day, was largely irrelevant in a Hobbesian world. Wilsonian appeals for self-determination of peoples, collective security, and a reformed international morality had won few successes during the 1930s; and in 1948 Morgenthau published his *Politics among Nations* to remind disillusioned Americans that the essence of life is politics and that the essence of politics is the pursuit of power.[13]

Emery Reves, whose mother was killed by Hungarian fascists during World War II, had a particularly bleak impression of man's motives and actions, but other major advocates of world government were inclined to agree that humankind was at least flawed by fundamental sinfulness. "Human nature is admittedly weak and inadequate," wrote Cord Meyer, Jr., the dynamic first president of the United World Federalists, "and the mature man will recognize that no sudden and spectacular improvement in the ways of the world is possible." Albert Einstein spoke of mankind's deeply embedded hates, fears, and prejudices, a state of mind unchanged for a million years; and even Norman Cousins, the instinctively liberal editor of *Saturday Review,* noted a "general aggressive tendency" in man's makeup and suggested that war "is an expression of his extreme competitive impulses."[14]

Conflict was thus perceived as an irradicable component of international society. Mankind would never be united in spirit and interest, according to Reves; indeed, he doubted that such uniformity would be desirable. Differences of culture, religion, political philosophy, and economic methods would continue, and competition for scarce resources could not be terminated by idealistic appeals for self-denial. Vernon Nash, the major field worker for the United World Federalists, admitted that even world government would not end conflict—it could only be tamed by being institutionalized within a commonwealth of man.[15]

Without world government, nations had no choice but to prepare for war, and tragically those very preparations made war inevitable. In international politics, Meyer lamented, "any disagreement is a potential source of armed conflict, and each nation must rely, for the protection of its interests, on the amount of armed force it is able and willing to bring to bear in a given situation. We should frankly recognize this lawless condition as anarchy, where brute force is the price of survival." In other words, within the anarchic nation-state system, the efforts of each nation to increase its security would, when extended far enough, threaten the security of other states. In the resulting competition for allies, strategic bases, economic self-sufficiency, and superior armaments, the distinctions between offensive and defensive action became blurred, and nations could find themselves sliding rapidly toward a war no one intended or welcomed.[16] Scientist Leo Szilard recalled a useful analogy drawn from everyday experience:

> During the first World War the Hungarian writer, Karinthy, was sitting in his study attempting to write an essay on the causes of that war, when he was interrupted by a loud noise which seemed to come from the nursery. Opening the door, he saw his five children engaged in a free-for-all. "Who started this fight?" he said sternly to Peter, his eldest. "It all started," said Peter, "when David hit me back."[17]

This "realistic" outlook made it difficult for world government supporters to perceive Russia as the villain in the developing cold war. In his book *Peace or Anarchy,* published in 1947, Cord Meyer maintained that neither the United States nor the Soviet Union was immediately responsible for their rivalry: both were reacting in a natural, predictable manner to the imperatives of the nation-state system. Each nation was forced by the nature of global anarchy to attempt to surpass the other's power; each exaggerated the other's hostility in order to gain popular support; and each sought allies to obtain diplomatic assistance, markets, raw materials, and military bases—or to deny these to the other side. In the past, Meyer concluded, a nation with no expansive ambitions could achieve considerable security without threatening others, but now both great powers had to rely on offensive power for their security, a course that was bound to raise doubts about each other's intentions.[18]

It is important to emphasize that most proponents of world government agreed with Emery Reves's insistence that violent conflict among nations was not fundamentally caused by economic, social, ideological, or racial differences. (Such divisions were present within many peaceful societies.) The outbreak of war, Reves concluded, could be attributed to "the *single fact* that those differences are galvanized in separate sovereignties which have no way to settle their differences except through violent clashes." Similarly, Albert Einstein wrote: "For me the problem [of war] is a purely political one. As long as nations demand unrestricted sovereignty we shall undoubtedly be faced with still bigger wars, fought with bigger and technologically more advanced weapons." There would still be rivalry in a world federation, the scientist admitted, "just as there is rivalry in the United States between the East and the South, or between management and labor." But "law would be substituted for force, and the rivalries would express themselves through legal channels. The various parts of the federation could not make war on each other."[19]

Thus squarely within the tradition of classical realism, world government advocates concentrated their attention on the political interrelationships of nation-states. Statesmen representing those national collectives were seen to be the primary actors on the world stage, and much of their conduct was assumed to be predetermined by the imperatives of the international political system. Even under new supranational institutions, nation-states would retain much of their autonomy, and world government itself would be based upon the nation-state model. All this would have been perfectly understandable to Bismarck, Metternich, or Alexander Hamilton. Yet while one-worlders perceived the nation-state to be crucially important, they were also convinced that it was becoming increasingly obsolete. In order to justify their lofty political status, most national governments had been able to promise their citizens considerable physical security, economic development, and international autonomy. But conditions had changed, and now the nation-state system threatened what it had promised to promote.

Technology was the villain. In a world of sparsely populated countries separated by primitive means of transportation and communication, national governments could hope to provide their peoples with security and freedom, and in a predominantly agricultural world with plenty of space for new settlement, governments could hope to assure economic growth. But under the impact of science and technology, populations grew, frontiers vanished, industrial economies matured, distances diminished, and weapons became more lethal. For nation-states, the world was increasingly interdependent and dangerous.

While this was a gradual, evolutionary process, particular developments during the 1930s and 1940s dramatized the limitations of national sovereignty. Among the most important was the airplane, which by 1945 had become a major means of commercial and military transportation. Airplanes drew nations closer together physically, and even the vast oceans afforded diminished protection from foreign attack—as Americans learned at Pearl Harbor. As a result, political isolation became more difficult for great powers who still hoped to shape their own destiny. But airplanes had a psychological impact as well. Whatever the physical realities, which were difficult to calculate precisely, the world's peoples *seemed* closer and more vulnerable to each other's ambitions. Politicians and publicists never tired of describing the earth as "a shrinking planet," a place where once distant peoples had become nextdoor neighbors. In 1943 former Republican presidential candidate Wendell L. Willkie, recently returned from a global air tour of thirty-one thousand miles in forty-nine days, marvelled at how small and interdependent the world had become and concluded that the problems of other people now had to be of interest and concern to Americans. His best-selling book, *One World*, did not make a case for world government, but a few years later writers like Meyer would typically argue that "every scientific advance, every new means of transportation and communication makes the political map with its picture of boundaries separating absolutely independent nations a more dangerous anachronism."[20]

In 1946 Harris Wofford, Jr., in his book *It's Up to Us: Federal World Government in Our Time*, breathlessly announced that the air age had arrived. According to this Army Air Corps veteran who would soon become a leading world federalist, the airplane had revolutionized man's conception of geography and, subsequently, his political thought. "A generation which grows up in the noise of engines overhead, planes which can rapidly circle the earth, can hardly limit its political thinking to borders which they know any airplane can cross with no trouble at all." "If we take to the skies again in warfare," he concluded, "our civilization will probably collapse under the blow."[21] By that time, airplanes had delivered atomic bombs to Hiroshima and Nagasaki, and those new weapons raised additional questions regarding the rationality of modern warfare as an instrument of national policy, since the price to all participants, winners or losers, would be prohibitive. Consequently, if scientists were correct in insisting that there was no effective defense against atomic attack, then national governments could no longer fulfill their most important obligation, the safeguarding of the lives and property of their constituents. As Albert Einstein observed: "The nation-state is no longer capable of adequately protecting its citizens; to increase the military strength of a nation no longer guarantees its security."[22]

Nor could military strength, combined with isolationism or neutrality, guarantee a nation's freedom of action. For Americans, Pearl Harbor was a sobering experience that cast doubt on the capacity of the United States to determine unilaterally her own destiny, and for proponents of world government, America's reluctant involvement in two world wars in a single generation was conclusive proof that nations generally lacked control over their own affairs. Emery Reves recalled that the "United States of America, so unwilling to yield one iota of its national sovereignty, categorically refusing to grant the right to any world organization to interfere with the sovereign influence of Congress to decide upon war and peace, was in 1941 forced into war by the Imperial War Council in Tokyo."[23]

Self-determination of peoples, one of the major objectives of Wilsonian idealists, was thus an illusion. The very idea of national sovereignty was preposterous, according to Norman Cousins, because we have invested it with nonexistent powers. "We assume that national sovereignty is still the same as it always was, that it still offers security and freedom of national decision. We assume it still means national independence, the right to get into war or stay out of it." But the development of air power alone, he continued, aside from many other closer interrelationships among nations, "outdated traditional concepts of independence." No country is independent and sovereign in its decisions, concluded Reves. "Instead, each has become the shuttlecock of decisions and actions taken by other nation-states."[24]

This was considered to be true economically as well as militarily and politically. The Great Depression had demonstrated the integrated nature of the world economy and the frustrations inherent in unilateral efforts to achieve recovery. In March 1945 a long article in *Fortune* magazine explained how technology had not only created modern weapons but also unified the world into one economic nexus. Yet a basically anarchic political system prevented the establishment of a stable, orderly economic environment and the creation of adequate legal machinery to make contracts among men and groups possible and binding. Emery Reves maintained that free exchange of raw materials, manufactured goods, and investment capital was essential to an industrial economy, and both Cord Meyer and Albert Einstein believed that atavistic economic nationalism was a threat to peace. In Meyer's view: "In an economically interdependent world, each attempt to solve pressing economic problems in exclusively national terms is itself a cause of developing conflict. Every step on the part of one nation to assure itself the self-sufficient productive capacity . . . essential to national security conflicts with the corresponding security measures of other nations."[25]

These arguments, designed to establish the economic and military obsolescence of the nation-state, led to a secondary conclusion—the widely shared belief that world government was inevitable. The same technology that had made a world state necessary also made it administratively possible, and somehow necessity would prove to be the mother of invention. Norman Cousins recalled that prior to World War II the Germans had recognized that the world had become a geographic unit and had sought to organize and control it. Other great powers would try to do the same unless postwar opportunities were utilized to create a properly constituted and representative world government. If such a government were not established by a process of agreement among nations, Einstein warned, it would come anyway in a much more dangerous form, "for war or wars can only result in one power . . . dominating the rest of the world by its overwhelming military supremacy."[26]

World government alone could save civilization from the ruin of war and its imperial result—alternative solutions would not suffice. Using argu-

ments familiar to nearly all advocates of a world state, Vernon Nash devoted most of his book, *The World Must Be Governed*, to discrediting
supposedly more realistic reforms of the nation-state system. Relying on
some vague spiritual rebirth was futile, he wrote, since prejudice and
injustice would not suddenly disappear, nor could human nature be fundamentally changed. To call upon powerful nations to maintain order would
not work because their power would be misused either for aggrandizement
or to perpetuate a favorable status quo. Political alliances, much like Hollywood marriages, had never proved durable, and regional federations
would only provide bigger players for the deadly game of power politics.
As for the United Nations, it was totally weakened by the veto, which
reduced the organization to a loose association that few would support,
especially since action against a major power, or the ally or client of a major
power, would probably mean war. That problem could not be eliminated
through pious appeals for members to fulfill their obligations: the United
Nations was structurally flawed. Here, Nash approvingly quoted E. B.
White of the *New Yorker*, who indicated that if he had to bail out of a plane,
he preferred "to be harnessed to a parachute rather than to clutch a chest of
drawers, strictly on the score of the parachute's superior design." The
world had to have a parachute; nothing less would do.[27]

Not even half a parachute. While gradual progress toward world government through functional agencies was an appealing idea, there was no
reason to believe, Nash lamented, that agreements regarding postal systems, transportation, or even trading relationships would turn nations
away from their basic preoccupation with their own security. Functional
cooperation, mostly in noncontroversial activities, would not produce a
higher level of government capable of preserving peace. As Norman Cousins suggested, a deep political canyon had to be leaped, and Nash warned
that one could not jump over such a space with a series of small steps. He
denied the gradualist claim that there was no canyon, but only a wide
desert valley that could be crossed by slow, weary plodding. There had to
be a world state enjoying sovereign powers in essential tasks of government. Alas, there was no easy road to Damascus.[28]

To this point in their argument, proponents of world government could
understandably perceive themselves as champions of rationality. For if it
were true that the nation-state was increasingly obsolete and that the
nation-state system would in all likelihood father another major war, then it
was reasonable to conclude that the system had to be fundamentally
changed. It could be demonstrated historically that balances of power,
alliances, and collective security arrangements had never assured lasting
peace, and it could be argued philosophically that human beings were
unlikely to become unselfishly dedicated to the general welfare. Thus it
was imperative, particularly in the atomic age, to create new, supranational
institutions capable of domesticating inevitable political conflict. Logically,
there was no alternative.

"Who are the realists?" radio commentator Raymond Swing asked his listeners. Were they the traditional practitioners of realpolitik, or were they people who recognized that war itself had to be abolished? Were they the enthusiastic champions of the new league created in San Francisco in July 1945, or were they the atomic scientists who believed that the dramatic use of atomic weapons in early August necessitated new, supranational institutions? After Hiroshima, what did realism and practicality mean? In Swing's judgment:

> Nothing can be called more impractical than to be destroyed. All of man's conservatism is now evoked. If we are to conserve, if we are to spare and save, we must abolish war. Those who say to you [that] we must merge national sovereignty into a world sovereignty . . . are not radicals. They are the practical men and women of our time.[29]

Similarly, Vernon Nash approvingly quoted the English publicist Ralph Barton Perry: "We must be visionary and utopian if we are not to be unprecedentedly base; in order to be realistic we must be loftily idealistic."[30]

In this context, realism had two meanings—it could refer to either the analysis of problems or the achievability of results. The two meanings, however, were closely related, since advocates of world government were convinced that their analysis was sound and that reason, judiciously mixed with fear, would make their goals achievable. Educator Robert Hutchins described the atomic bomb as "the good news of damnation," news that would "frighten us into doing what we know we should be doing anyway," and Hutchins's colleague at the University of Chicago, G. A. Borgese, argued succinctly that because world government is necessary, "therefore, it is possible." Logic, combined with man's instinct for self-preservation, would somehow prevail.[31]

Perhaps, but at this stage the case for world government became increasingly vulnerable to accusations of utopianism. One could easily construct a convincing argument that the nation-state was losing its traditional political and economic usefulness and that supranational institutions theoretically offered the best hope of preventing another world war, but it was not easy to explain precisely how those institutions would be created or what they would look like. What was world government? What powers would it enjoy, and how would it exercise them? Could these powers be successfully limited? In short, what sort of government would be strong and independent enough to maximize the chances of peace and prosperity, yet not so strong as to be unobtainable or arbitrary?

For most defenders of world government, the ideal solution to these problems was federalism. Typically, Cord Meyer hoped that a conference of member countries would amend the United Nations Charter to establish a government with sufficient power to prevent nation-states from arming themselves for war. Under a federal system with laws enforceable against individuals, the central government would severely limit the size of national armed forces, prohibit the production or possession of particular weapons, and monopolize potentially dangerous uses of atomic energy.

The central government, Meyer suggested, would have its own military forces, assured sources of financial support, and an inspectorate to help enforce its laws; but the government's power would be moderated through internal checks and balances. A legislature, with representation weighted in favor of the great powers, would establish administrative rules for implementing the government's security powers, would investigate and publicize the work of the inspectorate, and would have power of impeachment. An executive, in the form of a commission elected periodically by the assembly, would direct the inspectors, police, and atomic development authority. A judiciary would have compulsory jurisdiction over individuals and would settle constitutional arguments. Finally, a police force, distributed to various strategic areas, would have the power to arrest individuals and prevent national rebellions against the central authority. Officers would be continuously rotated and investigated, and there would be a limited number of soldiers from any single nation.

All nations would have to join this new government, Meyer concluded, and none could secede. In time, that government would expand its activities to encourage freer trade and assist poorer nations, although only if legislative representation were based on levels of economic and educational development as well as on population. But, basically, Meyer's world state would remain a security organization that would leave most governmental tasks to the member states.[32]

Most American supporters of world government advocated a similar type of federalism, the granting of strictly limited powers to a world state essentially concerned with international peace and security. This was a form of government familiar to Americans and one that seemed to offer the best opportunity for achieving order among the world's diverse cultures and political systems. Considerable national autonomy would be lost, but in compensation nations would escape the burdens of huge defense budgets and would enjoy a far better chance of avoiding major war.

A vocal minority of one-worlders, however, dissented from this limited, minimalist conception of world government. Denying that peace was merely the absence of war, they claimed that order and stability had to rest on justice. Vernon Nash envisioned a government that would promote the general welfare by freeing the channels of trade and ensuring a more equitable distribution of the world's wealth. Similarly, a group of University of Chicago academics, who in 1947 drafted a model world constitution, suggested that everyone should enjoy the basic right to claim "release from the bondage of poverty and from the servitude and exploitation of labor, with rewards and security according to merit and needs." Peace and justice, they agreed, would stand or fall together.[33]

These advocates of broad governmental powers were better at proclaiming worthy objectives than at suggesting how they could be obtained, yet the maximalists had not cornered the market on vagueness. Nearly all promoters of world government devoted little time to describing the nature of their final product. This would have been a difficult task and probably ill timed. "Nothing is more futile than to work out detailed plans and prepare drafts for a constitutional document of a world government," advised Emery Reves. Every individual or group who attempted to do so would produce a different draft, a pointless exercise until there was a consensus regarding first principles, a set of standards for safe and effective world government. After the need for a world state was established and agreement was reached on its essential characteristics, then useful debate could begin on the specifics. This was a reasonable argument, perhaps, but also a costly one politically. Before traveling very far down the road toward supranationalism, people wanted to have a relatively clear idea of their destination.[34]

Equally foggy was the one-worlders' conception of how world government could be achieved. Generally, hope was placed in an active, enlightened elite of opinion leaders and policymakers who would lead the nation and the world toward some sort of constitutional convention. Here again, there was considerable drinking at the well of classical realism, a school of thought that emphasized the central importance of elite-dominated diplomacy in the grand style of the eighteenth century. Favorable public opinion might be necessary to provide a conducive environment, but most essential were creative acts of statesmanship. The Founding Fathers would once again spend the summer in Philadelphia.[35]

Examples derived from American constitutional experience were extremely seductive. "There were thirteen American nations in the Revolution against England," observed Norman Cousins, and "they came out of that revolution as former allies rather than as partners in a continuing enterprise." The new states were characterized by different and frequently conflicting systems of political, economic, and social organization. They were ethnically and religiously diverse, and local prejudices were intense. State governments squabbled over boundaries, levied duties against each other's goods, and discounted each other's currencies. Each government jealously protected and promoted its sovereign independence, unchecked by any central authority. Their confederation was but an early version of the League of Nations.[36] Fearing the collapse of the new republic into warring fragments and believing that greater unity was essential to economic prosperity, America's leading statesmen met together to create a new federal government with sufficient power to impose order and economic cooperation. Courageously, they rejected incremental change—continued experiments with functionalism or minor tinkerings with their ineffectual confederation. Instead, they made the necessary leap to a fundamentally new system of government, a federal system with adequate centralized power to enhance the chances of lasting peace.[37] And they did this without much assurance of popular support. Lionel Curtis quoted George Washington's statement to the delegates in Philadelphia after his election to the presidency of the constitutional convention: "It is too probable that no plan we propose will be adopted. Perhaps another dreadful conflict is to be sustained." Yet rather than surrendering to popular prejudices, Washington advised the delegates to rise above them, to provide creative leadership: "If to please the people, we offer what we ourselves disapprove, how can we afterwards defend our work? Let us raise a standard to which the wise and honest can repair."[38]

Leadership, determination, strength of will—these were the qualities required to overcome the inertia of traditional nationalism. "Man is left," Norman Cousins believed, "with a crisis in decision. The main test before him involves his *will* to change. . . . That he is capable of change is certain." Equally hopeful, Vernon Nash recalled that "radical changes in man's political relations have been made in the past when he has found his status to be intolerable." And despite his pessimistic view of human nature, humanist Albert Guérard, who helped write the Chicago draft of a world constitution, maintained that change is the only reality, even the possibility of sudden change: "love at first sight, conversion, crisis, revolution, catastrophe, adventure, miracle."[39]

Conversions, perhaps even miracles, would have to come suddenly, most one-worlders argued, since time was quickly running out. Soon, other nations besides the United States would have the atomic bomb, and the resulting deadly combination of nuclear proliferation and rising international tensions could push humanity beyond the point of no return. There was simply not time to wait patiently for diplomacy and functional cooperation to nurture a more integrated community, a process that would not necessarily produce world government in any event. Already bound together by new technologies in transportation and communication and by considerable economic interdependence, the world's peoples would surely come to realize that they also shared a common interest in survival.

For the apocalyptic advocates of world government, the choice for mankind was terrifyingly narrow—peace or war, one world or none. The atomic scientists had awakened Americans to the dangers of modern weaponry, and in order to preclude another world war fought with such weapons, the case for world government was being skillfully presented by the movement's major spokesmen—Emery Reves, Cord Meyer, Norman Cousins, Raymond Swing, Vernon Nash, and Albert Einstein. Arguments for the obsolescence of the nation-state and for the necessity of world government seemed realistic, logical, and fundamentally unanswerable. But the next task would be the most difficult: to mobilize public opinion behind the supranationalist program and to encourage American political leaders to make that ten foot leap over the canyon of nationalism and war, a leap largely into the unknown.

III.

THE POLITICS OF SALVATION

"Man will never write,"
they said before the alphabet came
and man at last began to write.
"Man will never fly,"
they said before the planes and blimps
zoomed and purred in arcs winding their
circles around the globe.

"Man will never make the United States of Europe
nor later yet the United States of the World,
"No, you are going too far when you talk about one
world flag for the great Family of Nations,"
they say that now.

—Carl Sandburg, "The People, Yes," 1936

Cord Meyer, Jr., was born in Washington, D.C., in November 1920, the twin son of a wealthy State Department foreign service officer. The family fortune had been established many decades earlier by a paternal great-grandfather who, after immigrating from Germany, eventually founded a wholesale grocery business and a sugar refinery. Meyer's grandfather was an early real estate developer on Long Island who became deeply active in Massachusetts politics, and his son (Cord's father) married Katherine Thaw, the daughter of a New York physician who devoted his life to poetry and social reform. Meyer was thus born into a financially comfortable and socially secure family that had demonstrated sustained interest in public service.[1]

After a happy Long Island–Northampton childhood, Cord and his brother Quentin were educated at the English School at Glion, Switzerland, and at St. Paul's, in Concord, New Hampshire, where Cord played mid-dling hockey, edited the school's literary magazine, and graduated second in his class. By the age of eighteen he had already become a good writer, a stimulating conversationalist, and a passionate champion of the view that "the world would be a fair place if only people would see clearly, shoot straight, and hit hard." "The cold and faded oyster of cynicism," noted one of his masters, "drove him to absolute fury."[2]

In the fall of 1939, just as war began again in Europe, Meyer entered Yale to major in philosophy and literature. Plunging enthusiastically into his

29

studies, he was inspired by excellent teachers to read widely, perfect his writing skills, and reexamine many of his intellectual presuppositions. Professor Maynard Mack exposed him to the grace and wisdom of English poetry; Robert Calhoun introduced him to the history of Western philosophy; and Nicholas Spykman "explained in his thick [Dutch] accent and with a skeptical objectivity the workings of the nation-state system from the time of the Greek city-states to modern times and the inevitability of competition and armed conflict between sovereign nations in the absence of any enforceable supranational law." Sensitive, intelligent, and highly motivated, Meyer wrote poetry, helped edit *The Yale Lit*, and seriously considered and debated the moral and philosophical implications of the escalating world war. In 1942 he graduated *summa cum laude* in English literature and was awarded the Alpheus Henry Snow award for "the senior adjudged by the faculty to have done most for Yale by inspiring his classmates." Meyer's future in any of his family's traditional pursuits—business, politics, or academic life—seemed to be at his command.[3]

The war, however, intervened—almost fatally. Shortly after Pearl Harbor, Meyer joined the marines and, after his Yale graduation, entered basic training camp at Quantico, Virginia. By June 1943, after further training in Samoa, he became the leader of a machine gun platoon, and in late February 1944 he and his men met the Japanese at Eniwetok. This first encounter with war both hardened and inspired him. While willing to kill or be killed, he was unnerved to find on the still warm bodies of the enemy the letters and pictures that offered "disturbing proof of mutual humanity." In late March he wrote home:

> I really think I should like to make a life's work, if possible, of doing what little I can in the problem of international cooperation. We cannot continue to make a shambles of this world, and already a blind man can see the short-sighted decisions that point inevitably to that ultimate Armageddon, World War III.[4]

On July 21 he was on Guam, dug into a foxhole across from an unseen enemy, an adventure he would later dramatically relate in "Waves of Darkness," a prizewinning short story published in *Atlantic Monthly*. The loss of the youngest member of his platoon angered him against war in general, and the artillery shells screaming overhead were symbolic reminders of the purposelessness of much of war's destruction: "One moment you lived and the next you were snuffed out like an insect—no courage, no skill, no strength could make one iota of difference."[5]

Waiting in the darkness for an inevitable Japanese attack, Meyer suddenly felt a strange detachment as if he could look down on this awful spectacle while no longer involved in it. Below he could see his countrymen in their foxholes "with their backs to the sea, each one shivering with fright yet determined to die bravely." Nearby were poor Japanese peasantry "being herded into positions like cattle, to be driven in a headlong charge against the guns." Surely there was some mistake—civilized human beings did not slaughter one another. Perhaps he could rise from his foxhole and explain the matter reasonably to both sides:

> Fellow human beings [he would begin]. There are few of us here who in private life would kill a man for any reason whatever. There are differences between us, I know, but none of them worth the death of one man. Most of us are not here by our own choice. We were taken from our peaceful lives and told to fight for reasons we cannot understand. Surely we have far more in common than that which temporarily separates us. The only certain fruit of this insanity will be the rotting bodies upon which the sun will impartially shine tomorrow. Let us throw down these guns that we hate. With the morning, we shall go on together and in charity and hope build a new life and a new world.[6]

Soon rifle fire "interrupted his imaginary eloquence." The Japanese attacked, and Meyer sustained grenade wounds that almost took his life. Lying in his foxhole, bleeding profusely, and aware that he had lost at least one eye, he nearly abandoned all hope. He considered the pointlessness of man's strivings given "the certainty and conclusiveness of death." Man was only "a poor creature struggling for a moment above a forever escaping stream of time that seemed to run nowhere."[7]

But then, still on his back and barely conscious, he saw a star. He now knew that he still had one good eye, and this realization evaporated his indifference. "Light was life, and the possibility of hope both intoxicated and appalled." He looked again. The star remained and "flooded his being like the summer sun. Another appeared, and another, until the whole tropic sky seemed ablaze with an unbearable glory. Gently he permitted the torn lid to shut. Warm on his cheeks and salty in his mouth were the tears of his salvation."[8]

Some of Meyer's letters home describing his war experiences were published in the October 1944 issue of *Atlantic Monthly,* where they attracted the attention of Harold Stassen, one of the American delegates to the approaching United Nations conference in San Francisco. In April 1945, after Meyer had recovered, returned home, and enrolled in Yale Law School, Stassen selected him as a conference aide. Meyer readily accepted, abandoned his legal studies, and headed west—along with his new bride, Mary Pinchot, a brilliant Vassar graduate who shared his hopes for a reformed postwar world. The couple was married in Mrs. Pinchot's Park Avenue apartment by Reinhold Niebuhr.[9]

Meyer was deeply disappointed in the results of the San Francisco deliberations. Committed to the Security Council veto, the major powers refused to surrender any sovereignty to the United Nations, a decision that, in Meyer's judgment, left the organization powerless to preserve a lasting peace. "This is a step in the right direction," he told a *New York Times* reporter, "but there will have to be amendments to make it work"—a view shared by two members of the press corps with whom Meyer had long conversations, E. B. White and Emery Reves. In late May Meyer's gloom was reinforced by the news of his twin brother's death on Okinawa.[10]

After the conference Meyer prepared his *Atlantic Monthly* article, "A Serviceman Looks at the Peace," which explained his reservations regarding the United Nations Charter. Once again, he called for an effort to make it "the symbol and instrument of a just order among men," although he realized that nationalistic sentiments remained powerful and that the world's peoples could not agree on the common principles and values essential to world government. "We live in a tragic age," he concluded, "where the moral and intellectual resources of our time do not seem adequate to meet either our problems or our obligations."[11]

But in August the news of Hiroshima left him with a greater sense of urgency and of hope. "I knew then," he said, "that the question of world government was no longer a matter to be talked about for the future. I knew then that it must come about immediately or we will all be finished." Yet "the very destructiveness of the new weapon put a new and powerful argument in the hands of those who were prepared to use it." Perhaps this common threat would counter the ideological differences and narrow nationalisms that blocked progress toward a world state.[12]

Shortly after Meyer's criticisms of the United Nations Charter appeared in *Atlantic Monthly*, he was invited to attend a conference in Dublin, New Hampshire, to consider ways of strengthening the United Nations. The idea for the conference originated with Clarence Streit, leader of the popular Federal Union movement of the late 1930s that advocated a merging of American and British sovereignties in order to better defend democracy from its fascist enemies. One of Streit's major supporters, former Supreme Court Justice Owen Roberts, agreed to preside over the meeting scheduled for mid-March at a location near the summer home of Grenville Clark.[13]

Clark's involvement as secretary lent the gathering the kind of establishment respectability that would help arouse public interest. Heir to a banking and railroad fortune, he had attended Pomfret School and Harvard, helped found, in partnership with Elihu Root, Jr., a prosperous Wall Street law firm, organized the Plattsburg training camps that privately prepared officers (mostly Ivy Leaguers) for service in World War I, drafted and championed the World War II selective service law, and was instrumental in installing his friend Henry L. Stimson as secretary of war and law associate Robert Patterson as Stimson's assistant. Intelligent, determined, tactful, ruggedly handsome, and a good friend of America's movers and shakers (including both Theodore and Franklin Roosevelt), Clark enjoyed a formidable reputation as a powerful man behind the scenes of government, a man who got things done:

> One evening at the Harvard Club [related his law partner, Elihu Root], someone proposed offhand the question to a group of alumni, "Suppose you were lost in the Arabian Desert, running out of water, running out of ammunition, and the Arabs were hostile. Who would you like to have

appear on the horizon?" Four men instantly and simultaneously responded, "Grenny Clark."[14]

Clark was also legalistic, thoroughly Burkean in his abiding reverence for the law. He was a stout defender of civil liberties during the 1930s, opposed Roosevelt's court-packing plan in 1937, and initially drafted a proposed constitution for world government in 1940. "If you think you have an idea, put it in a statute," he liked to say, and after Hiroshima, he had some definite ideas about transforming the United Nations into the kind of organization that could assure world peace.[15]

A distinguished group of Americans came to Dublin as either participants or observers. In addition to Roberts and Clark, there were Robert Bass, former Governor of New Hampshire; Norman Cousins from the *Saturday Review*; Thomas K. Finletter, who would become Truman's secretary of the air force; Pulitzer prize-winning journalist Edgar Ansel Mowrer; Michael Straight, soon to be editor of the *New Republic*; Charles Ferguson, an editor of *Reader's Digest*; John K. Jessup, an editor of *Life* and *Fortune*; Beardsley Ruml, chairman of the Federal Reserve Bank of New York; and Donovan Richardson, managing editor of the *Christian Science Monitor*. The Dublin Conference Declaration, which was printed in full in the *New York Times*, was signed by Clark, Bass, Cousins, Finletter, Mowrer, and Straight, along with the leaders of various world government organizations and several talented young servicemen who were about to launch successful careers—Kingman Brewster, Alan Cranston, and Cord Meyer.[16]

The declaration stated that, due to atomic weapons, international warfare had to be abolished if civilization were to continue. Peace, however, required order, and there could be no order without law legislated and enforced by world government. In place of the inadequate United Nations, there "must be substituted a World Federal Government with limited but definite and adequate powers to prevent war, including power to control the atomic bomb and other major weapons and to maintain world inspection and police forces." To facilitate progress toward that goal, the declaration asked Americans to amend appropriately their own Constitution and to request that their government seek amendments to the United Nations Charter through either diplomatic negotiation or the calling of a new world constitutional convention.[17]

Following the conference, Clark retired to consider specific changes in the United Nations Charter, a task that would preoccupy him for the rest of his life. However, as Clark's assistant, Alan Cranston served as chairman of the Dublin Conference Committee, which sought to nurture the political progress of world government. In this capacity, he helped organize a meeting at Princeton to discuss the implications of the atomic bomb, and he soon met personally with Paul-Henri Spaak, Andrei Gromyko, Jawaharlal Nehru, and President Truman.[18]

Meanwhile, although Cord Meyer returned to Harvard to earn a graduate degree in government, he did not abandon his Dublin commitments.

He joined several world government groups, became a member of the planning board of the American Veterans Committee, and began to promote his world federalist ideas on public platforms. Merle Miller, who heard him speak before a university audience in 1946, concluded that, although his oratorical style was imperfect (too fast and too spare of gesture), he was passionate and persuasive—perhaps the best speaker of his generation. A good-looking ex-marine, confident and articulate, Meyer charismatically won thousands of young converts to the world government cause:

> World government is possible. It is possible in our time. We can and we will make it happen, and by doing so we shall achieve peace not only for our children but for our children's children, a peace that will survive to the end of time.
>
> There is no safe and simple way of stepping out of the suspicious world of the present into the hopeful future. . . . We must take chances, and we must do it now. No one dare concede defeat until the first bombs fall, but everyone must realize the inestimable value of the time that remains. What is possible today may be impossible tomorrow. . . .[19]

In February 1947 most of the major world government groups met at Asheville, North Carolina, to compose their differences and create a single organization. Meyer attended that meeting and made such a good impression on his elders that some of them compared him favorably to Alexander Hamilton. When the United World Federalists considered candidates for their presidency, a nominating committee suggested nationally prominent officeholders such as William O. Douglas, John Winant, J. William Fulbright, and Robert Jackson, but the executive committee placed Meyer third on their list, just behind Justices Douglas and Jackson. When those two refused the job, Clark, Finletter, and W. T. Holliday, president of Standard Oil of Ohio, offered the position to Meyer who accepted provided those distinguished emissaries served as vice-presidents and assisted him in raising money.[20]

Nineteen forty-seven was a good year for Cord Meyer and the world federalists. United at last, the federalists were growing rapidly in paid membership and popular support. Their cause had attracted the attention of nearly every major national publication, and congressional interest was flowering. Meyer settled into the presidency of the United World Federalists, published his new book, *Peace or Anarchy* (which sold over fifty thousand copies), and was chosen, along with Richard Nixon, as one of the Junior Chamber of Commerce's ten most outstanding young men in the United States. At the age of twenty-six, holding his first real job, Meyer set forth to convince his fellow Americans that the security they had just won on the field of battle could only be preserved by accepting the authority of a world state.[21]

The Asheville meeting that led to the formation of the United World Federalists was initiated by the four most important world government organizations in the mid-1940s: Americans United for World Government; World Federalists, U.S.A.; Student Federalists; and World Republic. Along with several smaller groups, the first three would merge to form the United World Federalists, while World Republic would retain its independence along with its dissenting views regarding the proper ends and means of the world government campaign. Yet even among the merged organizations, differences of background and outlook would divide the movement and thereby sap its collective energy.

Americans United for World Government was the offspring of Americans United for World Organization, an amalgamation of various internationalist political groups achieved in 1944. By the spring of that year, it was clear that a unified political effort would be useful in promoting American membership in a new league of nations, and Americans United was created for that purpose. Under the direction of Ulric Bell, a journalist and former director of the prewar interventionist lobby, Fight for Freedom, Americans United labored for the defeat of isolationist senators, supported American participation in the Dumbarton Oaks Conference, and urged the amending of draft agreements regarding the great power veto in order to improve the UN's peacekeeping capabilities.[22]

In the fall of 1944 Americans United launched an advertising campaign in support of American membership in the UN. Assisted by such experienced publicists as author Robert Sherwood and *Fortune* magazine's Russell Davenport, the organization worked through established community groups and sought to influence public opinion directly through the mass media. Such efforts were intensified after the San Francisco Conference.[23] Americans United, however, hoped that the UN Charter would serve as a transition to a more perfect instrument, a reform necessitated by the atomic bomb. In late September 1945 the group concluded that: "Only the moral force of the masses of humanity, brought to bear through a form of democratic world government in which sovereignty is pooled by all . . . can now suffice to meet the crisis." A new convention of nations had to be convened to amend the charter in order to keep the peace and control the atom. "World organization cannot turn back. Those who advocate it . . . cannot argue for its further development without arguing for world government."[24]

By February 1946 "government" replaced the word "organization" in the full name of Americans United. Norman Cousins became chairman of the executive committee, and Raymond Swing presided over a board of directors that included writers James P. Warburg, William Agar, and Clifton Fadiman, labor leaders David Dubinsky and Philip Murray, journalists Edgar Ansel Mowrer and Rex Stout, atomic scientist Harrison Brown, and political figures such as Thomas K. Finletter and former Undersecretary of State Sumner Welles. During its first year the organization attracted a dues-paying membership of about five thousand dedicated to establishing a world government with adequate but limited powers to control atomic weapons and prevent aggression, and in support of those objectives Americans United attracted media attention, assisted friendly politicians, and lobbied Congress on behalf of proposed charter amendments drafted by Grenville Clark.[25]

World Federalists, U.S.A., had a broader purpose. Moving beyond narrow, legalistic solutions to armaments and security, World Federalists asserted that "there can be no permanent peace without justice, no justice without law, [and] no law without institutions to make, interpret and enforce it." They also advocated a constitutional convention called by national governments as a possible alternative to requesting the UN to amend its charter.[26]

Founded in Cleveland in late October 1945, the World Federalists typically absorbed some older, smaller groups, including Campaign for World Government, which had endorsed the constitutional convention idea as early as 1937. The World Federalists's Advisory Council attracted such luminaries as Mark and Carl Van Doren, Thomas Mann, Louis Bromfield, Margaret Mead, Lewis Mumford, and Owen Roberts, while leading world government publicists Emery Reves and Vernon Nash also lent their support. The organization's executive secretary was Otto Griessemer, a former Berlin lawyer who, several years after emigrating to the United States in 1936, had become the New York State director of Clarence Streit's Federal Union. By the mid-1940s, he had abandoned the nuclear union idea and had become editor of the world government movement's major publication, *World Government News*.[27] World Federalists, U.S.A., used political methods similar to those of Americans United—media education, electioneering, and legislative lobbying. Both were membership organizations of similar size, but World Federalists was better organized at the grass roots into local chapters and state branches. This organizational difference between the combined organizations would cause problems later as members debated whether it was best to concentrate politically on elites or on the voters generally.[28]

The Student Federalists began as part of the Streit movement just prior to World War II. At age fifteen, Scarsdale high school student, Harris Wofford, Jr., heard a radio discussion on Federal Union while he was soaking in the bath tub. Moved by the wisdom of Streit, Claire Boothe Luce, Dorothy Thompson, and Thomas Mann, Wofford traveled to New York to gain permission to form Federal Union's first high school chapter. After the organization's Peoria Convention in 1943, Wofford almost singlehandedly inspired the creation of fifty additional chapters of the Federal Union student affiliate, by then called Student Federalists. In the Air Corps in 1944, Wofford still found time to address the *Herald-Tribune* Forum, visit Eleanor Roosevelt, and continue his organizational activities. *Time* magazine was impressed enough to comment favorably on the students' enterprise, enthusiasm, and good breeding: "Student Federalists would be distinguished, if for nothing else, by the fact that it is one of the few U.S. youth movements that did not spring from left-wing yearnings or prompt-ings."[29]

In 1945, however, Wofford was discouraged. Swayed by Wendell L. Willkie's appeal for one world and disturbed by advances in military tech-nology, Wofford concluded that both Streit's union of democracies and United Nations collective security arrangements were inadequate policies for an extremely hazardous future. "The earth will be governed," he wrote, "or it will be blown up; united or destroyed." The November 1945 meeting of Federal Union exposed a deep division between those who still wanted a nuclear union and those who favored an effort to create world government. Wofford and his Student Federalists sided with the second view and became organizationally independent.[30] By early 1947 they had become an organization of thirty-five hundred members from about eighty high schools and colleges around the nation. Their program was similar to that of World Federalists, U.S.A., although their energies were devoted more to educating fellow students than to political action. Their new president Colgate Prentice, a former B-29 crewman, delayed his own education in order to tour the country speaking before college audiences on behalf of world government.[31]

Even more committed were the leaders and members of another, smaller student organization headquartered in Evanston, Illinois—Students for Federal World Government. Founded by student veterans at Northwestern University, the group restricted its membership to those prepared to do-nate at least one hour per week to the movement. Their president, Jack Whitehouse, who had served as an infantry sergeant during the war and spent eleven months in a British hospital, gave his life's savings to the organization and postponed his marriage until his term of office was due to expire.[32] In 1946 the group changed its name to World Republic and adopted the slogan "One Hope, One World." Operating at first out of an Evanston garage and then from a three-story business building downtown, twenty-six full-time volunteers raised over $50,000, collected food for war victims abroad, staged a large world government rally at Chicago Stadium, and sought ten million signatures for a petition demanding a world consti-tutional convention. It was their hope that the world's peoples could be more successful than their governments in demanding the creation of a world state able to build and maintain a durable peace based on social and economic justice.[33]

Ironically, those beliefs led World Republic adherents to shy away from the world government organizational merger that they helped so much to create. Concerned about inadequate coordination among supranationalist groups, World Republic suggested that they meet in Chicago in late No-vember 1946 to consider ways of achieving greater unity. At those meet-ings, representatives agreed on the desirability of democratic world government, federal in form and with laws applicable to individual cit-izens. Member nations would retain jurisdiction over their own internal matters while the central government would concern itself with world affairs, including control of atomic weapons and supervision of universal disarmament. The organizations also recognized the importance of justice to lasting peace and endorsed the constitutional convention as a possible means of creating a world state, but subsequent meetings at Asheville failed to convince World Republic delegates that most federalists gave such considerations high priority. World Republic thus remained aloof, and divided opinions among the remaining groups were papered over with rhetorical compromises.[34]

Still, despite those problems, the United World Federalists were off to a strong start after Asheville in their quest for permanent peace. The amalgamation produced an organization of about seventeen thousand paid memberships, fifteen state branches, hundreds of local chapters, a vigorous student movement, and a total anticipated income for 1947 of about $250,000. United World Federalists took over World Federalists, U.S.A.'s New York brownstone on 74th Street, just off Madison Avenue, and maintained another set of offices in Washington. With unity achieved and public interest in world government increasing, hopes were high for substantial success.[35]

The United World Federalists also had some significant supranationalist fellow travelers during the late 1940s. As earlier, the prestigious atomic scientists offered invaluable assistance, and relatedly the University of Chicago was willing to establish an intellectually respectable committee to draft a model world constitution. There were also some interesting lone crusaders like Ely Culbertson and Robert Lee Humber. None of these people were formally affiliated with Cord Meyer's empire, but their combined efforts helped build the momentum for world government that crested in the spring of 1949.

The atomic scientists' campaign of fear exhausted itself by mid-1946, leaving its champions floundering in search of a new sense of direction. Scientists were aware that their entropy was due in part to the essential sterility of their message, the constant preaching of gloom and doom without much indication of what could be done to save mankind. Harrison Brown, one of the trustees of the Emergency Committee of Atomic Scientists, observed that "we have no objective" and have become "bored with our own speeches." We have come to realize that educating people to the horrors of atomic warfare, although necessary, is not sufficient."[36]

Paradoxically, the scientists' movement also faltered because it was able to achieve its immediate goal, an American plan for international control of atomic energy. There was much initial enthusiasm for the Acheson-Lilienthal proposals, which envisioned a United Nations atomic development authority as an exclusive agency for the production and allocation of dangerous fissionable materials. That authority would own and lease property, engage in manufacturing, licensing, and research, and inspect the atomic installations of member states. In April 1946 the Federation of

American Scientists endorsed the proposals and recommended that they become the basis of America's negotiating position at the United Nations.[37]

Scientists hoped that the resulting Baruch plan, which included the abolition of the great power veto in atomic matters, would ultimately provide supranational control of the atom. If accepted by the Soviet Union, a supranational authority would be established, an embryo world government that would help preserve a lasting peace. Baruch himself mentioned sacrificing some national sovereignty in order to prevent atomic war, and Robert Hutchins instructed a radio audience that "any proposal for a world atomic authority is a proposal for world government."[38]

It soon became obvious, however, that both the United States and the Soviet Union were shaping their atomic control proposals in ways to achieve maximum national advantage and that agreement was highly unlikely. J. Robert Oppenheimer would sadly conclude that control could not be achieved because of Soviet-American distrust, and Harold Urey, one of Baruch's advisors, admitted that the United Nations authority would not have worked even if the Russians had accepted the American proposals. As Cord Meyer recognized at the time, enforcement of the authority's regulations against a rebellious great power was impossible without war, and control of atomic bombs could not be achieved while arms races continued for every other type of weapon. Furthermore, balanced locations of atomic plants and acceptable inspection systems would be difficult for Americans and Russians to establish so long as they were locked in escalating political competition. Eventually these observations became conventional wisdom, but in the meantime many scientists had complacently returned to their neglected research.[39]

Finally, scientists became less interested in politics as they shied away from the conclusion that seemed to follow logically from their arguments. If the avoidance of atomic destruction depended on the abolition of war itself, as so many believed, how could this occur without establishing a relatively powerful world state? But advocacy of world government took scientists far afield from their areas of expertise and made them vulnerable to harsh political criticism. "We started out like glamour boys," Brown noted, "with only one major critic—the Army, that was fun. Since then, the list of critics has lengthened, the glamour has disappeared, the shoe is pinching, and it is no longer fun."[40]

Most of the organizations of atomic scientists had considered world government during the fall of 1945, and although many individual scientists were converted—including Harold Urey, Harrison Brown, Leo Szilard, Arthur Compton, and Edward Teller—the organizations were publicly cautious. For example, at the founding meetings of the Federation of Atomic Scientists, members agreed that "some form of representative world government" would be required to control atomic weapons, but no such objective appeared in their official statement of purposes. According to J. H. Rush, the federation's secretary-treasurer, scientists realized that war would have to be eliminated, but they concentrated on control of

atomic energy as a dramatic, relatively simple problem not yet entangled in
old issues. Similarly, the World Government Committee of the Association
of Oak Ridge Engineers and Scientists discovered through polling that 90
percent of association members favored world government and cooperation
with groups working actively for world government. But when the committee asked the organization's leaders why there was no official advocacy, it
was told that promoting world government would lessen their prestige and
authority. As physical scientists, they would be taking a stand on an issue
well beyond their competence. Eugene Rabinowitch, editor of the *Bulletin
of the Atomic Scientists*, reported that the atomic scientists decided collectively to make control of atomic weapons the first plank in their platform,
since it was a concrete aim all could accept and was more likely to be
achieved if not tied to some vague ideal. Moreover, success in achieving
control might help create a good psychological climate for establishing a
world state.[41]

The major exception to this conspiracy of silence was the Oak Ridge
World Government Committee. This group first met about five weeks after
Hiroshima when they concluded that misuse of atomic power could destroy civilization and that international control was necessary to prevent
such misuse. After several more meetings the group concluded that "the
powers of the control body would have to be so broad that it could hardly
be established with a good chance of success under the existing Charter of
the United Nations." World government seemed required, and the committee proceeded to study it in depth. As good scientists, they collected
copious information on the subject, drafted reports and organization
charts, and even derived an equation to indicate the probability of a world
state being created. By January 1946 they were able to distribute a fifty-page
preliminary report to about one hundred prominent people.[42] Ultimately,
the committee published a small book, *Primer for Peace*, which argued that
effective world government would have to be universal, democratic, and
able to guarantee basic civil rights and liberties. It would require courts to
settle all judicial disputes, an executive able to enforce world laws against
individual citizens, and an elected legislature that would limit the type and
amount of armaments permitted to each national government. Finally,
economic and social justice would have to be encouraged at the national
level by assuring the right of referendum.[43]

Members of the Oak Ridge committee were thus driven by their scien-
tifically trained logic to argue the necessity of a "maximalist" world state
that would not have to marshal arbitrary power to police an unjust status
quo. Aware of the reluctance of national statesmen to preside over their
own emasculation, the scientists also concluded that the impetus for world
government would have to come from the people in general. As a result,
the committee remained aloof from the United World Federalists and
supported instead the peoples' convention approach advocated by World
Republic and many world government enthusiasts abroad.[44]

The other group of scientists that eventually advocated world government was the small, but prestigious, Emergency Committee of Atomic Scientists chaired by Albert Einstein. (Trustees included Harold Urey, Hans Bethe, Linus Pauling, and Leo Szilard.) In early June 1947 several officers of the committee met with Einstein at Princeton to discuss their future course, having already achieved their original purpose of awakening Americans to the atomic threat. Einstein believed that the committee should now devote less time to "trying to reach the masses" and more on educating influential people regarding the committee's long-range aim of establishing world government.[45]

Funded by the Rockefeller Foundation, a conference was held at Lake Geneva, Wisconsin, June 18–22, to which members of the Federation of American Scientists, the Atomic Scientists of Chicago, the Emergency Committee of Atomic Scientists, and other similar groups were invited. About twenty-five delegates attended and reached agreement on a statement later endorsed by both the Federation of American Scientists and the Emergency Committee of Atomic Scientists. Collectively, the scientists promised to continue publicizing the dangers of atomic weapons and the need for international control, but they added that, since current plans to avoid an atomic arms race had been slow and uncertain, more comprehensive schemes of world cooperation were necessary:

> As scientists we claim no special competence in the fields of economics and international relations. We have come, however, to recognize during the last year that the problems of atomic energy cannot be disassociated from general progress toward cooperation among nations.
>
> We recognize that our purpose—which is the permanent elimination of war—requires the establishment of a government of the world with powers adequate to maintain a peace based on the rule of law.[46]

So once again, although fewer in number and weaker of voice, the scientists rallied. Their endorsement of world government probably had much to do with their general intellectual dispositions as scientists. The Lake Geneva statement mentioned the importance of applying the scientific method to political problems, and as the Oak Ridge group discovered, rational, logical examination of the problem of controlling atomic weapons seemed to lead to world government. Similarly, scientists were accustomed to thinking for themselves, to testing theories and propositions rather than accepting them as assumed truths. As a result, they were unimpressed with extravagant hopes for national autonomy or collective security and were willing to advocate world government despite much popular skepticism. Finally, scientists were used to international collaboration and spoke often of a world-wide scientific community. They were thus prepared to believe that extensive cooperation among nation-states was possible, especially when the alternative was so grim.[47]

The atomic scientists were indirectly responsible for the activities of yet another world government group, the University of Chicago's Committee to Frame a World Constitution. Shortly after the University of Chicago's chancellor, Robert Hutchins, told a radio audience that the atomic bomb might be "the good news of damnation," news that might frighten people into "those positive steps necessary to the creation of a world society," two Chicago faculty members proposed that a committee be struck to draft a model world constitution. Professors G. A. Borgese and Richard McKeon admitted that this was a staggering assignment but insisted that it was both necessary and possible. It would also be the university's way of compensating for its substantial scientific support for the Manhattan Project. "There is more than symbolic value," Borgese and McKeon argued, "in the suggestion that the intellectual courage that split the atom should be called, on this very campus, to unite the world."[48]

The man who received this startling proposal was himself an unusual academic. Born in 1899, the son of a college president, Robert Hutchins attended Oberlin College before World War I, served as an ambulance driver with the Italian Army, and then returned to finance his way through Yale as a lumberjack and clothesline salesman. After teaching for several years, he entered Yale Law School, earned his degree in 1925, and became a full professor of law there by 1927. In 1928 he was dean (he recruited William O. Douglas that year), and the following year he was appointed president of the University of Chicago—at age thirty. Hutchins's career at Chicago was controversial. He demanded much of his faculty, reorganized the curriculum, advocated an integrated liberal education for undergraduates, and, most upsetting, abolished the university football team. (His own aversion to physical activity was legendary: "Whenever I get the impulse to exercise," he admitted, "I lie down until it passes over.")

Politically, Hutchins defended Sacco and Vanzetti, battled Hearst and McCormick, supported Norman Thomas in 1932 and then FDR until the president led America into war. Although not a member of the America First Committee, Hutchins opposed intervention for a variety of reasons: the unfortunate effects of the previous war, the pressing social problems needing attention at home, the threat that mobilization would pose to American democratic institutions, and the needless loss of many American lives. During the war he doubted that the Allies would be able to assure a durable peace. Ambition would remain, as would desperation and a willingness to gamble if the stakes were high enough. Lasting peace would have to rest on justice, a sense of common humanity.

In 1945, Hutchins was one of America's leading educators. His stewardship at Chicago had been extremely successful, and his educational philosophy influenced both undergraduate and adult instruction throughout the country. Brilliant, ruggedly independent, mentally tireless, and handsome enough to be likened to Tyrone Power, he was an important convert to the world government cause.[49]

The idea of designing a consititution for world government appealed to him. While hoping that he and his twelve associates ("an apostolic figure," according to Borgese) could produce a useful document, he was certain that simply by discussing the problem they would stimulate public support for a world community. The lawyer and academician merged in Robert Hutchins to give him a serene confidence in both the significance of legal documents and in the efficacy of intellectual debate.[50]

Borgese, author of *The City of Man* and involved for thirty years in European and global planning, thought it important to give some concreteness to the vague descriptions of world government so characteristic of the movement. He considered the Dublin Conference resolutions to be "as poorly written as they were superficially thought," and he claimed that millions "have been waiting eagerly for voices more articulate than whistles in the dark." While aware that his constitution would not likely be implemented, he hoped it would provide tangible architecture for a world state, and should the world be blown up, a copy or two of the constitution might still exist "to help the survivors to survive."[51]

The committee that began its work in November 1945 was an impressive collection of philosophers, anthropologists, political scientists, and legal scholars. The best known among them were Hutchins, philosopher Mortimer Adler, Dean James Landis of Harvard Law School, former New Dealer Rexford Tugwell, and theologian Reinhold Niebuhr. As months passed, the membership changed somewhat. Niebuhr withdrew as his doubts increased about the value of the enterprise, and Landis became chairman of the Civil Aeronautics Board. Meanwhile others were recruited—Stringfellow Barr, president of St. John's College, and Harold Innis, a historian and political economist from the University of Toronto. The bulk of the labor fell to Borgese, Adler, Tugwell, McKeon, philosopher Erich Kohler, Wilbur Katz, dean of the Chicago Law School, and Stanford humanist Albert Guérard, a distant relative of Voltaire.[52] The committee held thirteen meetings of two or three days each from November 1945 to July 1947. It left a documentary record of four thousand pages and published the *Preliminary Draft of a World Constitution,* fully reprinted in the *Saturday Review of Literature* and the *Bulletin of the Atomic Scientists.* The committee's work was thus completed just after the United World Federalists emerged from Asheville.[53]

The Chicago Constitution turned out to be far more complicated than its designers originally intended. It began with a preamble (written in blank verse) that announced the end of the age of nations and its replacement by the era of humanity based upon justice. Next was a declaration of rights and duties, which included common civil liberties along with the more controversial "right" to be released from the bondage of poverty. This section also stated that the four elements of life—earth, water, air, and energy—were to be the common property of the human race.[54] Grants of power to the central government included the maintenance of peace, the administration of territories still too immature for self-government, control of armaments, the collection of taxes, the regulation of commerce, the administration of a world bank and other appropriate fiscal agencies, the supervision of immigration, the regulation of federal transportation and communication, and the furtherance of the rights and duties of man. A popularly elected federal convention would, through a complex regional process, select a legislative body that would in turn elect a president as chief executive officer. The president would appoint a chancellor who, with his cabinet, would handle day-to-day administration. Other bodies included an elaborate court system, a House of Nationalities and States to safeguard local institutions, a syndicalist Senate to mediate disputes among occupational associations, an Institute of Science, Education, and Culture, a powerful Planning Agency, and an ombudsman to protect minority rights. A Chamber of Guardians, chaired by the president, would control the armed forces.[55]

The Chicago Constitution unambiguously envisioned a maximalist world government that would, like a global New Deal, provide minimum standards of welfare and increased social justice. For example, all world citizens would be guaranteed free education to the age of twelve and various forms of social security later in life. According to Borgese, the committee did not want to create mere police power but rather sought to remove the causes as well as the instruments of war. He frankly stated that the United States and other wealthy nations would have to pay a price to "lead and save" the world because building a supranational structure depended on a "renunciation of privilege."[56]

About the time the committee completed its deliberations, Borgese convinced Robert Hutchins to subsidize a journal devoted to the problems of world government. For several years thereafter, the thoughtfully edited monthly *Common Cause* reported the progress of the movement at home and abroad and was especially good at discussing the philosophical and theoretical issues involved in creating supranational institutions. Here was a rich source of intellectual energy from which more politically oriented world government advocates could draw.

This is not to suggest that the Chicago Constitution itself was very popular, particularly among those who believed that it envisioned governmental powers so broad that no nation-state would accept them. Ely Culbertson spoke for many when he observed that, although he had read many proposed constitutions for the world, he had never seen "anything so childish and at the same time ferocious; so grimly utopian and yet so ominous" as the Chicago draft. "The national state," he continued, "has become the all-pervading reality of the political structure of the world, and the framers of the Chicago Constitution are engaged in a Children's Crusade when they attempt to build their world state by waving a magic wand and 'abolishing' the national states by so drastically reducing their sovereignty." Culbertson believed that he had a better plan.[57]

He was essentially a loner, a man without institutional ties or any significant base of power, but his status as a celebrity assured him a hearing. A fascinating character, Culbertson devoted most of his turbulent life to two powerful passions—rescuing men from tyranny and war and playing the game of bridge. Born in Rumania of an American father and a Cossack mother, he spent his early years in Europe where as a teenager he became, in his own words, one of "humanity's emancipators." He considered himself a revolutionary, as did the Russian Czarist officials who jailed him for antigovernment activities in the Caucasus where his father worked as an oil developer. In jail the young man learned from his fellow inmates how difficult it was to revolutionize and how easy it was to play cards, and he spent most of the next forty years earning his living at bridge while in his spare time he tried to fathom "the real *forces* that move people." Foregoing his revolutionary activities, he became a self-styled "social engineer" specializing in the problem of reforming the violent nature of international politics.[58]

Culbertson's research and reflection culminated during World War II in the publication of *Total Peace*, a book devoted to America's proper role in world affairs. Frankly assuming that foreign policy should be based on national interest and defining America's primary interest as defending what she already possessed, he concluded that the United States should use its power to help establish a supranational system of collective security to defend the status quo. Assuming also that force dominated relations among states, he suggested a plan that would balance force against force and thereby guarantee peace. Law could not assure peace, since there was no international law backed by force. The United Nations was no effective substitute for power politics, and he feared that a powerful Chicago-style world government would become tyrannical. Thus he proposed a peacekeeping system utilizing both national power and the collective force of a new world federation, a system based on a "synthesis of nationalist and internationalist doctrines."[59]

This "quota force" plan called upon the United Nations to assign each country a quota of powerful weaponry, just enough for its own defense. No nation would possess more than 20 percent of the world's armaments, and an international force composed of troops from small countries would be as powerful, but no more so, than the strongest states. The UN would, by majority vote (no veto), use the international police force and as many national military establishments as possible to resist any aggression, although aggression would be unlikely, since any one nation would lack a preponderance of power. The UN would also control atomic weapons and prevent national preparations for war.[60]

Culbertson organized the Citizens Committee for United Nations Reform to stimulate public interest and support for his ideas. Members of his national council included Roger Baldwin, director of the American Civil Liberties Union; Max Eastman, a roving editor for *Reader's Digest*; Edward Skillin, editor of *Commonweal*; Professor Sidney Hook; socialist leader Norman Thomas; columnist Dorothy Thompson; and liberal journalist Oswald Garrison Villard. Many businessmen were also on the council, including the president of Armco and the vice-presidents of Lambert Pharmacol and Eastman Kodak. Membership in the organization was never large, but public interest was considerable. The quota force plan was discussed on half a dozen major network radio programs, and magazine articles appeared in *Reader's Digest, Newsweek, Esquire,* and *Scholastic.* The plan was also fully endorsed by the American Legion.[61]

The other major lone crusader for world government during the 1940s was a Greenville, North Carolina, attorney, Robert Lee Humber. Serving in an artillery company during World War I, Humber was appalled by the horrors of war and resolved to help abolish it as an instrument of national policy. At Harvard and as a Rhodes Scholar at Oxford, he studied history and government, and in Europe, where he worked for an oil company, he was able to travel widely and observe the League of Nations at first hand. He returned to the United States in 1940, in part to promote his "Declaration of the Federation of the World," a resolution he hoped would be adopted by a majority of state legislatures.[62]

In a lengthy preamble the declaration stated that an integrated international community existed but lacked the necessary governmental institutions to regulate commerce, protect life and property, and assure freedom and permanent peace. This was one of those "supreme moments in history," the preamble concluded, "when nations are summoned, as trustees of civilization, to defend the heritage of the ages and to create institutions essential for human progress." Consequently, he urged state legislatures to resolve that all peoples be united in a world federation and that state representatives in Washington request the president "to initiate the procedures necessary to formulate a Constitution for the Federation of the World, which shall be submitted to each nation for its ratification."[63]

In his grassroots approach, Humber first tried to convert his hometown citizens of Greenville and, after succeeding at that, took his case to the North Carolina legislature. Passage of the resolution in March 1941 proved to be easier than expected, as legislators were easily overpowered by his idealism and logic. One assemblyman who objected that the matter required further study was squelched by another who argued that "the progress of civilization cannot wait for my colleague's intellectual development." Encouraged, Humber proceeded to win similar victories in New Jersey, Maryland, Connecticut, Rhode Island, Alabama, Utah, Oklahoma, New Hampshire, Florida, Georgia, and Missouri—twelve states by the spring of 1947.[64]

His energy proved inexhaustible. Paying his own expenses, he would come to a state and address countless civic clubs, women's groups, and college audiences before descending on the state capital for extensive lobbying. He traveled constantly, sometimes scheduling forty successive days and nights of meetings and speeches. And consistently his speeches were eloquent and moving—the Minnesota Senate gave him a standing ovation.[65] By 1947, Humber had visited nearly every state, and nearly all of them were at least considering his resolution. His efforts were endorsed by Justice Owen Roberts, Wendell L. Willkie, and educator Nicholas Murray Butler, who told Humber: "If I were a young man I would not go into education. I would devote my life to the realization of world federalism." Thus all by himself, the "Grassroots Crusader" had achieved much, even among hardened state politicians in the nationalistic American South, yet another clear sign that the world government movement was beginning to hit its stride.[66]

It was roughly from 1947 to early 1949 that the movement attained its peak of popularity and influence in the United States, from local communities to the committee rooms of Congress. World government became a major issue of discussion in the national media, was selected as the national debating topic for high school and college students, and received official endorsement from dozens of major political interest groups. As measured by increased membership in world government organizations and by frequent independent opinion polls, public support for one-world ideas was considerable, especially among the wealthier, better educated, and presumably more influential segments of the population. About 150 congressmen and senators cosponsored world government resolutions, and even President Truman approved of supranationalism in principle.

Locally, federalists focused their efforts on World Government Days or Weeks, during which citizens were deluged with petitions, pamphlets, speeches, radio announcements, and official proclamations. In 1947 such campaigns were waged in Norwalk, Connecticut; Scarsdale, New York; Princeton, New Jersey; and Sauk Center, Minnesota (the model for Gopher Prairie in Sinclair Lewis's *Main Street*). Later, similar tactics were followed in larger cities, including San Francisco, Corpus Christi, Miami, Chicago, and Mayor Hubert Humphrey's Minneapolis. In Cleveland, over 200,000 people signed a petition in support of establishing a world state, while in New England, thirty-nine town meetings passed world government resolutions. There was even room for the bizarre enthusiasms of youth, as Palo Alto high school students demonstrated on roller skates and enacted the results of an atomic attack by overturning a few old cars on one of the city's major streets.[67]

At the state level a total of twenty legislatures had passed Robert Humber's resolution by July 1949; Massachusetts and Connecticut had approved referenda in favor of world government; and six states had recommended a federal convention to adopt a constitutional amendment permitting American participation in a world state. This last tactic was devised by Alan Cranston, chairman of the northern California branch of the United World Federalists, who hoped both to answer constitutional objections to joining a world government and to provide the president with a clear mandate to negotiate with other nations. Cranston was successful in California, although only after some old-fashioned political logrolling.[68]

Nationally, interest groups that collectively represented millions of Americans endorsed some form of supranationalism. Among veterans groups, the American Legion liked the Culbertson plan, while the Amvets and the American Veterans Committee unambiguously supported a world federal government. Also explicitly in favor of a world federation were the Young Republicans and Young Democrats, Americans for Democratic Action, the Junior Chamber of Commerce, the General Federation of Women's Clubs, the National Grange, the Farmers' Union, the Cooperative League, the United Automobile Workers, the Brotherhood of Railway Trainmen, and about half a dozen major Protestant religious denominations. Many more organizations, such as Kiwanis, the National Education Association, and the American Association of School Administrators, took a somewhat vaguer position supporting charter amendments to enable the UN to enact, interpret, and enforce world law.[69]

These resolutions both reflected and reinforced a powerful current of public opinion in favor of stronger global institutions. Immediately after World War II, when American public attention concentrated on control of atomic weapons, 72 percent favored the creation of a world organization strong enough to prevent any nation from making atomic bombs, and 78 percent approved the Baruch plan. By April 1948 Baruch's failure combined with generally deteriorating relations with the Soviet Union had convinced Americans that the prevention of war itself was the nation's most important problem, one that necessitated reform of the United Nations. More specifically, 83 percent desired an international conference to create a more powerful UN, and majorities also favored a much enhanced UN role in preventing aggression, controlling atomic energy, and regulating international commerce. Only 20 percent of the American public believed that an unreconstructed UN could prevent war during the next twenty-five years.[70]

Support for the general idea of world government was extensive throughout the late 1940s. In November 1945 a National Opinion Research Corporation (NORC) poll determined that over 50 percent of its respondents believed that world government offered a better chance than any United Nations force to prevent the use of atomic bombs in another war, and in September 1946 *Opinion News* reported that various major polling organizations had found a majority of Americans in favor of strengthening the United Nations sufficiently to create world government. For example, when George Gallup asked if Americans wanted to reform the UN into a world government powerful enough to control the armed forces of all nations, 54 percent responded affirmatively, 24 percent negatively, while 22 percent held no opinion. (A year later, the respective percentages were fifty-six, thirty, and fourteen.) Gallup also discovered that the greatest support for a world state, 58–59 percent, came from the college educated, especially persons listed in *Who's Who,* although the well educated offered higher negative responses as well.[71]

Realistic advocates of world government discounted those pleasing statistics to some extent. In the first place, Americans were not convinced that world government could ever be established—a NORC survey found twice as many pessimists as optimists on that issue. More important, some general support for world government evaporated when Americans were asked about specific sacrifices of their freedom of action. A poll taken in April 1947 revealed that while 74 percent of Americans urged the United

States to help establish an international police force, only 14 percent wanted it to be larger than America's own military establishment. Meanwhile, about 65 percent endorsed universal military training.[72]

But despite such reservations one-worlders were delighted with the polls. In a remarkably brief time the public had apparently outgrown a legacy of nationalism and isolationism to become surprisingly receptive to the idea of world government. Just beneath that receptivity lay large pools of ignorance and misunderstanding, but presumably the federalists' educational endeavors would assure proper enlightenment. In any case, 56 percent public support for the principle of world government would surely impress legislators in Washington, perhaps enough to facilitate passage of resolutions that would force the president to convert his own supranationalist ideas into tangible policy. Unless unforeseen events altered the public mood, the future looked promising.

The world government movement's congressional strategy borrowed heavily from the recent experiences of United Nations advocates. During the early years of World War II, internationalists, wishing to avoid a repetition of Woodrow Wilson's debacle, sought to commit the Senate well in advance to supporting American membership in a new league of nations. As a result, Senators Joseph Ball, Harold Burton, Lister Hill, and Carl Hatch introduced a congressional resolution, probably somewhat in advance of contemporary public opinion, to inspire senatorial and presidential action. The "B_2H_2" proposal called upon the United States to request the Allied powers to form an international organization that would prosecute the war, occupy liberated territories, facilitate the peaceful settlement of disputes, and deter aggression by means of a UN police force.[73]

This effort in March 1943 was deemed premature by the Roosevelt administration. The public's views were uncertain, and an inevitable congressional dogfight would distract domestic attention from the war effort and emit confusing signals to America's allies. The State Department thus encouraged the Senate Foreign Relations Committee to stall the Ball resolution while drafting a more general, less controversial measure of its own. This is indeed what occurred, but at least Ball and his colleagues had created momentum by galvanizing public support and stirring the administration into positive action.[74]

By the fall of 1943 the Italian surrender raised hopes of victory in Europe and inspired serious thought about the political shape of the postwar world. Also, the Gallup poll demonstrated that 78 percent of the American people approved Congressman J. William Fulbright's resolution proposing American participation in creating "appropriate international machinery with power adequate to establish and maintain a joint and lasting peace among nations of the world." This proposal, vaguer than B_2H_2, easily passed the House by a vote of 360 to 29, an action that inspired immediate Senate approval (85 to 5) of the similarly worded Connally resolution recommending American membership in an "international organization, based on the principal of sovereign equality . . . for the maintenance of international peace and security." A cautious President Roosevelt now had a mandate to help construct new arrangements for collective security.[75]

By 1947 similar political techniques were being employed by proponents of world government. Largely through the efforts of Edgar Ansel Mowrer and Raymond Swing, agents of the United World Federalists, a bipartisan group of six senators and ten congressmen introduced a resolution stating that "it is the sense of Congress that the President of the United States should immediately take the initiative in calling a General Conference of the United Nations pursuant to Article 109 for the purpose of making the United Nations capable of enacting, interpreting, and enforcing world law to prevent war." Twenty-seven additional resolutions for UN reform, including one embodying the Culbertson plan, were introduced by the spring of 1948.[76]

With public opinion polls so overwhelmingly in favor of strengthening the United Nations and with congressmen receiving "stacks of mail" regarding the issue, the House decided to schedule hearings. In an attempt to forestall this, Secretary of State George C. Marshall and Undersecretary William Lovett met at Blair House on the evening of April 27 with Republicans John Foster Dulles and Senator Arthur Vandenburg but, through oversight, neglected to invite House Foreign Affairs Committee chairman, Charles Eaton. In retaliation, the miffed congressman ordered the hearings to proceed.[77]

Cord Meyer presented the federalist case before the committee. While conceding the need for military preparations and containment of Soviet expansion, he nonetheless argued that such policies were perilously insufficient. Rearmament could not offer much protection against modern weaponry and ultimately could not prevent war. Furthermore, containment as an exclusive policy was likely, due to the weight of military competition, to force the Soviet Union and the United States into open conflict. A sounder basis for international security was required, and since the United Nations was inadequate, it had to be given sufficient power "to keep the peace under binding and enforceable world laws." (Meyer avoided the term "world government" lest it frighten potential supporters of his resolution's indefinite phrasing.)[78]

For about ten days the committee took testimony from a long series of witnesses either championing or opposing world federal government, the Culbertson plan, and Clarence Streit's revived proposal for a federation of Western democracies. Two conclusions could be drawn from the proceedings, neither of which was immediately encouraging to the world government cause. First, as the cold war matured, congressmen were increasingly preoccupied with the Soviet threat and tended to view reform of the UN as a means of enhancing the non-Communist nations' ability to offer an effective, unified response. Even Meyer and Finletter, whose testimony on behalf of the United World Federalists emphasized the need for universal membership in world government, noted the advantages to the United States of a partial federation should Russia refuse to cooperate. Second, the

Truman administration was not receptive to any American initiative proposing fundamental changes in the UN Charter. As George Marshall's testimony clearly indicated, the State Department doubted that world government had substantial, well-informed public support or that other nations, particularly the Russians, would accept supranational reform. Also, pursuing such a dubious goal could both destroy the existing international organization and direct energies from more essential tasks of repairing the European economy and containing Soviet power.[79] Marshall also said, however, that he was not opposed in principle to charter revision provided that it "would generally strengthen the work of the United Nations" and that it was "strongly supported by the Congress and the American people with full knowledge of its implications for the United States." So although the secretary's testimony did much to confine the committee's recommendation to innocuous suggestions for improved voluntary peacekeeping measures, an encouraging challenge was thrown to world government advocates to demonstrate the breadth and depth of their public following.[80]

As if responding to the challenge, the world government movement soon proved its increasing popularity and influence. By October 1949, when the House held a second round of hearings on reform of the United Nations, the 1948 elections had revealed considerable political interest in supranationalism, the list of respected Americans in favor of world government had become impressively long, and the United World Federalists had nearly doubled its membership. In response, about one-third of the House and Senate sponsored a new resolution specifically advocating the creation of a world federation.

In the 1948 presidential election the Progressive party was the most enthusiastic proponent of a world state. The party's vice-presidential candidate, Senator Glen Taylor, had introduced the first Senate resolution on behalf of world government in October 1945, and presidential nominee Henry Wallace was sympathetic enough to suggest abolition of the Security Council veto and the establishment of a UN police force. Less ambiguously, the Progressive platform stated that "the only ultimate alternative to war is the . . . adoption of the principle of just enforcement upon individuals of world federal law, enacted by a world federal legislature with limited but adequate powers to safeguard the common defense and general welfare of all mankind."[81]

The Republicans also had a candidate for the party's presidential nomination who had once defended world government. Harold Stassen, former governor of Minnesota and one of America's representatives at the San Francisco conference, had been a forthright supranationalist from 1942 to 1945 and had argued for major UN reforms since that time. Stassen lost to Thomas E. Dewey, no special friend of one-worlders, but the Republican platform did urge a stronger UN including modifications of the veto.[82]

Similarly, the Democrats called for the "development and growth of the U.N., including international control of atomic weapons and the creation of international armed forces." The party's nominee, President Truman, was generally sympathetic toward the idea of world government. He had told a Kansas City university audience in June 1945 that nations would have to get along with their neighbors and submit their differences to legal settlement. "It will be just as easy for nations to get along in a republic of the world," he predicted, "as it is for us to get along in the republic of the United States." A year later he informed Congress that the United Nations ought to be developed "as the representative of the world as one society," and John Hersey reported that Truman always carried in his wallet a copy of Tennyson's "Locksley Hall":

> Hear the war drums throb no longer,
> See the battle flags all furled,
> In the Parliament of Man,
> The Federation of the World.

Someday, the president told Hersey, we will have universal law.[83]

All of these party platforms and many of the candidates' speeches recommended substantial development of the United Nations in the interests of lasting peace. There was political expediency here and enormous caution. (The Democrats favored "such amendments and modifications of the Charter as experience may justify.") Yet the judicious bending of the trees was a sign of a brisk political wind, and one can sense as well considerable sympathy for the logic of the supranationalist case and the seductive appeal of its ultimate promise.

Congressional candidates also adjusted to the public mood. When *World Government News* asked them if they would support the transformation of the UN into a federal world government with powers adequate to keep world peace and with direct jurisdiction over individuals, 107 Democrats, 33 Republicans, and 21 Progressives responded affirmatively, nearly 57 percent of those who replied. More significantly, eighty-seven congressmen and senators in the newly elected Congress were identified by the *News* as receptive to some form of world government, a group including both John Kennedy and Richard Nixon.[84]

This growing congressional interest in supranationalism was reinforced by endorsements from respected, often influential, individuals from outside Washington who were willing to defend publicly the world government cause. By October 1949 their numbers were cumulatively large. Important writers included John Hersey, Lewis Mumford, Robert Sherwood, Edna Ferber, Sinclair Lewis, Clifford Odets, Edna St. Vincent Millay, Louis Bromfield, Upton Sinclair, and James Thurber.[85] The labor movement was represented by Walter Reuther, Philip Murray, and David Dubinsky; and business by Harry Bullis, president of General Mills, Owen D. Young, former chairman of the board of General Electric, and Robert Gaylord, chairman of the executive committee of the National Association of Manufacturers.[86] Among leading political and military figures were former Secretary of War Henry L. Stimson, General Claire Chennault, General of the Army Douglas MacArthur, and Governors Chester Bowles of Connecticut, G. Mennen Williams of Michigan, and Luther Youngdahl of Minnesota.[87] Even the entertainment industry weighed in with Darryl Zanuck, Douglas Fairbanks, Jr., and a successful young actor named Ronald Reagan.[88]

Many of these people actively supported the United World Federalists, which achieved its greatest notoriety and popularity during the late 1940s. Paid memberships rose from twenty-three thousand in May 1948 to over forty thousand by March 1949 as over seven hundred local chapters provided political support for well-organized lobbying activities in Washington. Five hundred delegates attended the organization's general assembly meeting in Minneapolis in November 1948, where $65,000 was raised toward an anticipated budget of $550,000 and where a confident Cord Meyer was reelected as president. There was a feeling in the crisp Minnesota air that 1949 would be a crucial year, a time when the growing momentum of the world government movement might achieve some significant objectives before all doors were slammed shut by the worsening cold war.[89]

This optimism was encouraged by the progress of supranationalism abroad. Indeed, according to the *Congressional Digest*, the world government movement was more advanced at the official level in Europe than in the United States. New constitutions in Italy and France provided for the surrender of national sovereignty if world government were created, and federalist parliamentary groups existed in many European states. In England one hundred members of Parliament supported the Movement for World Federation led by Henry C. Usborne, a thirty-eight-year-old Labour party M.P., and the leaders of both major parties—Clement Attlee, Ernest Bevin, Winston Churchill, and Anthony Eden—all endorsed world government in principle.[90] Churchill told the House of Commons on August 16, 1945, that during the next several years of American atomic monopoly, "we must remold the relations of all men of all nations in such a way that men do not wish, or dare to fall upon each other for the sake of vulgar, outdated ambition, or for passionate differences of ideologies, and that international bodies by supreme authority may give peace on earth and justice among men."[91] Soon thereafter, Bevin, Foreign Secretary under Attlee, endorsed Usborne's idea of a popularly elected constituent assembly chosen to draft a charter for a world state:

> I feel we are driven relentlessly along this road: we need a new study for the purpose of creating a world assembly elected directly from the people of the world as a whole, to whom the governments that formed the United Nations are responsible and who, in fact, make the world law which they, the people, will then accept and be morally bound and willing to carry out. I am willing to sit with anybody . . . to try to devise a franchise or a constitution for a world assembly with a limited objective—the objective of peace.[92]

Henry Usborne was a Cambridge-educated engineer and plant manager from Birmingham whose father had served in the Indian civil service in the Punjab. Admittedly more at home with blueprints than with political studies, Usborne combined both in his plan for inviting the world's peoples to bypass recalcitrant national governments in designing a world state. He envisioned as many nations as possible electing one delegate for each one million of population to attend a convention in Geneva in 1950. Those delegates would create a supranational authority that would control atomic energy, administer a world bank and food board, and enforce peaceful relations among member states. Ideally, enough nations would then ratify the Geneva constitution to enable world government to be established by 1955.[93]

Beyond his considerable support in Britain, Usborne gained a parliamentary following in Italy, France, Belgium, Luxembourg, and especially the Scandinavian countries. In the United States the plan was approved by the United Federalists and actively promoted by World Republic, the Emergency Committee of Atomic Scientists, the Oak Ridge scientists, and by a Nashville attorney, Fyke Farmer, who persuaded the Tennessee legislature to authorize the election of three delegates from that state. And the founding conference of the World Movement for World Federal Government, held in Montreux in 1947, enthusiastically embraced the people's convention idea, partly from suspicion of any American-dominated limited revision of the UN Charter.[94]

Popular support abroad for world government is difficult to gauge. Cord Meyer claimed that there were organized movements in thirty nations, but most of those groups were small. The major exceptions were in England, Germany, Scandinavia, and France. Indeed, in France a great surge of intellectually respectable public interest centered around an improbable American political guru, Garry Davis.[95]

Born in Bar Harbor, Maine, and raised in Philadelphia, Garry was the son of society band leader Meyer Davis. The younger Davis enjoyed an easygoing life on the fringes of Broadway before becoming a bomber pilot in World War II. On his seventh bombing mission he was shot down and interned in Sweden, but escaped and returned to the United States where he resumed his acting career and joined the postwar peace movement. In 1947 he became a member of the United World Federalists but abandoned the organization as a "cocktail-time plaything." Determined to make a dramatic personal gesture on behalf of world government, he returned to Europe, renounced his American citizenship, and declared himself a citizen of the world.[96] In September 1948, when his temporary French residency was about to expire, he caught the imagination of the French people. Walking into the "free territory" donated by the French government to the UN, Davis pitched his tent and appealed to the UN to recognize him as a world citizen. After one hundred French police hustled him out, the resulting publicity earned him an extension of his visa and the assistance of a Garry Davis Solidarity Committee. On November 19 he interrupted the UN General Assembly with a speech from the gallery demanding a world constituent assembly, an action that inspired tens of thousands of Frenchmen to demonstrate on his behalf. By late December Davis had the support of Albert Camus, André Gide, and Jean-Paul Sartre and was granted a fifty-minute audience with President Auriol. Moving to an inexpensive Left Bank hotel, "Le Petit Homme," as his admirers called him, established a World Citizens Registry and was soon receiving over four hundred letters a day.[97]

Young, pleasant, shrewd, and theatrically dressed in his old Air Corps flight jacket, Davis became a symbol of the common man's uncomplicated desire for peace. Surrounded by romantic intellectuals and courted by French Communists seeking to harness his popularity, he nonetheless hoped to kindle an international moral crusade, a new faith to counter the "empty platitudes which are prescribed daily by diplomats and [other] national representatives." Speaking for peace, world government, and a Europe freed from cold war pressures, he struck a responsive chord among peoples bone weary from the hardships of war.[98]

A definite sense of accomplishment at home and abroad thus lent hope to the American world government cause by the summer of 1949. In Luxembourg 250 delegates from eighteen nations attended the second annual conference of the World Movement for World Federal Government, and permanent headquarters were established in Paris. In the United States, supranationalism remained a major topic of media interest, and many important newspapers, including the *New York Post, New York Herald-Tribune, Boston Globe, Christian Science Monitor, Wall Street Journal, Cleveland Plain Dealer, Detroit News, Chicago Sun-Times,* and the *San Francisco Chronicle,* had editorialized in favor of world government. Opinion polls still demonstrated that over 50 percent of the American people supported world government in principle, and 22 percent had taken some sort of public action to facilitate the creation of a world state. At least to the movement's most serious advocates and critics, it seemed as if the mandate Marshall had requested was being delivered.[99]

Predictably, Congress responded. By late summer, over 120 congressmen and nineteen senators sponsored a resolution providing that a fundamental objective of American foreign policy should be to support the United Nations and seek "its development into a world federation open to all nations with defined and limited powers adequate to preserve peace and prevent aggression through the enactment, interpretation, and enforcement of world law." The House sponsors included many members of both parties and a majority of the Foreign Affairs Committee, the most sizeable legislative bloc ever to sponsor a major foreign policy measure in Congress, according to the *Christian Science Monitor.* Hearings were scheduled for October, only about one month after the Soviets successfully tested their first atomic bomb.[100]

United World Federalists testimony at the hearings was more politically astute than the year before. Their new president, Alan Cranston, focused

on the escalating cost of America's preparedness program and its con-
sequent dangers to the nation's economy, while Cord Meyer argued that
passage of the resolution would enhance the influence of the United States
in world affairs by providing a popular positive program for peace, a
realistic program for international order that would "test the true intentions
of other governments." More pessimistic about the chances of immediately
achieving world government, Meyer spoke of first steps on a long and
difficult road, mentioned the need for a negotiated settlement of specific
Soviet-American differences, and suggested the possibility of an interim
partial federation enjoying predominant world power.[101]

In short, without losing sight of their ultimate objectives, world government advocates were becoming more gradualist and more willing to adapt
to the increasing American nationalism generated by the cold war. In his
testimony on behalf of the federalist resolution, Congressman John Davis
Lodge of Connecticut noted that the previous year's appeal for an immediate conference to amend the UN Charter had been abandoned as too
ambitious and that a period of exploration and preliminary negotiation
would be required. And after emphasizing the necessity of political and
military action to defend the West against Soviet aggression, Thomas K.
Finletter explained the practical as well as the moral reasons for supporting
the federalist plan for peace. "I just do not believe," he testified, "that it is
within the nature of the American people to be able to carry out this
defense program unless it is . . . part of a total framework of which the end
is world peace."[102]

These subtle shifts in the United World Federalists' position were welcomed by the State Department. After referring to a "cooperative understanding reached on your visit to my office," America's UN representative,
Warren Austin, praised Meyer's warnings against precipitate action that
might destroy the United Nations and his desire for thorough study and
consultation between the legislative and executive branches regarding the
powers the United States would be willing to grant to the UN. The department refrained from sending critical representatives to the hearings, a
decision that led the UWF legislative director to predict House passage of
the resolution in early 1950. From both conviction and expediency, the
federalists had derived a strategy that appeared to promise success.[103]

By spring, however, it was clear that the moment of greatest opportunity
had passed. President Truman had offered no support, and at Senate
hearings in February, the State Department had opposed all of the resolutions under consideration. Deputy Undersecretary of State Dean Rusk
warned that institutional changes alone would not solve basic political
problems and that ambitious efforts to reform the UN would "unleash
divisive and disruptive forces of diverse interests and cultures at the very
moment when solidarity is of the greatest possible urgency." Assistant
Secretary of State John Hickerson also urged caution in what he termed this
"great national debate." The proposed federation, he feared, would not
necessarily be a way to achieve a more closely integrated world community,

and he wondered if Americans were willing to accept the authority of supranational legislatures and courts or to be taxed by a world state.[104] Unencouraged by the administration or the House leadership, the Foreign Affairs Committee soon turned to other business, and the Senate committee proved unable or unwilling to convert two weeks of conflicting testimony regarding a half dozen resolutions into a useful final report. As angry opposition to supranationalism exploded across the nation, as congressional supporters drifted away, and as the morale of hard working one-worlders disintegrated, the UWF resolutions remained stalled in the two committees. Then, in June, came the coup de grace of the world government movement—the sound of gunfire in the barren hills of Korea.

When the Korean War began, Cord Meyer was still chairman of the United World Federalists' executive committee, but he had resigned the presidency the previous fall. He did so partly for personal reasons. "After two years of itinerant speaking and organizing," he recalled, "I had ceased to enjoy my role as Cassandra. My repetitive warnings of approaching nuclear doom echoed hollowly in my head, and I came to dislike the sound of my own voice as I promised a federalist salvation in which I no longer believed." He had neglected his family, longed to resume his education at Harvard, and wished to escape his reputation as a remote, intense, even fanatical advocate of the federalist cause. On January 3, 1950, he confided to his journal:

> To be always talking and thinking about an imminent catastrophe is unbecoming and in a certain sense rude and barbaric.
>   The difficulty is to avoid on the one hand the unproductive and inhuman fanaticism of which I have perhaps been guilty and on the other the amused and contemptuous objectivity of some of the Harvard professors who are able to be so disinterested only because they lack sympathy for their fellow men. To be able to admit the probability of one's defeat and yet to be able to fight on without bitterness or fanaticism is the real accomplishment.

Perceived as arrogant, argumentative, teutonic, and an unrelenting advocate of his ideas, Meyer needed time and space to regain a sense of perspective.[105]

He also needed time to reconsider his postwar intellectual assumptions. Stalin's imposition of totally subservient Communist regimes on Eastern Europe cast doubt on the likelihood of Russian acceptance of supranational authority; the proliferation of atomic weapons and fissionable materials made supranational control of atomic energy increasingly difficult; and Communist party tactics in domestic politics throughout the world produced second thoughts about granting "substantial power to a United Nations that might in time come to be heavily influenced by a communist voting bloc." In Meyer's judgment, the supposition that common fear of another major war would bridge wide differences of ideologies, institutions, and competing national interests proved to be erroneous. There was no good news of damnation.[106]

With the world government movement collapsing around him, Cord Meyer returned to Harvard to improve his understanding of the Soviet-American rivalry and to ponder "the complex play of economic and political forces behind the flow of international events." He attended classes, read widely, and labored on a new book about the origins of the cold war. After examining available documents and memoirs, he became convinced that the Soviets were primarily responsible for the breakdown of the war-time alliance and that Stalin did not believe in the possibility of peaceful coexistence with the West. The world was not one, and Western civilization would have to struggle to survive.[107] By the spring of 1951, Meyer was ready to enlist in this new cause, "the worldwide effort to contain the outward thrust of Soviet power." In Washington, he met with friends in the State Department, but they told him that they could not offer an appointment to someone so politically controversial. Soon thereafter, he scheduled an interview with Allen Dulles, a man he had frequently met on the tennis courts at the Long Island houses of mutual friends. The interview went well, and in October, Meyer began his long, successful career with the Central Intelligence Agency.[108]

IV.

COLLAPSE

> Things have gotten so bad that if you say
> you prefer liberty to death you are accused
> of nationalism. If you speak of the Stars and
> Stripes, you are accused of waving the flag.
> Better hands than mine have waved the
> flag. I will not sit idly by as an attempt is
> made to raise the flag of a world federation
> above the flag of the United States.
>
> —California State Senator Hugh
> Donnelly, 1949

> During 1949, I became convinced that our
> attempts to transform the United Nations
> had been overtaken by events that could no
> longer be ignored or explained away.
>
> —Cord Meyer, *Facing Reality*, 1980

The collapse of the world government movement occurred with dramatic suddenness. From early 1947 to the fall of 1949 world government was an important intellectual and political issue in the United States, a cause that enlisted thousands of activists from many walks of life. While learned theoreticians presented the case for supranationalism and pin-striped Washington lobbyists promoted federalist resolutions in Congress, young mothers attached to their baby carriages reflectors flashing "I believe in world government," and Yale students placed in campus mail boxes live turtles with the warning "Unite or Die" painted on their shells. Eight thousand people attended a Madison Square Garden rally in June 1949 in support of American membership in a world state, an impressive and politically useful demonstration of public sentiment. Meanwhile, in Europe, the world movement also appeared to be gaining momentum—in 1949 its president, Lord Boyd Orr, was awarded the Nobel Peace Prize. But appearances, both at home and abroad, proved deceptive. During the winter of 1949–50, public interest in world government withered and congressional support began to slip away. By spring the movement was, in the words of one of Cord Meyer's associates, "a stalled bus."[1]

The United World Federalists were noticing some engine trouble in early 1949, even as their congressional campaign was enjoying so much success. Total UWF membership fell slightly from April to June, and the organization's renewal rate was alarmingly low at 40 percent. Finances were also a serious problem: in April Meyer reported a deficit of $28,000 and indicated that, unless many members donated additional money, the work of the national office would have to be substantially curtailed. Considerable funding had come from a few wealthy sponsors who were no longer willing to bear that burden.[2] Membership leveled at about thirty-eight thousand throughout 1950 but then plunged to twenty-eight thousand by June 1951. Financial difficulties remained severe, and the flight of the young and marginally committed reached crisis proportions. In May 1950 the student division of UWF convened a policy review conference to consider the implications of the worsening cold war and the failure of its movement to win much public support outside the United States. Soon thereafter, most of those students founded their own independent organization in reaction to the cautious conservatism of their federalist elders who were trying to neutralize intense nationalistic criticism. By June 1951 UWF membership was reduced to twenty-two thousand.[3]

Similar difficulties affected other world government organizations. The World Government Committee of the Association of Oak Ridge Engineers and Scientists was moribund by 1947, and the Emergency Committee of Atomic Scientists decided in November 1948 to dissolve on January 1. Members of the Emergency Committee complained of high administrative costs and found it increasingly hard to reach agreement on policies regarding the United Nations, partial (less than universal) federation, and global unification. Ely Culbertson folded his tents in 1950, and World Republic limped along on extremely small budgets. *Common Cause* expired in 1951 when Robert Hutchins left Chicago for the Ford Foundation; *World Government News* was abandoned the same year by the United World Federalists; and the *Bulletin of the Atomic Scientists* turned away from supranationalism toward more practical articles about civil defense and military preparedness. Active participation in the world government movement was rapidly being reduced to stubborn true believers and rugged eccentrics, people who, despite much political adversity, still insisted that federalism was the best, and perhaps the only way to prevent another major war.[4]

The World Movement for World Federal Government was also in trouble. There were no large membership organizations abroad comparable to the United World Federalists, and consequently the World Movement was dependent on American financial assistance. Those subsidies gradually dwindled to the point where the movement's headquarters in Paris struggled to survive on about $1,200 per month. Living under the constant threat of dismissal, its small staff had to seek private loans in order to purchase office supplies. The student affiliate was in a similar state of financial crisis, its members resorting at their world meeting in Amsterdam to auctioning their personal belongings. Meanwhile, Garry Davis's World

Citizens Registry fell into administrative chaos as his money ran dry and as he diverted his energies to other tasks such as a proposed pact among all the world's peoples not to answer any government's call to arms. In late 1949 Davis bade his friends and associates farewell in a small Paris café and shortly thereafter returned to the United States (via Ellis Island) to regain his citizenship. By 1951 the World Movement, burdened with dissension and ineffectual leadership, could not even obtain consultative status at the United Nations.[5]

The weakening of world government organizations, combined with emotional attacks from their growing number of critics, soon had devastating political effects, particularly at the state level. In the spring of 1949, even as additional states were approving the Humber resolution, it was defeated in New Mexico, Delaware, Vermont, and Texas. In early 1950 Georgia was the first to *repeal* the resolution after an angry campaign by the Daughters of the American Revolution led in Georgia by Mrs. Julius Talmadge, a relative of the governor. Rhode Island and Louisiana soon followed suit, and Humber's retreat became a rout in 1951. Meanwhile, an Oklahoma referendum on world government was defeated by a four to one margin, and the Tennessee legislature rescinded its provisions for the election of representatives to a world constituent assembly. In California in early 1950 the state's request for a constitutional amendment to facilitate American membership in a world state, a measure that had passed the assembly unanimously and the state senate by a vote of twenty-two to twelve, was rescinded by both houses in a surge of patriotic hysteria. Before debate began in the senate, the chambers were darkened, and spotlights were thrown on a large portrait of Washington behind the dais and on a nearby American flag fluttering dramatically under the influence of a hidden electric fan. A year later, a resolution was introduced in the senate to investigate the United World Federalists.[6]

Hardships were also experienced in Congress. State Department opposition, the Korean War, and sagging public interest had combined to bury the United World Federalists' resolution, and in subsequent congressional elections in 1950, world government was not a decisive factor in the victory or defeat of any candidate. A new, diluted resolution was introduced in the House, but despite its harmless appeals to support and strengthen the United Nations, the measure attracted only sixteen cosponsors, some of whom were enthusiastic cold warriors who wanted to seize the ideological initiative from the Soviets. Even while participating in the Korean War, the United States could vaguely appeal for lasting peace.[7]

These concessions in purpose clearly demonstrated how weak the world government movement had become. It began in the mid-1940s pledged to the immediate establishment of a world state as the only viable alternative to suicidal nationalism. But by 1950 the movement envisioned the gradual pursuit of supranationalist objectives within the United Nations, a process useful for "testing Soviet intentions" and for enhancing America's ideological reputation in the cold war's struggle for the hearts and minds of the uncommitted. The reasons for this collapse into nationalistic gradualism are worth exploring, as they reveal much about the nature of the movement and the conditions that caused it to advance or recede. Also, many of the political and theoretical problems that confronted world government advocates during the late 1940s would plague later supranationalist reformers who tried to modify fundamentally the nation-state system.

Politically, one of the most difficult problems for proponents of world government was how to sustain a movement based essentially on fear. Fresh memories of world war and the terrific destructiveness of atomic weapons fueled the supranationalist cause during the 1940s, but with diminishing efficiency. Uncomfortable with such fear and eager to retreat to the more immediate concerns of everyday life, Americans assumed that appropriate defensive weapons would be developed, that the United States would generally maintain a commanding lead in military technology, and that the very horror of renewed warfare would help prevent it. Also, predictions of "one world or none" began to lose force the longer the world managed to muddle along between those starkly posed alternatives. As a member of the House Foreign Affairs Committee observed in 1949: "There is growing in the minds of the people of this country a reaction against being pushed by even the atomic bomb." The "bogeyman approach" is wearing thin, for "every day that the Russians have the atomic bomb and every day it has not been used is a day that makes people feel that the reasons given [for world federation] are that much less valid."[8]

Hard to maintain, fear was also a difficult emotion to guide or direct, for how can severely frightened people be encouraged to consider calmly and logically the case for a world state? Fear can easily be paralyzing and cause its victims to hold fanatically to traditional means of achieving security. Fear is also likely to produce irrational responses, desperate measures to relieve debilitating anxiety. Indeed, such measures may appear reasonable if other courses of action are perceived as either futile or disastrous. In this regard one of the sad ironies of the world government movement was that its theoreticians indirectly made an excellent case for preventive war. For if the proliferation of atomic weapons among sovereign nation-states posed an inevitable threat to civilization and if supranational control of such weapons proved impossible to achieve, then a logical alternative was for the United States to defend forcibly its atomic monopoly. As relations with the Soviet Union worsened, it could be argued that Americans should defeat the Russians before their encroachments on vital Western interests threatened the survival of the planet. As scientist Philip Morrison concluded in 1949, the horrors of Hiroshima had inspired demands for total security, demands that implied American domination of all other major nations.[9]

However improbable that objective, there were enough public references to a *Pax Americana* during the late 1940s to cause considerable unease among world federalists. In October 1946 Bertrand Russell insisted that "if utter and complete disaster is to be avoided, there must never again be a great war, unless it occurs within the next few years." While Russell preferred voluntary world government, he believed that the next best course would be an American effort to "compel the rest of the world to disarm and establish a world-wide monopoly of American armed forces."[10] Similarly, James Burnham, author of *The Managerial Revolution*, wrote in 1947 that only the United States or the Soviet Union could effectively control atomic energy, and to do so, one of the two nations would have to control the world. Since the Soviets, according to Burnham, were already seeking global hegemony, the United States would have to do the same in order to assure its own independence and to protect civilized society from total destruction. Burnham's book, *The Struggle for the World*, was widely reviewed, and his basic argument was given mass circulation by *Life* magazine.[11]

Signals from the American military were also unsettling. In May 1948 General George C. Kenney, commander of the Strategic Air Command, told an audience in Maine that present peace was "little more than a superficial armistice" and that war with the Soviet Union was inevitable. In July Air Force General Carl Spaatz lamented that "we who profited so much from the airplane and the atomic bomb now stand to lose most by it." Once other nations obtained atomic weapons and effective delivery systems, Americans would be highly vulnerable and could only protect themselves with the most powerful armed forces in the world. And in August 1950 Secretary of the Navy Francis Matthews, speaking in Boston, bluntly advocated "preventive war." Later apologizing to President Truman, he said that he had heard so many military officers talk about preventive war that he had repeated the phrase without realizing how much it deviated from administration policy.[12]

Thus, although fear was a necessary ingredient of supranationalist success, it lacked both durability and predictability over a long period of time. Increasingly nervous about the less desirable implications of their own arguments, world federalists warned against preventive war and watched helplessly as America's sense of insecurity led to massive rearmament. In a speech to the UWF General Assembly in October 1950 William O. Douglas prayed that world federalist arguments would not be utilized for unworthy ends, and soon thereafter federalists believed it necessary to state officially that any proposed effort to "seek peace by launching an atomic attack is not only wholly immoral, but . . . would alienate our allies and bring in its wake the chaos and destruction on which dictatorship thrives."[13]

Paradoxically, while federalists complained that fear could generate dangerous irrationality, they also worried that the world government movement was too rational to become politically popular. The successful promotion of world government required the maintenance of several delicate balances—despair and hope, ideals and self-interest, emotion and reason. The last of these was especially troublesome, for although reason and logic lent enormous intellectual strength to the federalist case, they could not in themselves attract a mass following. Few if any great political movements have been inspired by syllogisms.

In late 1946 Bertrand Russell suggested that if a campaign for world government were to progress it would require the enthusiasm of a great moral crusade. Without that, nothing could be achieved, for "although from a purely rational point of view, self-preservation is a sufficient motive for all that needs to be done, self-preservation alone will not overcome the obstacles of rational thinking that are presented by ancient habits of hatred, suspicion, and envy." The atomic scientists, specialists in merchandising fear, had come to a similar conclusion. Harold Urey wrote that "a great human problem can be solved only by great and glorious ideas that cause men to lose their individual selfish and narrow desires in a great emotional and intellectual crusade." And Albert Einstein concluded that the scientists could not "arouse the American people to the truths of the atomic era by logic alone. There must be added the power of deep emotion which is a basic ingredient of religion. Unless the movement for a 'peace based on law' gathers the force and zeal of a religious movement, it can hardly hope to succeed."[14]

The world government movement, however, never became an emotional crusade. Some of the younger leaders were capable of impressive enthusiasm and self-sacrifice. Some of them donated nearly all their time and savings, postponed education and marriage, and firmly believed that they offered the only hope for humanity's salvation. But most older members of federalist organizations were much more cautious and restrained. Concerned mostly with publicity and lobbying efforts in New York and Washington, UWF stalwarts were embarrassed by youthful exuberance until finally, in 1951, the student federalists regained their original autonomy. For the UWF's competent, establishment style of leadership, heavy emotion was both bad politics and poor taste.

The world federalists' message was also a hindrance to mass crusading. It was one thing to promise Liberty, Equality, and Fraternity or Peace, Land, and Bread—those were the types of blood-coursing slogans that moved people. But it was quite different to demand Support and Development of the United Nations into a World Federal Government with Limited Powers Adequate to Assure Peace. There simply were not enough lawyers out there to constitute a mass movement.

The scientists' campaign of fear did arouse deep emotions about the dangers of atomic warfare, but as early as mid-November 1945 the *New Yorker*'s cliché expert, "Mr. Arbuthnot," was satirizing the dulled sameness of their argument. "In the stillness of the New Mexico night," the bomb "ushered in the atomic age." This age could prove "a boon to mankind" or "spell the doom of civilization as we know it." Atoms could be "harnessed" or "unleashed"; humanity "stands at the crossroads"; the bomb "has made current weapons of war obsolete" and "has made world unity essential." Hair-raising enlightenment was quickly disintegrating into atomic *déjà vu*.[15]

Even worse, the federalists' case was frequently misunderstood. Opinion polls demonstrated that the public's enthusiasm for world government was poorly informed, and a *New Republic* reporter investigating the 1948 Connecticut referendum on transforming the United Nations into world government (which passed by a twelve to one margin) discovered that many voters believed that they were merely registering their support of the UN and world peace.[16] In Congress the UWF resolution attracted a bewildering array of adherents with many different motives and interpretations of the measure's essential meaning. Some, like Congressmen Brooks Hays and Walter Judd, hoped that proposals to reform the United Nations would at least embarrass the Russians and at most enable the organization to help contain Soviet expansion. Similarly, Congressman John David Lodge assured the House Foreign Affairs Committee that the UWF resolution did not envision an international union of states; rather, it was merely an attempt to deny nations the sovereign right to wage aggressive war.[17] No wonder that Secretary of State George C. Marshall requested evidence that the public and its representatives fully comprehended the vague, general propositions they so readily endorsed.

Because the federalist case was potentially so complex in describing the nature of world government and how it might be achieved, its champions consistently sought a more understandable and less controversial simplicity. This strategy made their case less vulnerable to criticism from inside and outside the world government movement, since internal disputes could be papered over with bland generalities and external critics found few fixed positions toward which they could direct their fire. However, the trade-offs for deceptive simplicity were a reputation for vagueness and a tendency for fellow travelers to fill half-empty generalizations with their own preferred plans and objectives. "Reforming the United Nations into a body capable of formulating, interpreting, and enforcing world law" could mean anything from the powerful world state envisioned by Hutchins's constitutionalists to the minimal centralization proposed by Grenville Clark, anything from universal world government clearly superior to its member states to a restructured United Nations freed from troublesome Russian membership and dominated by Western powers determined to counter Soviet "aggression."

This vagueness, which remained a dominant characteristic of the world government case, left so many important questions unanswered. How could a world state be created? Was there a sufficiently developed global community to provide the necessary foundations for world government? Would the Soviets cooperate? How could democratic values and institutions be preserved by a government partially composed of totalitarian regimes? What powers would the new government enjoy, and how could members prevent the evolution of a tyrannical superstate? How much influence would the United States have, and what price would Americans have to pay for permanent peace?

In his testimony before a Senate subcommittee in February 1950 Deputy

Undersecretary of State Dean Rusk agreed that nations had not yielded enough freedom of action to ensure the safety of all and that man's technical capacities were beyond effective political control. But he warned against sacrificing modest gains in international cooperation in pursuit of "whimsical fashion" or "glittering formulae for perfection." He wondered whether supranationalists were acting from sober reflection or from hysteria and whether they or the American public understood the implications of their proposals. "There would be a very great danger," Rusk believed, "in our raising with other governments major questions of American sovereignty unless we knew exactly what it is we wanted, and unless we were completely convinced that that was what we did want and were willing to follow through with it and pay the costs."[18]

Assistant Secretary of State John Hickerson agreed and asked even more precise questions regarding voting arrangements, assurances against tyranny, taxation, the process of disarmament, the feasibility of a supranational armed force in an otherwise disarmed world, the extent of legal authority over United States citizens, and the changes required in the American Constitution. He insisted that discussion of international organization would be most fruitful when it concerned itself "specifically with objectives to be sought, practical steps toward these objectives, including organizational forms, and possible effects of such steps on the United Nations. Proponents of world government would have to demonstrate that "what they propose offers a better chance of obtaining our objectives and has a real chance of general acceptance. Perfection of constitutional form does not necessarily increase our chances of grappling successfully with the security problems confronting us."[19]

Federalists could not effectively respond to these questions by suggesting that they be left to a world constitutional convention. Americans were being asked to make a huge leap of faith—to authorize their representatives to meet with nations largely indifferent or hostile to any surrender of sovereignty in order to create some sort of world government that would provide the United States with maximum security at minimum cost. But why should Americans be willing to mount such a dubious expedition toward such an ill-defined objective at the possible sacrifice of existing international collaboration within the United Nations?

World government advocates had two major responses to such skepticism. Primarily they argued that whatever the disadvantages were in procedural uncertainties and commitments to sacrifice indefinite amounts of national authority, the alternative was immeasurably worse. Risks on behalf of peace, even great leaps of faith into the political unknown, were worth taking. Yet, as already indicated, doomsday descriptions of atomic warfare lost persuasiveness as people learned to coexist with cold war competition that continuously stopped short of major conflict. Perhaps Americans did not have to choose between one world or none.

The other increasingly common federalist response was that the quest for world government, however vaguely defined or difficult to achieve, was justified because it served the immediate and long-term interests of the United States. Conviction as well as expediency motivated this nationalism, which was successful in enlisting badly needed political suppport. But, as a trade-off, federalist objectives were even further beclouded: it was far from obvious why a movement so dedicated to restricting national sovereignty was so devoted to the interests of its own sovereign nation. Nationalism was a dangerously unreliable weapon for supranationalists to wield.

Federalist nationalism first manifested itself in arguments favoring United Nations control of atomic energy. Advocates of an atomic development authority were well aware that, as a highly industrialized, urbanized country with complex, integrated systems of transportation and communication, the United States had more interest than most other nations in preventing atomic war. Furthermore, federalists realized that the Baruch proposals were tailored to fit particular American concerns. In a carefully staged progression toward UN control, the United States would have retained her monopoly of weapons until the last stage. Meanwhile, the Soviets would have had to open their closed society to foreign inspection, forego development of the weapon most likely to overcome America's geographic isolation, and allow other nations to make decisions regarding Russia's peaceful uses of atomic power. Also, as Leo Szilard had once indicated to President Roosevelt, if control systems broke down, the advantages in an atomic arms race would go to the most technologically advanced state, the nation best able to harness its scientific knowledge and sophisticated production facilities to produce new weapons in the shortest possible time. In the 1940s these advantages were enjoyed mostly by the United States.[20]

In addition to supporting atomic control policies that incidentally favored American national interests, world government advocates were also aware of the economic advantages of carefully designed supranationalism. In considering the severely limited powers of their proposed world state, United World Federalists suggested that taxation be limited to a fixed percentage of national income and that the central government have no authority to utilize national resources or exercise control of key industries. Further safeguards would come from basing federal representation on the education levels and economic strength of member states as well as on their relative populations. Thus protected against arbitrary redistribution of wealth, Americans could concentrate on taking full advantage of a world economy freed of restrictions imposed in the name of national security. *Modern Industry* told its readers in 1946 that "if lasting peace can be assured only through World Government, then management has intensely practical reasons for supporting this [idea]—beyond all the vital reasons which apply to the average citizen. Industry's access to raw materials, world markets, foreign scientific and industrial discoveries and personnel depend upon the assurance of lasting peace." The American economy, by far the world's largest and most efficient, had much to gain from supranationalism's promise of political stability and freer trade.[21]

Much more welcome, however, was the promise of more political and economic freedom at home, an escape from the heavy taxation and big government that appeared to threaten free enterprise democracy. When UWF president Alan Cranston testified before the House Foreign Affairs Committee, he described himself as a businessman (California homebuilder) concerned about the economic consequences of the arms race. The enormous cost of military preparedness would produce large government deficits and a corresponding increase in inflation, a process that would destroy capital and threaten the livelihood of America's middle classes. Moreover, businessmen would increasingly become salaried administrators of state contracts, men subject to constant government interference. In agreement, *Modern Industry* warned that "if nations live under the permanent threat of war, each sovereign state will inevitably become more and more totalitarian; . . . the surest way to end free enterprise is to allow the threat of war to hang over our heads." Massive debts, high taxes, and government erosion of civil liberties and traditional economic freedoms could encourage communism at home even while it was being so expensively resisted abroad.[22]

In short, unlike nations that were less affluent or less pleased with the international political status quo, the United States had a large vested interest in stability and peace. Economically powerful and territorially satisfied, Americans had little to gain from war and much to lose from even having to prepare for it. As Robert Hutchins argued, the United States had so much more to protect than other nations and thus needed to promote change in order to conserve.[23] All peoples shared an interest in survival, but Americans also hoped to survive as a rich country of substantial economic and political influence. Self-interest and the common good neatly coincided.

The key to sustaining that coincidence was to design a world state that would emphasize stability and order rather than distributive justice. Most world federalists advanced such plans as being more achievable: the great powers, whose consent was essential to creating world government, would lose few privileges, while diversity in political, social, and economic life would be preserved. Perhaps so, but nations unable to sit at the head table could hardly be expected to embrace a supranationalism that would entail, in Harold Lasswell's words, a "minimum change in existing power relationships," and any world state firmly committed to preserving the political and economic status quo would invite civil war.[24]

The point here is not to accuse one-worlders of hypocrisy, although the political Left did that at the time. (Virtually all reformers are in some way self-interested.) But so much regard for American interests limited the movement's potential appeal abroad and undercut federalist claims to be citizens of the world. Tragically, the arguments required to gain support in the United States alienated people elsewhere, and the kind of world state the great powers were most likely to accept was unlikely to endure. These were dilemmas that most federalists only dimly understood.

Unrecognized by most American one-worlders was an even more subtle form of nationalism—a pervasive provincialism or ethnocentrism that flavored nearly all arguments on behalf of a world state. Most American supranationalists were liberals of some sort, steeped in traditions of democratic government, civil liberties, the rights of property, and the rule of law. Also, Americans were mesmerized by their own historical experience in creating a nation from thirteen autonomous units differing substantially in social and cultural characteristics, economic systems, and political power. As a result, American models of world government were predominately constitutional, federal, libertarian, procedurally democratic, and sharply suspicious of excessive governmental power. Typically, Grenville Clark spent most of his retirement trying to universalize American constitutional principles, and Carl Van Doren devoted an entire book (*The Great Rehearsal*) to the instructional qualities of the Philadelphia Convention.[25]

The American experience did contain valuable lessons for world government, but drawing and utilizing those lessons in a sophisticated manner required qualities that Americans have seldom enjoyed in abundance—an awareness of the particular social and economic context of their own political institutions and an appreciation for the value and appropriateness of institutions evolved elsewhere. One-worlders were not necessarily worldly, and supranationalists were not by definition liberated from cultural nationalism. These realities limited their effectiveness.

The paradoxical provincialism of the world government movement did not pass unnoticed by domestic critics. Reinhold Neibuhr charged American liberals with infantile lack of maturity in "trying to solve the complex problems of our global existence in purely legal and constitutional terms." This was, in his judgment, "a dubious inheritance from the whole 'social-contract' theory of government" that assumed that "men and nations create communities by the fiat of government and law." Similarly, in his book *From Many One*, historian Crane Brinton doubted that the world would be unified under American federalist principles or that human suffering could be banished through the creation of perfect legal instruments. Questioning the relevance of America's early constitutional history, he reminded his readers that Americans in 1787 had much in common, including political and military experiences that prepared them to cooperate on behalf of shared interests. This was Walter Lippmann's view as well: the colonies had been part of one empire, had already enjoyed a sense of community, and had come together at Philadelphia to form "a more perfect union."[26]

There was also skepticism abroad. From Japan it was reported that, while the idea of world government enjoyed general support, the theory of world federalism was not well understood. The Japanese had no experience with federalism, and in the Japanese language the term "government" was interpreted to mean only the executive branch of government, without reference to parliament or courts. An article in *Common Cause* suggested that American enthusiasm for limited government was not widely shared among peoples immediately concerned with various forms of colonial or neocolonial domination, and G. A. Borgese believed that "the Eastern mind" was far better able to comprehend and appreciate appeals for social justice than demands for civil liberty. Even in Europe, American principles were greeted with suspicion. Harold Urey was told by a Belgian judge that "the Federal system will be interpreted in Europe as an American system, . . . another way in which the United States imposes its institutions on the world. The Belgian people are very much afraid that the United States will impose its laws on Belgium."[27]

Some world government advocates were conscious of their cultural biases and tried to compensate. In their desire to reach the peoples of Asia, Africa, and Latin America, members of World Republic moved away from limited eighteenth-century federalism toward a functional suprana-tionalism that would use centralized governmental power to address various global social and economic problems. Members of the Chicago Committee to Frame a World Constitution also were partially successful in liberating themselves from American constitutional precedent—although their legalism was bound to Western liberal tradition, and they seemed determined to impose upon the world an only slightly modified version of Franklin Roosevelt's New Deal. It was difficult even for academics to think like citizens of the world they wanted so much to create.

Nationalism of a less theoretical, more immediately practical sort also emerged by the late 1940s. To understand this, it is essential to realize that the world government cause was not in the mainstream of the American peace movement. Few advocates of a world state were pacifists, and most feared that pursuit of peace as an end in itself might encourage aggression and war. In general, they had a dark view of human nature, assumed the inevitability of political conflict, and realized that, in the absence of world government, Americans had vigorously to defend and promote their interests within the anarchic nation-state system.

For the most part, these people did not ignore the reality of increasing Soviet-American antagonism. They favored military rearmament, supported United States participation in the Korean War (while regretting its necessity), and increasingly perceived their own supranationalist ideas as useful weapons in the cold war. In this context, Cord Meyer's conduct becomes easily explicable. His shift of employment from the United World Federalists to the Central Intelligence Agency was not, as some have charged, a sellout of the peace movement. Rather, it was a political realist's logical step once it became clear that traditional politics among nations were not being fundamentally reformed.[28] By the early 1950s, the world government cause in general was moving in Meyer's direction. In October 1950 the United World Federalists officially asserted that the United States had the opportunity "to assume the moral leadership of the world, to seize the initiative from communist imperialism and to join together in a unified front all nations truly seeking peace. This dynamic moral offensive is . . . indispensable to defense against communist aggression."[29] Mere advocacy of strengthening the United Nations into a world federation, according to Alan Cranston, would create for Americans an immediate "situation of strength" by providing a moral purpose "capable of rallying the allegiance of men of good will everywhere in the world."[30] And similarly, a UWF statement regarding the underdeveloped world sounded as if it had been written by Dean Acheson or John Foster Dulles:

> Communism feeds on desperation. The seething millions of the earth are easy prey to the rising Red tide. The free world needs a weapon.
> An idea greater than any creed of Marx or Lenin exists in the world today. It is the idea of a world organization for peace and security under law. With this idea, America can offer in terms of reality her friendship and cooperation to the world.[31]

The United World Federalists went beyond words to become active cold warriors when they broke lances with the Soviet peace campaign of the early 1950s. Designed to mobilize popular support abroad against Western military preparations, particularly the stockpiling of atomic weapons, the Russian "ban the bomb" campaign infuriated United World Federalist leaders. Cranston told his Executive Council that the Soviets wished to seize the peace issue for their own purposes and warned his lieutenants to be on guard against possible infiltration. The UWF condemned the Stockholm Peace Petition as false propaganda designed "to weaken the free world's resistance to Communist aggression," a cynical attempt to neutralize American power without providing realistic plans for effective international control. UWF members were urged not to sign the petition, and the Communist-dominated Partisans of Peace were excluded from the Rome Congress of the World Movement for World Federal Government.[32]

By this time, Ely Culbertson's approach to world government was even more closely linked to American cold war diplomacy. For although his Quota Force plan appeared to offer reasonable, achievable means of establishing supranational control of atomic weapons and prevention of major war, the proposal in practice would have been decidedly weighted against the Soviet Union. Since the envisioned United Nations police force, required to be no larger than that of any single great power, would need assistance in countering aggression, even major states would find that their apportioned strength would make them vulnerable to hostile associations or alliances. This would have been particularly dangerous for the Russians because, with the UN veto eliminated, the United States could theoretically have controlled about 80 percent of global military power—in effect creating an anti-Soviet collective security alliance sanctioned by the supranationalist trappings of a reformed United Nations.[33]

In congressional testimony, Culbertson described his plan as "a solution to the Russian problem," which he defined as "the issue of how to stop fourteen Godless fanatics from building atomic bombs." Possession of the bomb, he predicted, would enable them to utilize their hundreds of divisions to conquer both Europe and Asia, a strategy feebly resisted by an American State Department committed to "peace in our time." Only a revised United Nations could avert a third world war by controlling atomic weapons and by convincing Kremlin leaders that their ambitions would be opposed by overwhelming counterforce. At that point, the Soviets would "find it to their advantage to join the rest of the world, and the rest of the world will find it to its advantage to have them join." Effective world government would be established.[34]

But what if the Soviets refused to cooperate in their emasculation? If Russia did not submit to an atomic development authority, the UN would, according to Culbertson, give her an ultimatum: "either to stop atomic armament by submitting to the reasonable international control and inspection prevailing for all other states, or to evacuate her industrial centers in expectation of immediate atomic coercion. It is far better to have a showdown with Russia now, while we still have the overwhelming superiority, than five years from now, when they become stronger." But the famous card player offered ten-to-one odds that an ultimatum would not be necessary. The Soviets would cooperate:

> Once we are unified under an authority of higher law with a world judge, with a world policeman; once we are organized without Russia but not against her, . . . firmly determined to stop any actual or potential aggressors, Soviet Russia will find herself outside. She would be facing in a position of defiance the organized might of the world. . . . She would have no choice but to join.[35]

Culbertson's cold warriorism was unusually blatant, but in 1950 his full-bodied nationalism was shared by many within the world government movement. By that time, innocent provincialism and pragmatic efforts to design a world state that would not demand too much of the United States had yielded to strident promises that proposals to reform the United Nations, whether successful or not, would be useful weapons in a growing Soviet-American confrontation. This appeal made political sense in Washington and helped protect federalists from harsh domestic criticism, but at a price—the alienation of some peace advocates at home and abroad and, more seriously, reduced justification for the continued existence of any *world* government movement. Culbertson's odds to the contrary, the world seemed incapable of being unified.

Ironically, the maturing nationalism of the world government movement did not ultimately offer much protection from more extreme domestic nationalists, American superpatriots from the political Right. For example, the Hearst newspapers published large cartoons of wild-eyed, long-haired one-worlders peddling their idealistic patent medicines to state legislatures and hoisting world government flags above the Stars and Stripes in the public schools. "World government would enable foreign countries to write our laws, commandeer our defenses, tax or confiscate our resources and try our citizens before alien tribunals," editorialized the *San Francisco Examiner.* "To elevate another flag beside our own would be only the first step toward repealing the Declaration of Independence and nullifying the Constitution of the United States." Under a world state, Americans would "enroll themselves as a fragment of a nondescript horde under an ensign of universal subjection."[36]

Similarly, Colonel Robert McCormick's *Chicago Tribune* warned that United World Federalists' objectives "would reduce Americans to a minority who might be subject to a world constitution drafted by the backward masses of China, Russia, [and] India, . . . which either are without political and economic liberty or subscribe to very different ideas about it from those accented by the Americans." The paper reported that the federalist cause, "ostensibly a movement for establishment of a world government," was filled with radicals and wealthy Eastern liberals while "quietly in the background are veteran followers of the Communist party line." Indeed, the *Tribune* recalled that since Alan Cranston, as an employee of the Office of War Information, had tried to suppress any criticism of Russia, it was hardly surprising that his more recent objectives did not "differ materially from [those of] the party leaders convicted under the Smith Act." It seemed incredible that while the government went out of its way "to prosecute leaders of the Communist party for seeking the overthrow of the United States, . . . leaders of movements which would achieve the same result in a different direction are given a respectful audience by congressmen."[37]

An analysis in *Public Opinion Quarterly* of militant opposition to world government found a prevalence of conspiracy theories involving socialists, Communists, Jews, and the British, plots designed to destroy American sovereignty and world power. Federalist leaders were usually perceived as Communists or fellow travelers, and the rank-and-file were described as gullible innocents—naive students and veterans, impractical intellectuals, and mothers with draft-age sons. Soviet opposition to world government was dismissed as "part and parcel of the grand deception," and even a federation excluding Russia was suspect because "obviously it would be far easier for Russia to infiltrate, undermine and finally to destroy one government, than a score or more of independent governments." Simple arithmetic indicated that supranationalism would mean "abject submission to World Communism," wrote Merwin Hart, president of the National Economic Council. The yellow, brown, and black races, "controlled by Soviet Russia," would soon dominate any world state.[38]

At a time when McCarthyism was beginning to play a major role in American politics, charges of disloyalty were commonly leveled at all types of one-worlders. The Daughters of the American Revolution distributed a leaflet on world government entitled "Selling America Down the River," and their magazine claimed that the movement was "the key to Russian domination of America." Myron C. Fagan, director of the Cinema Education Guild, spoke of the "traitorous audacity" of the United World

Federalists, and conservative publicist Joseph Kamp devoted a book to the argument that the "subversive" schemes of world government advocates constituted "disloyalty if not outright treason."[39]

Some representatives of the American government shared those suspicions. In June 1946 the chairman of the House Committee on Un-American Activities investigated supposedly subversive actions by atomic scientists at Oak Ridge. After discussions mostly with military officers in charge of security, the chairman and his assistant expressed concern that scientists opposed any supervision, favored international control of atomic energy, and actively supported "some form of world government." Two years later, the committee investigated the United World Federalists and found that sixteen people whose names appeared on UWF literature were affiliated with other organizations cited as "Communist-front and/or subversive." Former UWF vice-president Thomas K. Finletter was criticized in Congress when he sought confirmation as President Truman's Secretary of the Air Force, and *Newsweek* reported in February 1953 that government loyalty investigators were asking many prospective government employees if they ever had been members of the UWF.[40]

World government advocates tried to defend themselves. They protested government harrassment, emphasized Communist condemnation of their objectives, and toughened their organizational membership requirements. United World Federalists' literature in 1950 assured the public that the group did not advocate a world organization dominated by Russia, that it was not a front for Communists or fellow travelers, and that it was not on the Attorney General's list of subversive organizations. While some members had supported groups during the 1930s and 1940s that were later declared subversive, all those people (according to the UWF) had resigned from the fronts once their questionable nature became apparent. Meanwhile, UWF had adopted a strictly worded resolution excluding all Communists and Fascists from membership.[41]

But these defenses proved inadequate. A broad coalition of veterans and patriotic organizations established the Sovereignty Preservation Council to lobby against state and federal measures sympathetic to supranationalism, an effort partially funded by the Veterans of Foreign Wars' American Sovereignty Campaign Fund. In Texas the United World Federalists was banned from the campus of Texas Tech, and a public high school teacher was forced to sever his UWF affiliations in order to retain his job. A motion picture studio even found it prudent to abandon plans to film the life of Indian peacemaker Hiawatha lest the story be regarded as Red propaganda. This was hardly an environment conducive to the healthy growth of the federalist movement or to retaining the support of the marginally committed. Membership rolls shrank, and nervous politicians headed for cover.[42]

Why were federalists targeted for such emotional and abusive criticism? To some degree, it was a product of success. Their popularity in public opinion polls, the support of over twenty state legislatures, and the endorsement of so many congressmen and senators meant that the world government movement came to be taken as a serious threat by American nationalists. Skillful political organization by the United World Federalists produced anxiety among those already concerned about American membership in the United Nations and about the growing menace of "world Communism." Federalists also suffered during this politically conservative period in the United States from being associated with the Left. World Republic, for example, was dominated by young idealists who sought a vaguely defined social justice and was funded by the liberal eccentric Anita McCormick Blaine. The wealthy eighty-two-year-old daughter of Cyrus McCormick, Mrs. Blaine lived alone in a gabled brick mansion on the Near North side of Chicago. Surrounded by musty, oversized furniture and still fond of Victorian dress, she looked, according to a *Newsweek* reporter, as if she had just stepped off the set of a gaslight play. Moving left as she grew older, she broke with the Republicans in 1920, supported Franklin Roosevelt during the Great Depression, and then backed the Progressive party of Henry Wallace. In 1948 she donated one million dollars to her World Government Foundation and announced that Wallace would be one of its trustees.[43]

Her choice alienated world government stalwarts, despite their desires to tap the foundation's rich resources. Spokesman Upshur Evans of the United World Federalists assured all interested parties that his organization had no present or anticipated connection with Blaine, while Ely Culbertson commented acidly that "anything Wallace is associated with is a red herring—doubled and redoubled." It was bad enough that only the leftist Progressive party had unambiguously endorsed world government in 1948, but now to have Wallace directly associated with supranationalism was both embarrassing and dangerous. Furthermore, Blaine's foundation was funding, and therefore profoundly influencing, the World Movement for World Federal Government.[44]

Robert Hutchins's Chicago Committee was also an embarrassment. Dominated by New Deal enthusiasts and world government maximalists, the Chicagoans produced a model constitution guaranteed to anger conservative American nationalists. The *Chicago Tribune* ridiculed the constitution's lush prose, poetic symbolism, and soaring idealism and denounced Marxist commitments to rescuing mankind from exploitation and managing property for the common good. Here, in the *Tribune*'s judgment, was a brave new world less interested in guaranteeing democratic freedoms than in assisting backward peoples to redistribute America's money.[45]

The United World Federalists was dominated by men like Cord Meyer and Grenville Clark, paragons of establishment respectability and political moderation, but some of its Advisory Board members were suspect among conservatives. Especially so were Philip Murray, president of the CIO, James G. Patton of the National Farmers Union, Rex Stout, one of the founders of *New Masses*, politically active scientists Albert Einstein and Harold Urey, and many writers once associated with supposedly "pro-Communist" organizations—Louis Bromfield, Clifton Fadiman, Dorothy Canfield Fisher, Thomas Mann, Lewis Mumford, Quentin Reynolds, Upton Sinclair, Raymond Swing, and both Carl and Mark Van Doren. Indeed, any UWF member with an activist liberal record from the 1930s and early 1940s contributed to the organization's undeserved reputation for radicalism.[46]

This reputation persisted, despite bitter criticism of the world government movement by the Left. In 1949 the socialist newspaper *Labor Action* argued that the United World Federalists failed to recognize the fundamental economic causes of war ("the efforts of each rival ruling class to integrate the world for itself"), the impossibility of federating Western liberal democracy with Russian totalitarianism, and the need to achieve a socialist reorganization of societies as a prerequisite to peace. Even more negatively, the Communist *Daily Worker* charged in March 1950 that world government, "whatever it may mean to many honest advocates of peace, is, in reality, but a reflection in the area of political ideology of the aspirations of American foreign policy to dominate the world." Among the proponents of world government, "one will find as fine a collection of monopolists, military men, and anti-Soviet careerists as can be found anywhere, together with university presidents, National Democratic and Republican Committeemen, and churchmen, the whole adding up to a sponsorship both very 'respectable' and most obviously non-radical." But conservatives were unimpressed: they were sure that leftists were at the heart of a world government conspiracy and that their objectives would intentionally or unintentionally serve the interests of the Soviet Union.[47]

This last belief points to another reason why one-worlders were so vulnerable to nationalist criticism. Given the existence of a basically anarchic international political system, it was highly likely that opposition to narrow nationalism in the United States would indirectly serve the narrow nationalism of America's competitors, particularly the Soviet Union. If all major powers could simultaneously agree to subordinate immediate selfish interests to a common long-term interest in peace and survival, then those individuals who labored for supranational objectives could avoid charges of naiveté or disloyalty. But if the Soviets were hostile toward world government and meanwhile continued to expand their political influence, then efforts within the United States to promote the national self-denial essential to creating a world state could be perceived as dangerous.

There was no satisfactory escape from this trap. As the cold war worsened, supranationalists faced a terrible dilemma. They could continue to urge moderation in American political and military policies in hopes that reason would prevail in both East and West, a strategy that could play into Soviet hands, or federalists could argue that their objectives were valuable instruments of cold war diplomacy, a position that essentially destroyed the *raison d'être* of the world government movement. Federalists wanted a world state, but they did not want, and did not dare, to weaken the United States in order to achieve it. Most refused to risk becoming the hand-maidens of Soviet diplomacy.

Realism prevailed, perhaps inevitably, as world government appeared much less achievable. The Russians were categorically opposed to a world state; European support dissipated; and American statemen uncom-promisingly insisted that the supranationalist movement diverted Amer-ican attention from more useful and important pursuits. Against those odds, it was difficult for world government leaders to inspire their troops.

Soviet reaction to world government was similar to that of the American Left. Radio Moscow drew attention to corporate executives within the movement and darkly warned of American "war-mongers" trying to pro-mote global domination "under an atomic aegis." A statement from several Russian scientists, publicly replying to Albert Einstein's appeal for a world state, was more reasonable, yet no more positive. While conceding the good intentions of Einstein and other intellectual idealists, the scientists argued that such liberal-minded people did not understand the implica-tions of what they proposed. Supranationalist ideas, the Soviets continued, originated with capitalist monopolies that "find their own national bound-aries too narrow. They need a world-wide market, world-wide sources of raw materials and world-wide spheres of capitalist investment." National self-determination was therefore a progressive force that permitted nations to maintain their political and economic independence. In a world parlia-ment, capitalist monopolies would exercise predominant influence through their control of their own nations and of colonial and neocolonial dependencies. Thus, instead of promoting peace and cooperation, world government "would only serve as a screen for an offense against nations which have established regimes that prevent foreign capital from extorting its customary profits. It would further the unbridled expansion of Amer-ican imperialism and ideologically disarm the nations which insist upon maintaining their independence." Reprinted in the *Bulletin of the Atomic Scientists*, this unemotional yet firm rejection of world government dis-heartened Americans like Einstein who desperately sought some sign of Russian sympathy and open-mindedness.[48]

Soviet intransigence also helped weaken the movement in Europe. As the cold war continued, the European Left lost interest in a world state, and committed supranationalists concentrated on European federation as a more obtainable objective that would also enhance European self-deter-mination in a bipolar world. European union had long been a dream of continental idealists and empire builders, and now it made especially good sense politically and economically. American proponents of world govern-ment generally denigrated partial federations as merely a grander form of nationalism: the basic problem of colliding sovereignties in an anarchic state system would be left unsolved, and larger units could presumably mobilize even greater military power. But these objections carried little weight.[49]

Never robust, the Euro-American World Movement for World Federal Government was reduced to a skeletal force easily dominated by anyone willing to pay the bills. As the Blaine Foundation ceased to do so, the United World Federalists filled the vacuum in order to ensure that they were not embarrassed at home by the world organization. By the time of the Rome Congress in 1951 UWF leaders were able to prevent cooperation with the Soviet peace offensive or endorsement of impractical plans to lift the world's peoples out of hunger and poverty. But such effortless manipulation only dramatized the World Movement's weakness and could hardly be used to inspire support among Americans who doubted that other peoples would embrace world government even if the United States proposed it.[50]

State Department officials made much of Soviet opposition to world government and the general waning of interest in supranationalism abroad. In a speech delivered to a UWF audience in July 1950, Francis H. Russell, Director of the Office of Public Affairs, asserted that "the Soviet Union does not have, and has never had, the slightest intention of joining in any plan of world federation." He predicted that any American effort to champion such a futile cause would bewilder other nations, distract "the free world" from its vital efforts to contain Soviet power, and "create doubts concerning our wholehearted support of international cooperative efforts in their present available form." Any premature request for world government could hinder practical day-to-day efforts to deal with immediate problems; the best would become the enemy of the good.[51]

These were powerful arguments that did much to erode domestic support for world government. It was increasingly difficult to counter the admonitions of people like Reinhold Neibuhr who believed that the establishment of world government would have to await the gradual evolution of a world community based on mutual trust, common standards of justice, and the acceptance of self-restrained majority rule. Such evolution was difficult in an environment of global Soviet-American conflict requiring the West to protect its civilization from Russian encroachment. No political program could offer Americans perfect security against either war or tyranny, Neibuhr concluded, and no sympathy could be extended to utopian escapes from essential efforts to deal prudently and responsibly with the inevitable insecurities and ambiguities of the postwar world.[52]

Relatedly, supranationalists were discomfited by charges that, in the name of perfectionism, they were undermining support for the United Nations. UN representative Warren Austin told the story of a Vermont farmer who was asked by a passing motorist how to get to Montpelier. After considerable thought, the farmer judiciously replied: "If I were going to Montpelier, I wouldn't start from here." One-worlders, in Austin's judgment, refused to take the world as it was, refused to start with the

United Nations in order gradually to improve it. Austin demanded support for the UN, including specific, constructive criticism of it as "the living, growing organism that it is, and not merely as a stepping stone into a cloud-cuckoo land of mutually inconsistent possibilities." Clark Eichelberger, president of the American Association for the United Nations, also resented federalist descriptions of the United Nations as hopelessly inadequate, even a hindrance to the progress of genuine supranationalism. These people, Eichelberger complained, viewed world government as the only path to salvation and did not hesitate to weaken the United Nations "by calling for changes which today are quite impossible."[53]

Here was another cruel trap for world government proponents, a situation tactically analogous to that of political radicals forced to deal with moderate domestic reform. As an established organization modestly contributing to international order and hoping to develop into a stronger agent of collective security and functional cooperation, the United Nations drew potential support away from the federalist cause. Federalist praise for the UN was therefore expensive politically and fogged the essential difference between international collaboration and a genuine world state. Yet to dismiss the UN as inherently inadequate was to risk alienating its many champions, the very people most likely to be converted to more fundamental change. The dilemma was never satisfactorily resolved, as enthusiastic spokesmen for internationalism and supranationalism continued to accuse each other of living in a fool's paradise.

By the early 1950s the world government movement was generally perceived as being irritatingly irrelevant, a terrible fate politically. It was discomforting to be at the center of controversy and unpleasant to be accused of treason, but it was fatal to be patronizingly tolerated, or even ignored. For a cause that depended on gathering momentum, it was a serious matter not to be taken seriously.

The movement had been beset by significant liabilities from the outset—theoretical vagueness, cold rationality, excessive nationalism, reliance on ephemeral fears of atomic war, and a vulnerability to charges of disloyalty. World federalism was always a fragile plant requiring a perfect ecosystem within which to flourish. Briefly it enjoyed such favorable conditions, but for too short a time to sink stabilizing roots.

International events were the most critical determinants of federalist fortunes. The movement was born in the aftermath of war and atomic destruction when relations with the Soviet Union, a former ally, were still unclear. Initially, deteriorating relations with the Soviet Union, prior to testing of its first atomic bomb, lent helpful urgency to the federalist cause: the United Nations was not working; time was running out; world government, including supranational control of atomic weapons, seemed for many the only hope. But soon relations worsened beyond probable repair. The Czechoslovakian coup and Stalin's hostility toward Tito in 1948 indi-

cated that the Soviets demanded total subservience within an ever widening sphere of influence, and 1949 delivered a series of shocks—Berlin,
China, and the Soviet atomic bomb. A year later came the Korean War,
which, as Cranston observed, squeezed the federalists "between those who
think it too early and those who think it too late to adopt our aims."[54]

The harsh conflicts of the cold war called into question the achievability
of world government, an issue also raised by uncompromising Soviet
hostility toward supranationalism. A universal world state, once seen by
federalists as a prerequisite to lasting peace, now appeared beyond reach,
and pressures on the American government to subordinate narrow national interests to the promotion of a world state seemed unwise. The
pervasive nationalism of world federalism was given freer reign, a process
encouraged by the tireless efforts of cold war patriots to silence suspected
sources of treason.

The world government movement was being forced toward compromises
and concessions that ultimately destroyed its distinctive personality. As
United World Federalists supported substantial rearmament, American
membership in NATO, and intervention in Korea, and as advocacy of world
government was subordinated to vague appeals for UN reform and functional cooperation, federalists surrendered their most important weapon—
their relentless, unanswerable logic. They now seemed to be saying that
great power confrontation could be avoided, that nation-states could avert
conflict through judiciously maintained balances of power, and that world
government could be approached gradually step by step. Sacrificed in this
process was the valuable federalist critique of the nation-state system,
including a sharp, unambiguous distinction between *inter*nationalism and
*supra*nationalism. It became difficult to distinguish United World
Federalists from defenders of the United Nations, a confusion unlikely to
inspire much federalist loyalty as they braced themselves against vigorous
nationalist attacks.

Unfortunately, these compromises and concessions earned few tangible
rewards. Diluted federalist resolutions remained stalled in Congress; the
UN Charter's provision for constitutional review in 1955 was largely ignored; and functionalism came to be more effectively championed by
organizations with little interest in a world state. Meanwhile, professional
patriots maintained their assault, and the United World Federalists' membership continued to dwindle. Lost in the political wilderness, the group
nearly expired in the mid-1950s and presently exists only as a shadow of its
former self. As a veteran federalist later observed, the movement collapsed
in the early 1950s and has never recovered, "despite the fact that Norman
Cousins, when he is not otherwise occupied, does from time to time issue a
manifesto on the subject."[55]

The movement's decline exacerbated its internal divisions, and those
divisions accelerated the decline. At UWF general assemblies, controver-
sies raged over how much emphasis to place on the immediate establishment of a world state, whether a partial federation should be sought if

world government were impossible to achieve, what supranational powers were essential to assure a durable peace, whether positions should be taken on foreign policy issues generally, and how much attention needed to be devoted to Washington lobbying (VIP's) as opposed to local field work (grass roots). By the time the dust settled, a popular field representative, Vernon Nash, had been fired, ties with *World Government News* had been broken, rebellious students had bolted, and many important council members had resigned. Nash subsequently concluded that UWF faltered primarily because of the arrogance of a small, self-perpetuating group of minimalist insiders who crushed all dissent. As a result, too many activists, the "sparkplugs" of healthy branches and chapters, withdrew in protest.[56]

But Nash was largely confusing cause and effect. The organization had suffered serious divisions from its founding in early 1947, but these had not precluded impressive progress over the next several years. The movement stalled in late 1949 and early 1950 because of cold war tensions, Soviet unilateralism, hysterical American nationalism, State Department hostility, and federalist theoretical deficiencies, not because internal divisions were deeper or more irreconcilable. It was true, however, that loss of political momentum, quickened by McCarthyism and Korea, generated heated debates over the prerequisites of organization survival, debates that helped convert gradual decline into sudden collapse.

Contemporary critics and later historians discovered many faults in the world government movement—simplistic ideas, Eastern elitist leadership, covert nationalism, self-defeating liberal pragmatism, and debilitating sectarianism. Yet there was also much to admire. Federalists cared deeply about the implications of atomic weapons and were prepared to go where their logic took them—to the position that supranationalism was a required ingredient of lasting peace. They wrote well, won many converts, and lobbied effectively in state legislatures and in Washington. They steered a reasonable course between fear and hope, specificity and generality, ideals and self-interest, the minimalism that seemed essential for acceptance and the maximalism that seemed necessary for endurance. They compromised partly from fear, but they also endured the slings and arrows of outraged nationalists. And finally, they consistently adhered to their basic political realism, even though forced to conclude that the same assumptions about political behavior that made world government necessary made it extremely difficult to achieve. They therefore faced the cold war squarely and accepted the reality of the political conflict they had hoped to avoid.[57]

The world government movement was not without accomplishment. It helped alert the public to the dangers of atomic energy and to the inadequacies of the United Nations. It encouraged an awareness that the nation-state was becoming obsolete, a vitally important development that mankind could not indefinitely ignore. By proposing fundamental changes in the nation-state system, it drew the heaviest nationalist fire and thereby helped modest new agencies of international cooperation achieve acceptance and respectability among a traditionally isolationist people. And it produced committed reformers, some of whom would hibernate through nationalistic winters to resume their efforts to give the world the blessings of peace, order, and good government.

In 1952, as the world government movement gasped for life, political scientist Frederick Schuman offered it both praise and hope:

> World government has become for this generation the central symbol of Man's will to survive, and of his moral abhorrence of collective murder and suicide. Some of the movements dedicated to this cause have already been corrupted by age-old evils. Others have displayed invincible ignorance toward the realities of power and the facts of life. Yet the only universalism of our epoch which proposes to give effective political expression to the timeless words of righteousness and wisdom is the universalism of the prophets of a global polity.
>
> If [the opportunity to create world government is] seized upon, no Millennial Golden Age will dawn. Men will not thereby become saints nor be magically liberated from unreason. They will still struggle with themselves and with one another for goals ignoble and noble, and find many of their conflicts desperately difficult of resolution. But the result, we may reasonably believe, will be an escape from an Inferno, wherein men like devils torture one another to death in a vain quest for salvation.
>
> It would be premature to conclude . . . that the Parliament of Man and the Federation of the World are beyond attainment. Assuredly, a generation that has achieved the means of self-destruction has also thereby achieved, if the will to live is still alive, the means of self-preservation and of a more abundant life for most of humanity than any of our ancestors ever knew.[58]

Part Two

Cold Warriors:
The Atlantic Unionist Movement,
1949–1959

V.

LOSING THE COLD WAR
THE NEED FOR A UNION OF THE FREE

> Our country *is* in danger. World War III *is* a possibility—this month, this year.
>
> —*Life*, April 9, 1951

> Stalin is winning the cold war. The Communists are closing in on us.
>
> —William Clayton, congressional testimony,
> January 23, 1950

> By federating all the Atlantic democracies . . . as the first step toward a free world government, the policy of Union of the Free puts more power behind freedom—gives it the overwhelming preponderance of power that peace and recovery require.
>
> —Clarence Streit, *Union Now*, 1949

In early September 1949 American high-altitude bombers began to detect abnormal levels of radioactivity in the atmosphere above the Pacific Ocean. Soon thereafter, similar discoveries over the North American continent confirmed what many Western scientists had fearfully predicted: the Soviet Union had successfully tested an atomic bomb. In a deliberately bland public announcement President Truman recalled that "ever since atomic energy was first released by man, the eventual development of this new force by other nations was to be expected. This probability has always been taken into account by us." By inference, what was foreseen and expected could be competently managed.[1]

Behind the public calm, however, the Truman administration was thrown into a state of alarmed confusion. In truth, predictions regarding the time required for the Russians to develop the bomb had varied widely, and 1949 had been at the low end of the scale. Meanwhile, American defenses, particularly conventional forces, had substantially deteriorated since 1945

85

due to popular pressures for demobilization and congressional insistence on fiscal restraint. The Soviets had retained a much larger armed force, and according to the president's National Security Council, "this excessive strength, coupled now with an atomic capability, provides the Soviet Union with great coercive power for use in time of peace in furtherance of its objectives and serves as a deterrent to the victims of its aggression from taking any action . . . which would risk war." In other words, once the Soviets achieved a rough balance of atomic power with the United States, the enormous Red Army would be able to intimidate the many weak nations along the borders of the Soviet sphere. The Kremlin would finally have the military capacity "to support its design for world domination."[2]

The American public was equally anxious after the Soviet atomic test. George Gallup found that most Americans expressing an opinion on the subject believed that Russian development of the bomb made war more likely, and *Time* magazine, in gauging the public's reaction to learning for the first time "how it feels to live under the threat of sudden destruction," reported that Americans were painfully aware that their atomic monopoly was gone and that the nation's concentrated industrial centers offered tempting targets for Soviet surprise attack. It was difficult to remain calm while the Atomic Energy Commission recommended dispersal of governmental agencies in Washington and as atomic scientists warned that nuclear weapons exploded upwind from the United States, one thousand nautical miles west of California, could destroy all life from Oregon to Maine.[3]

Public unease regarding the Russian bomb and the president's decision to develop a more powerful hydrogen weapon manifested itself in many ways, not all of them rational. Washington real estate firms advertised houses and lots "beyond the radiation zone." Boston architects designed a circular steel and concrete home designed to withstand heavy shock waves, while building contractors in most major cities tried to interest clients in expensive fallout shelters. Also, throughout the country, shrewd entrepreneurs sold worried customers lead girdles, aluminum pajamas, and medical antidotes for atomic contamination.[4]

Somewhat more sensibly, civil defense became a popular issue. President Truman appointed a civil defense chairman to administer a national effort, and the state of New York turned to General Lucius Clay, the successful coordinator of the Berlin blockade. Under his direction, New York City made detailed plans for a crisis, even including the installation of stretcher hooks in city buses and the use of Boy Scouts and pigeons as emergency messengers. A private Council on Atomic Implications published a *Manual for Survival* that, among other things, taught children how to take cover during an atomic attack, a technique soon routinely practiced in many public schools. Also privately, some major corporations began to prepare for atomic warfare. Standard Oil, for example, established alternative offices on a fifty-acre tract of land in New Jersey, thirty-five miles from its Manhattan headquarters in Rockefeller Center.[5]

Even the motion picture industry in 1950 and 1951 reacted to, and probably helped to reinforce, America's renewed sense of vulnerability. London Films distributed *Seven Days to Noon*, the story of a British scientist who threatened to detonate an atomic device in Central London unless the government renounced the manufacture of such weapons. Meanwhile, Twentieth Century-Fox offered salvation from outer space. In *The Day the Earth Stood Still* a league of distant planets sent their agent, Klaatu, to caution earthlings against developing atomic energy to the point where they could threaten other beings. With the help of a young war widow (veterans), her eleven-year-old son (youth), and the earth's most prestigious scientist (atomic scientists), Klaatu conveyed his demand that earthmen would have to reform their aggressive behavior or face severe punishment from a robotic, peacekeeping space patrol. More typical of the postwar interplanetary invasion films, *The Thing* described a terrible threat to America's normal peace and tranquility. A ferocious eight-foot vegetable that dined on human blood and multiplied by dropping seeds along the ground, The Thing was eventually dispatched by the military, but only after a long struggle during which human survival was at risk.[6]

By the fall of 1950 the threat of foreign invasion from a monstrous atomically armed foreign power seemed plausible to many Americans. In 1949 the Communist triumph in China appeared to deliver one-fifth of the human race into the Russian sphere. That disaster was closely followed by the Soviet atomic test and by a series of espionage cases that suggested that Western governments were riddled with Russian spies. In June 1950 North Korea, presumably with Russian permission, invaded and nearly conquered the South, and six months later American forces in Korea retreated before a massive attack by Chinese troops defending the security of their Yalu border. Psychologically reeling from that series of events, Americans pessimistically concluded that the Soviets sought world domination, that they were winning the cold war, and that the Korean conflict would escalate into World War III.[7]

Such fears were encouraged by bleak, almost panicked interpretations of Soviet intentions by political and military leaders in Washington. In its report to the president in April 1950, the National Security Council claimed that the Russians sought "the complete subversion or forcible destruction of the machinery of government and structure of society in the countries of the non-Soviet world and their replacement by an apparatus and structure subservient to and controlled from the Kremlin." The report (NSC 68) warned that "our free society finds itself mortally challenged by the Soviet system," a threat that could be successfully countered only by a strong, global defense of "free world" interests. The United States enjoyed a temporary overall lead in military power, but this gap was quickly closing as the Russians perfected atomic weapons and delivery systems and as Western nations neglected their conventional forces. In July 1950 the Central Intelligence Agency suggested that the Russians would be ready for a general war by 1952 when they would have a stockpile of as many as ninety atomic bombs.[8]

A surprising amount of this secret analysis leaked into the public domain. *Time* reported that General Omar Bradley, chairman of the Joint Chiefs of Staff, believed that 1950 would be a normal year, comparable to 1913, but that the danger of war would become acute in 1952. Economic Coordinator and former Secretary of the Air Force Stuart Symington argued that the United States was in greater danger than at any other time in its history, and Air Force General Hoyt Vandenberg predicted that war with the Soviet Union was "probably inevitable and perhaps imminent." In late 1950 *Time* informed its readers that many members of Congress feared that war was possible "at any hour" and that the nation was not yet adequately prepared to fight it. The Pentagon had a calendar, the magazine revealed, marked with an "X" for the date when the Russians would be ready to attack and a "Y" for the time when Europeans and Americans would have enough divisions to deter a Soviet invasion. "X" was predicted for 1952; "Y" for 1954.[9]

The administration's fear of the Russians was highly contagious. In October 1951 *Collier's* devoted an entire issue to a "Preview of the War We Do Not Want." Supervised by Associate Editor Cornelius Ryan, the 130-page edition included articles by Robert Sherwood, Edward R. Murrow, Lowell Thomas, Hanson Baldwin, Walter Reuther, and Arthur Koestler, all pretending to report the causes, development, and results of a world war with the Soviet Union. The war began in the Balkans, when Russia's satellite troops invaded Yugoslavia, and ended in Western victory after extensive destruction and loss of life on both sides. Russia was then reconstructed into a cooperative liberal democratic state happily introduced to the American way of life: drawings pictured Russians crowding into the "New World Theatre" to view a well-staged production of *Guys and Dolls,* while "fashion-starved Moscow women" jammed a sports stadium to witness their first style show. Such progress, however, followed in the wake of a terrible war, including the use of atomic bombs by both major belligerents. The magazine appealed for reasoned restraint from East and West before it was too late, mainly by cautioning "the evil masters of the Russian people that their vast conspiracy to enslave humanity is the dark, downhill road to World War III," a war the West would surely win because of the inherent internal weaknesses of unpopular dictatorship.[10]

The *Collier's* article was unusually dramatic, but its concern about approaching conflict with the Soviet Union was common during the 1950–51 period. In August 1950 *Time* began to include a new, regular feature section entitled "Background for War," which compared the relative strengths of the United States and Russia and considered the merits of various Western global strategies. One of the first articles carefully weighed the pros and cons of war in 1950, 1953, or several years later and concluded that the wisest course was "intensive preparation for a showdown by 1953." An earlier conflict could lead to the loss of Western Europe to the Russians, while "postponing preparations beyond a 1953 deadline is a disguised policy of drift; it is waiting for the atomic dust to settle on Chicago." For many Americans a "showdown" seemed preferable to the constant attrition of brushfire wars and the steady increase of Russian military might.[11]

Feeding on this fear and frustration, Senator Joseph McCarthy began his meteoric rise with his Wheeling, West Virginia, speech in late February 1950. In March the Senate voted to investigate his charges of Communist infiltration of the State Department, and soon thereafter the nation became preoccupied with eliminating Moscow's fifth column. In Columbus, Ohio, police cautioned teen-age clubs to beware of Communist agitators and to be suspicious of "any new member whose background is not an open book," while in Birmingham, Alabama, Police Commissioner Bull Connor threatened vaguely defined "Communists" with constant arrest, fines, and jail sentences. A member of the radio Aldrich family was dropped from the program after she was identified as a "leftie" in a right-wing publication, and even Maurice Chevalier was turned away from American shores as a potential security risk. (He had supposedly participated in a Soviet-sponsored European peace movement.) Meanwhile, McCarthy himself launched a well-publicized and popular effort to expose subversives in Washington. A Gallup poll in May 1950 found that 84 percent of respondents had heard of the Wisconsin senator and that 57 percent of those informed persons who were prepared to express an opinion believed that he was doing more good than harm.[12]

Not since Hiroshima had Americans felt so vulnerable and insecure. In 1950 and 1951 the "fall" of China, the Russian bomb, the Korean War, and mounting evidence of internal subversion led many to believe that war with the Soviet Union was highly likely. The world was clearly divided into two bitterly hostile camps, guns at the ready, waiting and preparing for a devastating atomic showdown.

The key to lasting peace seemed to be power, the power required to deter the Soviets and convince them of the futility of their global ambitions. Negotiations with the Russians were useless, Dean Acheson concluded, until the United States and her allies could deal from positions of greater strength. The Communist river was determined to flow—one could not argue with it, only dam it or divert it. Only Western power could provide deterrence and thus offer time for the Soviet system to decay and the dynamism of the Communist movement to weaken. Only a momentous democratic common effort could successfully counter Communist expansion from East Asia to West Berlin and thereby avert another world war. In the judgment of Secretary of Defense George C. Marshall, this was a fateful period in the history of the world, a period that reminded him of the critical years of the late 1930s.[13]

Recollections of the late 1930s were warmly welcomed by a man who thought he had the perfect remedy for the West's terrifying insecurities. Clarence Streit had founded a political movement prior to World War II to oppose the advance of fascism, a movement that sought to unify the democracies in a powerful federation. Streit's cause flourished briefly before it was silenced by gunfire along the Maginot Line, but he kept his hopes alive during the war. As the cold war worsened in the late 1940s, his audience began to return. According to *Fortune* magazine in 1949, "History is catching up with Union Now."[14]

The son of a farm machinery salesman, Streit was born in the small town of California, Missouri, in 1896. During his early years he read voraciously, argued incessantly, and began to absorb the energetic idealism of his mother, whose guiding principle was, "I can't, never did do anything." From her, the boy acquired a taste for romantic poetry along with a concern for the world's unfortunates. "He was always worrying about people who were bad off in India and other foreign places," his father recalled.[15] In 1911 the family moved to Missoula, Montana, where Clarence founded his high school newspaper. Attending Montana State University, he continued in journalism and used his college editorial position to oppose a student letter in April 1917 patriotically endorsing whatever war policies President Woodrow Wilson chose to adopt. Streit objected to the inclusiveness of the promise and would have preferred support of specific objectives— the encouragement of democracy, a magnanimous peace settlement, and the establishment of a league of nations. Inappropriately condemned as a pacifist, he enlisted in June in an engineering regiment that was quickly sent to France.[16]

A year later he was transferred to the Intelligence Service and in December 1918 was assigned to the Archives Division of the American delegation to the Paris Peace Conference. Concerned with security, he had access to considerable secret information related to the conference, such as position papers, minutes of meetings, and communications between the president and Washington. Disillusioned by what he read and heard, he sadly concluded that he was not witnessing a peace congress, "but an inter-allied Victory meeting, with indignation as the guiding general force and Individual Economic Interest as the chief counselor of each nation." Even the new League of Nations appeared tainted by those realities: it seemed an imperfect instrument tied to an even more imperfect treaty. In the spring of 1919, after helping to guard Wilson on his return to Washington, the unhappy young soldier left the army to resume his university studies in Montana.[17]

In 1920 he was awarded a Rhodes Scholarship but rejected Oxford in favor of marriage and a new job as a European correspondent for the *Philadelphia Ledger.* During the twenties, in his work for the *Ledger* and the *New York Times*, he traveled extensively while covering the Turco-Greek War, Mussolini's march on Rome, the Carthage excavation, and Balkan rivalries. Finally, in 1929, he settled in Geneva, where he served as the *Times*'s League of Nations correspondent for the next ten years.[18]

The period from 1918 to 1933 offered a series of good learning experiences for Streit. He noted the successful workings of parliamentary democracy in Britain, the traditional commitment to equality in France, the weighted legacy of absolutism in the newer democracies of Italy and Germany, the rise of totalitarianism, and the failures of the League either to prevent aggression or to create an effective positive instrument of international cooperation. In September 1931 he commented to his readers: "The world as seen from Geneva appears an Alice in Wonderland world, devoted to the propositions that all nations are created superior, the part is greater than the whole and the day is longer than the year." Even as the world order created at Versailles began to fall apart and as the democracies were thrown on the defensive by expansive totalitarian powers, nations in Geneva clung to their sovereignty and recklessly promoted their own particular short-term interests.[19]

As the years passed, his pessimism increased. The democracies seemed unwilling or unable to meet what was becoming a major historical crisis, and Streit increasingly wondered if he were reporting the demise of Western civilization. Nationalism had killed the League, yet no other strategy for containing the totalitarian challenge had emerged. What could be done?

In considering this problem, Streit divided the world into two parts, the democracies (including their dependencies) and the autocratic states. In so doing, he discovered that the fifteen democracies on his list controlled two-thirds of the world's trade and most of its wealth and natural resources. Essentially, the democracies owned the earth, yet they were being bullied by less powerful totalitarian states. The problem was that the democracies were not united: the same nationalism that was destroying the League was preventing democratic nations from pooling their wealth and power into a coordinated effort at collective self-defense. As a result, another war loomed on the horizon.[20]

Streit refined his arguments through five revisions of a book manuscript until he privately printed a limited edition of three hundred copies in 1938. His timing could not have been better, as the Czechoslovakian crisis dramatically taught democratic peoples the seriousness of their predicament. Soon thereafter, *Union Now* was concurrently published in the United States and Britain, and Streit's ideas were aired on American network radio, endorsed by the editors of *Fortune*, and given wide circulation by *Reader's Digest*. Streit resigned from the *New York Times*, returned to the United States for the national lecture tour, and established an organization, Federal Union, Incorporated, to promote his plan. By late 1939, *Union Now*, described by *Current History* as the outstanding book of the year, had sold ten thousand copies, and translations were available in Swedish and French. Sales would eventually reach 300,000.[21]

Streit labored tirelessly on behalf of his cause. During his first year in the United States he spent one-third of his nights in sleeping cars as he raced across the country to deliver his message before it could be overtaken by events. When France fell, after the period of "phony war" in Europe, he spent $2,000 on a *New York Times* advertisement proposing a provisional union of the United States and the British Commonwealth, an idea elaborated in another book, *Union Now with Britain*. Then, after America was deeply involved in the war, he revived his plea for a democratic union as the only means of assuring a durable peace.[22]

But the war forced him into well-ordered retreat. Federal Union limped through the early 1940s with a much-reduced membership—its 1943 convention in Peoria was described by *Time* as a drowsy affair held "in a do-gooder atmosphere of maiden ladies, ministers, matrons, high school students, and professors." Meanwhile, from his modest Washington headquarters, Streit wrote pamphlets, maintained correspondence with his most faithful followers, and tried to survive on a budget of about $12,000 per year. Unionists were attempting "to save the world on a shoestring," according to Federal Union board chairman, A. J. Priest, but at least the organization was being kept alive.[23]

Barely alive. After Hiroshima and V-J Day, Streit saw many of his remaining supporters move into the world government movement. A union of Western democracies seemed contrary to the spirit of the United Nations and offered only a gradual approach toward the global institutions many believed necessary to preserve peace and control atomic armaments. While Streit helped organize the Dublin, New Hampshire, meeting in October 1945 that energized postwar supranationalism, he could not agree to the final conference resolutions and thus kept Federal Union apart from world federalist organizations. Content to restate and defend his ideas in a new magazine, *Freedom and Union*, he impatiently waited for history to catch up.[24]

By 1950, it apparently had. Czechoslovakia, Berlin, China, the Russian atomic bomb, Klaus Fuchs, Alger Hiss, and the Korean War all appeared to demonstrate that the 1930s were being replayed. Once more the Western democracies faced a totalitarian power bent on expansion while democratic disunity discouraged an effective response. Once more world war loomed close. The appeal of one-worlders naturally waned as it became clear that the world was not one, and Streit's brand of supranationalism correspondingly regained its former popularity. For many frightened Americans in the early 1950s, a democratic union seemed the only way to preserve both domestic freedom and international peace as Western nations responded to an unrelenting Soviet challenge.

Peace and freedom—these had been Clarence Streit's fundamental objectives since the mid-1930s. He deeply valued both and did not welcome the prospect of sacrificing one in order to achieve the other. Also, he believed that the two goals were mutually reinforcing. In his judgment, free societies were essentially peaceful, and peace was a precondition of a free society. What he searched for and thought he found was an effective way to promote both, a way to counter aggressive, totalitarian power without resort to war or without abandoning domestic freedom to a highly mobilized garrison state.[25]

He agreed with Emery Reves and Cord Meyer that the world was in a state of anarchy and that atavistic nationalism was a serious threat to both peace and freedom. Logically, Streit could not deny that world government was an ultimate necessity. "We cannot," he reasoned, "give our world the tendons that mass production and consumption give it, the blood circulation that steamships, railways, automobiles, and airplanes supply, and the nervous system with which electricity permeates it, and expect it still to function as it did before we made it one organism." Modern technology and industrialism made nations, especially developed nations, increasingly interdependent, and failure to achieve a corresponding political unit was exacting a punishing price. According to Streit, the interwar failure to create institutions to deal effectively with major economic, financial, and monetary problems contributed significantly to causing the Great Depression and encouraging the rise of fascism.[26] He did not believe, however, that an acceptable form of world government was achievable during either the 1930s or 1940s. It was virtually impossible for the world's many democratic and autocratic powers to agree on any form of supranationalism, and even if they could, the result would endanger American freedom. A world state heavily influenced by peoples untutored in democracy would soon become tyrannical, and its probable efforts to redistribute global wealth could impoverish the West. World government was necessary, but it would have to be approached gradually and carefully, not in a state of panic.[27]

This was not to argue that leagues and alliances were effective, gradualist substitutes for world government. Internationalism was no answer to nationalism, only an extension of the same principle. In a league or alliance, nation-states retained their independence. Common action was thus slow, uncertain, and undemocratic, especially in an emergency, due to the need for unanimous consent and the ability of a minority of a league's population to thwart the will of the majority. In short, associations of nations did little to diminish international anarchy, and each member state was therefore required to rely on its own power to defend its vital interests.[28]

Nations were forced to strive unilaterally for security and self-sufficiency, a hopeless task with troubling implications for individual freedom. Again, Streit agreed with Reves that one nation's relative security usually caused another nation to feel insecure and that the quest for self-sufficiency produced great superstates that could exercise enormous control over their citizens' lives. Individual liberty was sacrificed to a national independence that proved to be largely illusory in an interdependent world of heavily armed great powers. Neither peace nor freedom was safe.[29]

In response to the problems of the existing nation state system, Streit proposed a union of democracies, a federation of the people most advanced and experienced politically that would serve as the nucleus of an eventual world state. In the late 1930s he suggested fifteen nations in the North Atlantic and British Commonwealth—the United States, United Kingdom, Canada, Australia, New Zealand, South Africa, Ireland, France, Belgium, Switzerland, Denmark, Norway, Sweden, Finland, and the Netherlands. These states shared a common cultural and political heritage, spoke mostly English or French, were somewhat concentrated geographically, and had all avoided war with each other for over one hundred years. In combination, they were immensely powerful. They ruled the oceans, governed half the earth, conducted two-thirds of international trade, possessed nearly all the world's gold and banked wealth, and controlled over 50 percent of every essential raw material. Together they could contain totalitarianism and prevent war by creating a decisive unbalance of power weighed in favor of the Western democracies. Peace would be guaranteed.[30]

As would freedom. Citing the American example, Streit denied that a democratic union would generate a mighty central state threatening the liberties of its citizenry. To the contrary, he maintained that an efficient, effective government of a prosperous and powerful democratic union could relieve individuals of the burdens presently imposed by weaker, frightened nation-states. Citizens would not lose their sovereignty; rather, they would agree to transfer some of it to another level of government. The powers of that government would be carefully delineated, and as in the American system, checks and balances would be used to counter arbitrary authority. Then, enjoying the blessings of federal union, individuals could travel freely, have access to open markets, pay lower taxes, and be required to offer less military service. Citizens would be freer than they were in their theoretically autonomous nation-states.[31]

The powers of the union would be those necessary to any central government in a federated nation. It would have the authority to grant citizenship and passports, represent the union in diplomatic negotiations, raise and maintain an armed force, create an internal free market, regulate foreign commerce, issue currency, establish weights and measures, administer a postal service, and operate or regulate other interstate communications. It was imperative that the central government have the authority to enforce its laws directly on the citizen, not via member states, but those powers would be constitutionally limited. Some powers would be granted to the federal government, others reserved to the states, and still others specifically denied to either in the interests of individual freedom.[32]

Regarding the structure of the democratic union, Streit suggested a division of powers similar to that of the United States along with some features borrowed from parliamentary systems. A bicameral legislative branch would consider laws within the union's jurisdiction, help elect an executive board, approve treaties and judicial appointments, and reserve the right to vote no confidence in the premier. Representation in the House of Deputies would be based upon population, one representative for every 500,000 people. (The United States would therefore have elected 258 of 554 deputies in 1940, although Streit expected party voting to transcend national identifications.) Every state would also elect two representatives to a federal Senate, with possibly two extra members for the United Kingdom and France and an additional six for the United States.[33]

The executive would consist of a board of five persons, each elected for a five-year term. Three would be chosen by direct popular vote of the entire union electorate; the other two would be selected by the House and Senate. The board would act as commander-in-chief of the armed forces, appoint judges, negotiate treaties, choose the premier, and have the power to veto new laws and to dissolve either house of the legislature. The premier would deal with most problems of day-to-day administration after the board recommended broad measures and policies.[34]

Finally, a federal judicial system would settle legal disputes between states, hear cases involving citizens of different states (or the citizen of one state and the government of another), and assure that state legal decisions conformed to federal standards. The federal supreme court would also see that both central and state governments adhered to their designated powers, a task that implied the right to declare unconstitutional legislation null and void. No government would be permitted to encroach on the rights of another or on the civil liberties of the union's citizens.[35]

Streit was convinced that this balanced federal system with its constitutionally enumerated divisions of power would provide effective, yet democratic, supranational government. Composed of the world's most mature democracies, the union would protect, not threaten, individual liberty, and the federation's probable economic growth would supplement political liberty with freedom from unemployment, poverty, ignorance, and disease. Free trade, a stable currency, lower taxes, political security, and the certainly of peace would create ideal conditions for the prosperity needed to sustain a successful democracy.[36]

All this was possible if democratic nations could abandon the seductive illusions of nationalism. Traditionally, Streit observed, men have achieved greater freedom by uniting. In the nineteenth century, nationalism was a useful means for achieving popular sovereignty and home rule as well as for creating the more comprehensive political and economic organizations necessitated by the new age of steam. But in the twentieth century, the destructive elements of nationalism began to outweigh the constructive as technology demanded larger units, as national security required too much centralized power, and as nationalism became married to totalitarian ideologies. Now once again it was time for democratic peoples to unite in defense of liberty.[37]

This advice seemed as wise to unionists in the late 1940s as it had in 1939. During that momentous decade the case for Federal Union remained basically the same, although Streit and his associates more thoroughly elaborated the benefits of federation and pursued their objectives with an even greater sense of urgency. Unionists feared that the United States was losing the cold war, that the West's deteriorating condition would lead to major conflict (perhaps atomic conflict), and that traditional nationalistic efforts to reverse this dangerous state of affairs would lead to the loss of individual freedom. Union, on the other hand, would produce victory at acceptable cost and concurrently offer unprecedented prosperity for member states.

By 1949, nearly all Federal Unionists were committed cold warriors. In his new edition of *Union Now,* Clarence Streit described the Soviet Union as a formidable dictatorship determined to enslave all mankind under its tyranny, and, similarly, one of Streit's major converts, Harold Urey, consid-

ered Russian leaders to be a "ruthless group of men" who "have no
intention of working with the rest of the world in any way whatsoever
except on the basis of a Communist conquest of the world." Former Undersecretary of State William Clayton warned that "Soviet Russia has separated
the world into two hostile camps," and the gigantic struggle between them
"is so universal and so explosive in nature that . . . it could result in
consequences too dreadful to contemplate. Indeed, the outcome of this war
may decide the question of man's freedom for a thousand years." And
Owen Roberts, retired Supreme Court justice, testified before a Senate
committee: "Our so-called peace seems little better than an armed truce.
Why is this? Because a nation that despises our ideas and our institutions,
and proposes to destroy them grows ever more powerful."[38]

These sentiments were widely shared among the American population
generally at midcentury, but unionists were especially militant anti-Com-
munists. In part, this was due to their almost mystical devotion to Western
civilization—its religious, ethical, and moral commitment to individual
freedom and its heritage of political and economic liberalism. Communism
challenged nearly every aspect of their creed. Relatedly, unionists exhibited
a siege mentality, a feeling that both at home and abroad the liberal values
of the eighteenth and nineteenth centuries were on the defensive. Most
unionists were free enterprisers and free traders who viewed suspiciously
any substantive growth of governmental power. They considered socialism
to be antithetical to individual liberty and a hindrance to economic growth,
and socialism seemed to be flourishing everywhere during the early twentieth century, even in the United States. An article in the first issue of
Streit's magazine, *Freedom and Union*, in October 1946 asked:

> How shall we preserve our freedom when the devoted efforts of a Roosevelt
> to free the forgotten man end by saddling him the more with burdens they
> were meant to lift? When they load him with heavier taxes than rich men
> paid before? Vex him with a bewildering bureaucracy? Habituate him even in
> time of peace to even greater government interference in his life, to even
> greater concentration of power in the executive and even greater dependence
> of the citizens on the state?[39]

This erosion of liberty was especially unfortunate, in Streit's opinion,
because he believed freedom to be "the best breadwinner the human race
has ever found." Wealth, he argued, comes more from freedom than from
capital. Economic growth is dependent upon new ideas, which in turn
require a receptive environment of economic incentive, political security,
and unfettered exchange of information. When productive people are not
thwarted by heavy taxation and bureaucratic interference, they can generate prosperity and rising living standards for all.[40]

Unionists were alarmed during the late 1940s because freedom seemed to
be diminishing in America and Western Europe, because communism had
expanded so dramatically after World War II, and because atomic weapons
made the democracies vulnerable to crippling attack. Streit calculated that

as a result of the war and its aftermath (including decolonization), the percentage of the world's population controlled by the democracies fell from 43 percent to 23 percent. Westerners were once the "lords of creation," Arnold Toynbee wrote, due to their technological superiority, opportunities to fill the world's empty spaces, and an ability to impose their political and economic ascendancy. But the tide was turning, and now the West was threatened with domination unless it could unite in its own defence.[41]

Streit's followers feared that the unilateral and cooperative efforts of Western democracies were dangerously ineffective. Tennessee Senator Estes Kefauver told his colleagues: "We are burdened by heavy taxation. Our armaments are expensive pyramids. Living standards are threatened in half the Atlantic community. Our economies are weakened. The area of freedom in the world has shrunk, and still shrinks." *Freedom and Union* warned that the continuous flow of American money into a weak, insecure Western European economy was creating rampant inflation, unacceptable levels of debt and taxes, and a trend toward a collective crash that would invite Communist expansion and increase the likelihood of war. Similarly, Owen Roberts informed readers of the *Saturday Evening Post* that the United States was forced to spend 18 percent of its citizens' income on national defense while the nation's debt rose to $258 billion. Americans were falling into bankruptcy, even while Europeans remained weak militarily and economically. The Russians might win the cold war without firing a shot![42]

Federal Union, it was suggested, would solve most of these problems. Through unified command and efficient division of labor, an integrated defense would provide more formidable power at reduced cost. A large, politically secure free trading area with a common monetary system would stimulate private investment in Europe, eliminate the need for American loans, increase living standards, and dampen the appeal of socialism and communism. Expanded markets for American products, combined with lower taxes, would help prevent the depression that the Soviets anticipated would bring the West to its knees. Also, a democratic union could assist colonial peoples to become independent democracies closely associated with the West, and as the union gradually increased its membership of experienced democracies, it would virtually become the world government demanded by twentieth-century national interdependence.[43]

Most important in the shorter term, however, Federal Union would enable the West to grasp the offensive in the cold war, to move boldly beyond mere containment policies that exhausted Western resources in economic assistance, rearmament, and brushfire wars. Union, according to Streit, would "bowl the enemy over with surprise"; it would "throw Communism into confusion" by demonstrating that democratic peoples knew what they wanted and were even willing to sacrifice their traditional national sovereignties in order to get it. Faced with a preponderant Western political force of considerable economic and ideological attractiveness, Soviet imperialism would stall, and in the words of Federal Union publicist

Livingston Hartley, "The lessons of history indicate that an autocracy which cannot advance is likely to be compelled in the end to retreat." Indeed, added Streit, "freedom can bring down the Communist dictatorship from within. Once the oppressed peoples see that the Union of the Free is no dream, but a living, growing giant, leading the way toward a Parliament of Man in which they may participate by overthrowing their oppressors and gaining their own freedom—what a means we then shall have to wreck dictatorship from underground!" Russia could not expect to remain "a desperate island in a sea of freedom."[44]

A democratic union would thus usher in "a golden age" in which money saved from excessive military expenditures could be used for more worthy purposes. Under what Senator Kefauver called a moral and ethical *"pax Americana,"* the United States would be safe, Europe free, the Soviets defeated, and the world eternally at peace. Here was a promise of security and prosperity without big government or high taxes, of victory over Communism without war, and of world government without any sacrifice of freedom. Here, in Clarence Streit and his movement, was a perfect marriage of small town midwestern idealism with cosmopolitan European interwar cynicism. In a world of power politics, overwhelming power would be safely and economically mobilized on behalf of peace and freedom.[45]

World government advocates had a similar vision, but faltered in explaining how to achieve a world state and then how to tame or restrain it. Streit believed that he had those problems solved primarily because he was proposing a union of democracies, not an unstable compound of political and social systems that included totalitarian dictatorships. The democracies had so much in common, including a common foe who instilled fear deep into the hearts and minds of Western peoples. Western cooperation was generally perceived as a vital need—only its extent remained in doubt. Moreover, once achieved, a union government was incapable of becoming an internal or external menace because such behavior was essentially uncharacteristic of democratic institutions.

The cultural and political homogeneity of the Western democracies led Streit and his supporters to see the Philadelphia Constitutional Convention as a useful analogy. As John Foster Dulles observed in his introduction to Federal Union's *The New Federalist:* "When our founders had only disconnected sovereignties with which to face the aggressive empires of their day, they found strength by adopting the principles of federalism." That experiment, defended so skillfully in the original *Federalist Papers,* "contains an unparalleled wealth of political wisdom upon which we should continue to draw." As did the world federalists, unionists recalled that the American nation was not easy to create despite common language, a shared British political heritage, and similar pioneering traditions. Yet formidable problems of ethnic and religious diversity, economic differences, and fierce provincial loyalties were overcome without more recent advantages of improved communications and over 150 years of experience with democracy and federalism. Streit believed that, at least among the democracies, unification was easier to achieve in 1947 than in 1787.[46]

He was convinced that democratic nations could meet in convention and, aware of the consequences of failure, agree to unite. Difficulties, apparently so numerous and insoluble, would be mostly transitional and therefore temporary. Many would prove illusory once it was understood that no one expected the immediate creation of a perfect instrument. Anticipating objections, Streit assured his readers that massive emigration from one part of the union to another would be unlikely, that defense forces could be gradually amalgamated under a council of commanding officers, and that assistance could be extended to persons injured by staged progress toward free trade. None of the problems of union were beyond the wisdom and patience of reasonable men, and democratic peoples were accustomed to achieving difficult objectives through discussion and compromise.[47] Moreover, these peoples were unlikely to create a common government that would endanger their traditional liberties. Experienced in constitutionalism, grass roots political organization, and respect for civil liberties and minority rights, the democracies would not facilitate the creation of a supranational autocracy. Nor would their common government contain totalitarian systems that would instinctively attempt to use democratic procedures in order to destroy democracy.[48]

Theoretically, unionists argued, a democratic union would also be internationally benign, because, according to constitutional historian James McLaughlin, "free people share the view of the desirability of law and order and the undesirability of promoting war as an instrument of national policy." Indeed, given their openness, deliberateness, suspicion of governmental (especially military) power, and respect for the rights of other peoples, democracies find it difficult to be successfully aggressive. Even the Russians would realize that.[49]

Free enterprise would reinforce this natural commitment to peace. Unionists maintained that socialists were wedded to nationalism and the growth of governmental power that could easily be used for aggressive purposes. Also, state support or ownership of business enterprises turned economic competition into international conflict as commerce became wrapped in the flag. Free enterprise, on the other hand, contributed to the internationalization of economic power through dispersed ownership and the need for multinational companies to placate the many states within which they conducted their business. Free peoples with free economies conditioned to free trade would be almost completely drained of aggressive warlike spirit.[50]

These were seductive arguments for many frightened Americans during the worst years of the cold war. With a persuasive combination of emotion and logic, idealism and realism, Streit offered security, peace, prosperity, freedom, and the nucleus of democratic world government all in one achievable plan. He promised the West more power at a time when it faced almost certain decline, and he promised Americans total victory at a price they could afford. His vision, at least in some form, was difficult to resist.

Once again, his timing was exquisite. By 1949, the brief for federal union had been thoroughly presented, and events favored its success. As the Soviet threat grew more menacing, as Western weakness seemed more consequential, as the danger of atomic war became more immediate, and as the United Nations demonstrated its inherent deficiencies, Americans demanded an effective, unified Western response. In Congress, hearings regarding international organization revealed considerable support for North Atlantic collective security arrangements or even for the transformation of the United Nations into a Western dominated anti-Soviet alliance. Even within the world government movement, there was increasing interest in a partial federation as an intermediate step between nationalism and a universal world state, and the United World Federalists began negotiating with Streit's group in the interests of accommodation and possible political collaboration.[51] With minimal dissent, the Senate approved the NATO treaty, which committed the United States to protecting European security, and soon thereafter America was contributing billions of dollars to the common defense. The times seemed favorable for renewed political efforts to achieve a supranational federation of democracies.

VI.

THE RISE AND FALL OF THE ATLANTIC UNION COMMITTEE

One world, embracing all mankind, we
shall not see in our time. But what we may
see, if we have the vision and the energy, is
the formation of a great western
community, at least a confederation of
federations of European and American
nations, determined to give the lie to those
who say that our civilization is doomed and
to give back faith and will to those who fear
that freedom is perishing where it
originated.

— Walter Lippmann, 1948

As a Senator I shall vote for the Atlantic
Union Resolution. In debating the North
Atlantic Treaty and the Military Assistance
Program in the Senate, I have consistently
emphasized the importance of a greater
degree of unity.

— Senator John Foster Dulles, 1949

The [Atlantic Union] resolution was not put
before Congress in 1953 because it was
opposed by Secretary of State John Foster
Dulles.

— Ambassador Livingston Hartley, 1965

Owen J. Roberts was a Philadelphia lawyer. Born into a prosperous merchant family in that city in 1875, he studied Greek at the University of Pennsylvania in the mid-1890s, earned his law degree in 1898, and, on the strength of his brilliant scholastic record, immediately accepted an appointment on the law faculty, a position he retained for the next twenty years. Concurrently, he served as assistant district attorney, lawyer for the Pennsylvania Railroad and other large corporations, and prosecutor of espionage cases in eastern Pennsylvania during World War I. In 1924 he was chosen by President Calvin Coolidge to be one of two special prosecutors in the Teapot Dome oil scandal, and although personally associated with many corporate interests, Roberts nonetheless thoroughly pursued the case until former Secretary of the Interior Albert Fall was sent to jail. As a result, the capable, scholarly Philadelphian became sufficiently honored and well known nationally to be nominated to the Supreme Court by Herbert Hoover in 1930.[1]

On the Court, Roberts generally held a conservative position, although he was unpredictable enough to be considered a crucial swing vote during the tense legal struggles of the early New Deal. He helped sink the Railroad Retirement and Agricultural Adjustment Acts but rose to the defense of the Wagner Act and Social Security. *Time* described him as "relatively impervious alike to New Dealers or conservatives, of greater physical and mental stamina than most leaders, with vast erudition, a natural oratorical voice trained to express sense rather than emotion, and an impressive presence." Ruggedly independent and pleasantly unassuming, he drove himself to work every morning in his dated La Salle and always arrived carrying his own lunch. Typically, the conservative judge's best friend in Washington was Frances Perkins, Franklin Roosevelt's liberal secretary of labor.[2]

In 1942 Roosevelt appointed Roberts head of a special commission to investigate the Japanese attack on Pearl Harbor, a politically charged task that he completed with considerable tact and fairness. Several years later, in 1945, he retired from the Court, leaving behind a solid reputation for integrity, thoughtfulness, and quiet competence. He was then seventy years old but was still healthy and energetic and had no intention of retreating to his hobbies of hunting, riding, and gentleman farming. The times seemed much too dangerous for such frivolous pursuits.[3]

Since the late 1930s, Roberts had been on the board of Clarence Streit's organization, Federal Union, and now in retirement he planned to devote most of his time to promoting a federation of democracies. (Indeed, he claimed that this was one of the reasons he had resigned from the Supreme Court.) During the late 1940s, he publicly endorsed American membership in the United Nations, favored the British loan, helped lead a citizens committee in support of the Marshall Plan, and welcomed a mutual defense pact among the nations of the North Atlantic. Then, in early 1949, he agreed to become president of the newly established Atlantic Union Committee, a group of prestigious Americans formed to win political acceptance of an impregnable democratic union.[4]

Joining him in this task was another man of considerable influence in Washington, William Clayton. An extremely wealthy cotton broker from Houston, Clayton had recently served as undersecretary of state for economic affairs, a position he aggressively used to pursue his ideas of free trade and American assisted world economic recovery. With Secretaries Edward R. Stettinius, James F. Byrnes, and George C. Marshall, Clayton concentrated his attention on projects that would simultaneously rehabilitate the Atlantic economy, assure American postwar prosperity, and contain Soviet military and political expansion. He was the chief architect of the Marshall Plan.[5]

Clayton was born on a cotton farm near Tupelo, Mississippi, and spent his boyhood in Jackson, Tennessee. Leaving school at age fourteen, he supported himself as a court reporter and as a secretary for guests at a local hotel, a job that introduced him to many important people, including William Jennings Bryan. Another guest, cotton factor Jerome Hill, sufficiently appreciated Clayton's abilities to take him to St. Louis and then on to a larger firm in New York. There, from 1896 to 1904, he avoided the city's many temptations and devoted all of his attention to learning the cotton business. Working long hours day and night, he dutifully sent most of his earnings home to his mother.[6] In 1904 he moved to Oklahoma to found a new cotton firm, Anderson-Clayton & Company, which grew rapidly as it assumed the assets of the failing enterprise Clayton had abandoned in New York. Headquartered in Houston in 1916, Anderson-Clayton established offices abroad, enjoyed a booming business during the war, and by the mid-1920s was servicing about 15 percent of the entire American cotton crop. The company continued to prosper even during the depression, although Clayton militantly fought New Deal efforts to regulate cotton production and support prices, policies he considered disastrous for the export business. From 1933 to 1935 he contributed $7,500 to the Liberty League.[7]

However, as the New Deal modified its farm policies and as Secretary of State Cordell Hull relentlessly battled for freer trade, Clayton returned to the Democratic party. In the late 1930s he supported reciprocal trade agreements, urged opposition to the economic nationalism of Adolf Hitler, and advocated enough military preparedness to help end a war so injurious to international commerce. In 1941 the Houston businessman joined the Roosevelt administration and a year later became assistant secretary of commerce.[8]

Throughout Clayton's career in public service, he seemed to subscribe to a philosophy similar to that of Charles Wilson, Eisenhower's secretary of defense: what was good for Anderson-Clayton was good for the country. During World War I, he served on the War Industries Board, Cotton Division; in the early 1940s he enlisted in the fight against German economic autarchy; and then in the State Department after the war he labored for freer trade, economic assistance to Western Europe, and the general recovery of the world trading system. In November 1945, *Fortune* magazine noted that although there was a global shortage of textile products, American cotton exports were in the doldrums due to a shortage of international credit:

> Until the world's shattered credit machinery is rebuilt and made to run smoothly again, international cotton merchants such as Anderson, Clayton cannot get the raw cotton from the gins to the mills. There is cotton, there are

merchants, there are ships, and there are mills as customers. But what, for example, is an Italian millowner going to use for money? Restoring international credit machinery is a task for government. The cotton merchants and the cotton mills and the ragged world must wait on the statesman.

As they waited, Undersecretary of State Clayton helped draft the Marshall Plan.[9]

In December 1947 Oveta Culp Hobby, executive vice-president of the *Houston Post*, sent Clayton a copy of Cord Meyer's book on the need for world government. Agreeing that a world state was both desirable and inevitable, Clayton joined the advisory board of the United World Federalists, but he soon decided that world government could not be created in time to prevent World War III. As the reins of world leadership slipped from Britain's grasp, peace depended on the United States rather than the Soviets seizing the initiative. The Russians were threatening much of the world with direct control or internal subversion and would retire only if defeated in war or if confronted by effective cold war resistance by democratic nations. The democracies would have to be unified to assure their own economic recovery and to guarantee their collective self-defense. In late 1948 Clarence Streit seemed to make more practical sense than did Cord Meyer—the welfare of both the United States and Anderson-Clayton demanded a federal union of the free.[10]

Clayton's subsequent sponsorship of the Atlantic Union Committee was a major coup for Streit. Tall, elegant, urbane, and good-humored, Clayton had the looks and manner of a polished Texas cowboy. He had many contacts in government and, as a successful businessman and administrator, could command a hearing from other corporate leaders. Also, he enjoyed the deep respect of both Marshall and President Truman. Even more than Owen Roberts, Clayton was at home in the corridors of political and economic power.[11]

Like Roberts and Clayton, the other major founder of the Atlantic Union Committee was a prestigious man of conservative background. Born in Glen Falls, New York, in 1891, Robert Patterson attended Union College in Schenectady and subsequently graduated from Harvard Law School in 1915. Soon thereafter, he joined Grenville Clark's law firm and took officer training at Clark's Plattsburg Camp during World War I. Sent to France in April 1918, the young lawyer rose to the rank of major and was decorated for "extraordinary heroism." Honorably discharged in 1919, he returned to a decade of successful corporate legal practice with the firm of Murray, Aldrich, and Webb.[12]

In 1930 President Herbert Hoover appointed the Republican Patterson to a federal judgeship, and nine years later Roosevelt elevated him to the circuit court. But he quickly leaped beyond that modest promotion to become assistant secretary of war under Henry L. Stimson. When Patterson learned of Stimson's offer, the aging soldier-judge was humbly peeling potatoes at the Professional Men's Training Camp at Plattsburg, where he was refurbishing his military skills. Laying aside his peeling knife, he went to Washington to help direct the war effort, and five months later, in December 1940, he was promoted to undersecretary of war. Good fortune was the product of good connections: he had known Stimson since World War I and was highly recommended personally to FDR by Grenville Clark, who was soon helping his protégé develop a new program of military conscription.[13]

Later in the war Patterson concentrated on procurement, earning a reputation for energy, efficiency, leadership, and a more tender regard for the interests of American industry than for wartime labor. As secretary of war from 1945 to his retirement in 1947, he unified the armed services under a single Department of Defense and lobbied energetically for larger military appropriations and universal military training. Consistently arguing that the best way to avoid war was to prepare adequately for it, he tried to assure Americans that their country would never become a threat to others: "This nation will never go on the warpath; no one can point to a case where a democratic nation, with free speech and a free press, made itself a nuisance or a menace to its neighbors." In Patterson's judgment, an innocent United States of America was called once again to resist the menacing expansion of a totalitarian power.[14]

Returning to his seventy acre farm along the Hudson across from West Point, Patterson resumed his legal practice, served as president of the Council on Foreign Relations, and lent his support to various citizens groups seeking a strong Western response to Russian aggression. Informal, modest, and well-respected, he brought considerable influence to the new Atlantic Union Committee, which now had soaring expectations of transforming Clarence Streit's dream into the dominant reality of the cold war. The need seemed obvious; Americans only awaited a call to action from men who had already earned their attention and respect.[15]

In late January 1949 a small group of leading citizens had met privately at the Barbizon Hotel in New York to consider the founding of a new political committee to promote a federal union of democracies. Citizens committees were then one of the most popular forms of political activism. Inspired by the success of the Committee to Aid the Allies in 1940 and of Americans United for World Organization during the war, citizens committees were formed to support the UN, the Marshall Plan, NATO, European unification, and tougher, less compromising cold war diplomacy. Typically as well, such organizations often sought congressional resolutions that demonstrated sufficient popular support to push cautious presidents into new diplomatic commitments. At their January meeting, the Atlantic union group defined its major purpose as mobilizing public opinion behind a resolution inviting the six nations about to sponsor the North Atlantic Treaty to meet in convention to explore the possibilities of federal union.[16]

Leadership of the Atlantic Union Committee was given to an impressive collection of solid citizens, the sorts of people likely to gain the respectful

attention of congressmen and State Department officials. In addition to
Roberts, Clayton, and Patterson, the board of governors would soon include editor and historian Herbert Agar, publisher Gardiner Cowles, scientist Harold Urey, and the editor of *Barron's*, George S. Shea. Among the
advisory council members were Warren Atherton, past National Com-
mander of the American Legion, former Attorney General Francis Biddle
and former Secretary of the Interior Harold Ickes, Congresswoman Clare
Boothe Luce, educators Sidney Hook and Milton Eisenhower, and editors
William Bohn of the *New Leader*, Russell Davenport of *Fortune*, and Pulitzer
Prize–winner Hodding Carter. Businessmen included Percival Brundage of
Price Waterhouse, Chester Davis, president of the Federal Reserve Board of
St. Louis, Paul Litchfield of Goodyear Tire, H. W. Prentis of Armstrong
Cork, and Harry Bullis, board chairman of General Mills and an influential
member of the National Association of Manufacturers.[17]

With Robert Patterson quickly retreating to a secondary role, tactical
planning for the committee devolved upon Streit, Roberts, Clayton, Walden Moore, Hugh Moore, and Elmo Roper. Walden Moore, a professor of
international relations at the University of Rochester, had worked for the
Red Cross and the League of Nations Association between the wars and
served with the Allied occupation government in Bavaria. Hugh Moore was
president of the Dixie Cup Corporation and had contributed generously to
various internationalist causes. As one of America's major public opinion
analysts, Roper was a regular columnist for both *Fortune* and the *New York
Herald-Tribune*.[18]

After a month's preparations, Owen Roberts and his colleagues publicly
announced the formation of the Atlantic Union Committee (AUC). William
Clayton told reporters that a democratic union was the "only way to stop
Russia short of war," the "only road to world freedom, world prosperity,
and world peace," while Robert Patterson warned that the West had to
unite in order to "convince the Kremlin that the democracies mean business." The North Atlantic Treaty would be a useful intermediate step to
prevent war and would bring the democracies closer together, but it would
not be adequate to assure a durable peace. The AUC supported the treaty,
Roberts indicated, but the committee would begin immediately to promote
a congressional resolution favoring a union of NATO members:

> Such a federation would offer three immediate benefits. It would strengthen
> the U.N. It would raise the standard of living and lower the cost of military
> security for all. When organized, the Union would admit other nations
> which protect individual liberty by law and practice representative govern-
> ment. In the meanwhile, it would make democracy so powerful that the
> Kremlin could not hope to start war with any prospect of success.[19]

The committee's decision to endorse NATO and thereby delay the introduction of the Atlantic union resolution was the result of a Clayton-Roberts
scouting expedition to Washington in February. After conferring with congressional leaders and Secretary of State Dean Acheson, the two men

decided that the United States was too far committed to NATO to change course during the spring. Also, in managing balky congressmen, Acheson was trying to divorce the NATO mutual security agreement from *any* immediate commitment of American military assistance; thus he hardly welcomed provocative proposals for democratic federation. Clayton and Roberts agreed to back NATO "as an emergency first step toward Atlantic Union" and believed they had in return Acheson's sympathy for their resolution to be introduced at a later date.[20]

The North Atlantic Treaty was initialed by its six founders on April 4, 1949, and was ratified by the Senate in late July. Meanwhile, AUC leaders began to woo the general public—plans envisioned a war chest of $400,000 and an eventual membership of one million organized "down to every last block in every town and city." Roberts, Clayton, and Patterson testified on behalf of the North Atlantic Treaty in hopes of generating good public relations and attracting Senate sponsors for their resolution, and Roberts was also busy cultivating support in the House of Representatives.[21]

These efforts achieved some success through June and July, especially in securing a firm commitment of assistance from Senator Estes Kefauver. Elected to Congress in 1939, Kefauver was an independent populist, a self-sufficient maverick who avoided close associations with either southern conservatives or northern liberals. In 1948 he ran for the Senate, despite the powerful opposition of the Crump political machine in Memphis, and in challenging Crump, Kefauver sought the help of Memphis banker and businessman Edmund Orgill, a man who had recently been converted to Atlantic union by Clarence Streit. The candidate gained Orgill's loyalty by reading *Union Now* and agreeing to support Atlantic union in Congress. As Orgill recalled:

> All of us . . . had been going around talking in favor of Atlantic Union at various meetings, and we decided one man in the United States Senate was worth a whole lot of us talking to civic clubs. We were impressed with Estes' House record too, but I would say it was Atlantic Union that decided us to risk Mr. Crump's displeasure by coming out publicly for him. And, you know, at the time of his death, Estes was still working for Atlantic Union. He was a man who never broke faith.

The candidate became senator, was genuinely converted to the Atlantic union cause, and agreed to introduce its resolution on July 26, 1949.[22]

The resolution requested the president "to invite the democracies which sponsored the North Atlantic treaty to name delegates, representing their principal political parties, to meet this year with delegates of the United States in a Federal Convention to explore how far their peoples, and the peoples of such other democracies as the convention may invite to send delegates, can apply among them, within the framework of the United Nations, the principles of free federal union." Seventeen other senators, including J. William Fulbright, Walter George, Guy Gillette, Lister Hill, John Sparkman, and Joseph McCarthy, joined Kefauver in sponsoring the resolution in the Senate, while four congressmen (Hale Boggs, George Smathers, Walter Judd, and James Wadsworth) concurrently introduced the measure in the House.[23]

In promoting Atlantic union, Senator Kefauver emphasized that it was impossible for the United States to "give positive assurance of our help to our European allies and at the same time preserve freedom of action by Congress." If the terms of the NATO treaty were strengthened to make the alliance automatic, then Congress would be disregarding constitutional principles concerning its right to declare war, and independent European states would be given a blank check guaranteeing American assistance regardless of their own diplomatic conduct. Yet reservations to safeguard American interests in these matters and preserve freedom of action would cast doubt on the certainty of the American commitment. In short, an alliance could not well serve the primary purpose of the nation's foreign policy, "to secure our free way of life without having to fight a recurring world war every generation." A much more effective instrument would be a federal union that would strengthen Atlantic unity, stimulate Western economic recovery, and offer more formidable power at reduced cost. "We cannot in this atomic age," he concluded, "rely on antiquated diplomatic niceties. We need not waste more precious moments awaiting the force of public opinion. . . . We do not kill time; time kills us."[24]

The State Department, however, was cautious. Failing to give the "green light" that Atlantic union leaders expected, Secretary Acheson declined to comment on the resolution and urged thorough study by Congress and the administration. The force of public opinion *would* therefore have to be marshaled, and Roberts now called upon the local AUC chapters being established throughout the nation to make their voices heard.[25]

The times seemed favorable to such an appeal: not only were Americans increasingly fearful of war with the Soviet Union, but Western unity in various forms was a popular proposition among political leaders in both Western Europe and the United States. In the aftermath of a second world war and in the preparatory stages of a third, Western democracies felt a strong need to stand together. The Marshall Plan was a reflection of that need, as was the North Atlantic Treaty. Among plans for Western integration, the most popular and politically successful were proposals for European unity—proposals centuries old, but largely unrealizable until Europe suffered two terrible civil wars within a single generation. After World War II, European states were weak, demoralized, and unlikely to regain their former grandeur. Their economies were shattered, their military establishments exhausted, and their empires shaken. Excessive nationalism was partially blamed for those disasters, and in a new age of large political and economic superstates, nationalism seemed doubly dangerous. Old rivalries might resume at the very time that individual European nations were unable to defend themselves from the great powers on their periphery.[26]

There were other reasons why European integrationists were optimistic during the late 1940s. Eastern Europe was severed from the West, leaving a more homogeneous group of states to consider political or economic union. A divided Germany removed the threat of Teutonic domination of any new federation, and a weakened Britain raised hopes that she would develop a more cooperative, continental outlook. Also, Western Europe shared a common fear of Communist imperialism and a common reliance on American protection. In theory, unity could assist European economic recovery, provide more effective defense against Soviet encroachments, and diminish dependence on the United States.[27]

Americans strongly encouraged European unification. The Marshall Plan demanded a common, European approach to economic recovery, and after negotiating the North Atlantic Treaty, the United States favored coordinated military preparations and the creation of a European Defense Community. It was assumed that these measures would in turn help produce political unity, a goal Americans considered highly desirable. A united Europe, with its large common market, would no longer need American assistance and would offer excellent opportunities for American trade and investment. Also, by integrating West Germany into a larger Europe, a federation could neutralize aggressive German nationalism while providing Western Europeans more effective defenses against internal or external threats from the Soviet Union.[28]

For a while after the war there seemed to be a good chance of achieving political unity. Many Europeans, including important former members of the Resistance, favored federation as one means of revitalizing their tired continent. Committees were struck, declarations pronounced, and meetings convened, culminating in the founding of the European Union of Federalists in 1946 and the assembly of the first Congress of Europe at The Hague in May 1948. That enthusiastic gathering was addressed by Winston Churchill who promoted his particular plans for European confederation. The former prime minister had suggested British union with France during the Nazi invasion of Western Europe in 1940 and in 1943 had proposed a postwar world community of closely associated regional organizations within the framework of the United Nations. To the degree that he spoke for Britain, Churchill seemed to suggest that that nation was willing to end its historical aloofness from continental affairs. Meanwhile, in France, public opinion polls demonstrated that 74 percent of French citizens favored a union of Western European countries, while 65 percent endorsed a "United States of Europe." Men like Jean Monnet and Robert Schuman worked tirelessly for unity, and even Charles de Gaulle desired a confederated Europe.[29]

Problems arose in translating theory into practice, especially since words like "federation," "confederation," "union," and "unity" meant such different things to different people. A Council of Europe Consultative Assembly met in Strasbourg in August 1949 under the presidency of Paul-Henri Spaak. French Premier George Bidault told the group that a united Europe could come about only "by giving up some sovereignty, and the assembly agreed to consider common European nationality and common political structures as well as issues of economic policy, social security, and public works. But the British now dragged their feet, as did the Scandinavian countries, wary of Franco-German ambitions. As a result, the federalist movement was confined to functional economic arrangements—the Schuman Plan (merging French and German coal and steel industries) and, ultimately, the Common Market.[30]

American leaders were unhappy with this lack of progress. Marshall Plan administrator Paul Hoffman leaned on the Europeans to integrate their separate economies, while Secretary of State Acheson demanded common European defense planning as a prerequisite to American military aid. A group of visiting American congressmen invited to Strasbourg bluntly asked their hosts why, after the United States had provided $12 billion of aid, federation remained such a distant goal. Congressman Walter Judd insisted that Europeans had "a choice between voluntary federation or union by involuntary compulsion [by the Soviet Union]," while Congressman Howard Smith grumbled: "I came to Strasbourg to hear how European unity can be achieved. I have heard nothing except how it cannot be done. At the end of a journey through different European countries you end up with all sorts of money and you can't even buy a cigar. There are too many passports, too many languages." There was even a citizens group within the United States established to encourage European federation, the American Committee on United Europe, led by William J. Donovan and Allen Dulles, both of whom had presided over American intelligence operations (mostly in Europe) during the war.[31]

Meanwhile, there was support in Europe for wider, transatlantic unity as well as purely European integration. Indeed, some Europeans saw the two ideas as being closely related. Paul Reynaud, president of the Economic Commission of the Council of Europe's Consultative Assembly, reasoned that while both objectives were desirable, European union would have to come first lest American mass production industries ruin their European competitors. George Bidault, on the other hand, believed that European unity depended upon broader associations with Britain and the United States, a view shared by smaller continental states jealous of their larger neighbors and by Europeans generally who were impressed by Europe's postwar weakness.[32]

Winston Churchill hoped for close transatlantic ties. In his famous Fulton, Missouri, "iron curtain" speech in March 1946, he appealed for a "special relationship" between the British Commonwealth and Empire and the United States:

> Fraternal association requires not only mutual understanding . . . but the continuance of the intimate relationships between our military advisors, leading to common study of potential dangers, similarity of weapons and manuals of instruction and inter-change of officers and cadets at colleges. It should carry with it the continuance of the present facilities for mutual

security by the joint use of all naval and air-force bases in the possessions of either country all over the world.

Several years later he publicly told General Eisenhower that if the English-speaking nations could unite, the rest of the democracies would soon follow.[33]

Churchill was promoting something more than a formal alliance and something less than a political federation. In his *U.S. War Aims,* published in 1944, journalist Walter Lippmann called it an "Atlantic Community," a description that became popular during the postwar period. "The Atlantic nations," he wrote, "should not have divergent foreign policies since all are involved if any one of them is at war with a great power. A house divided against itself cannot stand." Common policy would require what Englishman George Catlin called "organic consultation"—a "network of agreements and understandings that, as a matter of right, there will be a habitual exchange of information and views in the ordinary routine of the foreign offices, the war offices, and the departments and agencies which regulate international commerce." Sharing common values and common interests, the Atlantic nations constituted "a living community" that needed to think and act as one.[34]

Some Europeans, however, pushed well beyond vague appeals for community or confederation. Atlantic Union organizations were established in Britain, France, the Netherlands, Belgium, and Luxembourg. In late October 1949 the International Committee for the Study of European Questions, a group including Paul Reynaud and Maurice Schumann of France and Lords Vansittart and Brabazon in England, reported in favor of Atlantic union, and at a loftier level, foreign ministers Stikker of the Netherlands, Lange of Norway, Van Zeeland of Belgium, Sforza of Italy, and Morrison of Great Britain all endorsed a federal union of Atlantic democracies. Count Sforza envisioned "an association without limits" if the international situation further deteriorated, and Herbert Morrison anticipated the day when "there will be a common citizenship for all peoples in the North Atlantic community with all barriers to thought, travel, trade, and understanding swept away." Meanwhile, closer to home, the Canadian Senate in June 1950 passed with only one dissenting vote a resolution nearly identical to the one introduced by Senator Kefauver.[35]

Evolutionary developments in NATO would also encourage American Atlantic unionists. A North Atlantic Council was established to coordinate Allied defense policies, and in May 1950 it agreed to create "an integrated force under centralized command." (General Eisenhower became Supreme Commander in December.) Integrated defense policies soon required cooperation in related policy areas as well, which led to a Defense Production Board, a Financial and Economic Board, and a Temporary Council Committee to reconcile alliance defense requirements with the economic capabilities of its individual members. There was also an effort to breathe life into Article Two of the NATO treaty, which committed members "to eliminate conflict in their international economic policies and . . . encourage economic collaboration." In the fall of 1951 the Ottawa Conference of NATO foreign ministers promised more cooperation in economic and cultural matters, a pledge that, according to *New York Times* reporter James Reston, gave new life to the phrase "Atlantic Community." Both Reston and his colleague Anne O'Hare McCormick agreed that the Western democracies had ventured into uncharted waters and that "a new Atlantis might some day emerge from the narrowing seas."[36]

American unionists held some reservations about both European unity and the NATO alliance. William Clayton doubted that a European federation could be created in time to deter the Soviets, and he argued that Western European economies were too similar to combine into a prosperous free trading area. Streit was somewhat more charitable but worried that "a Western European Union cannot stand without far stronger economic aid and political guarantees than the United States can wisely give a sovereign state." Such a half-way measure would diminish chances of creating a larger union, and inevitable European desires for independence, perhaps even cold war neutrality, would divide the democracies and undermine their efforts to contain Soviet expansion. "Only with the inclusion of the United States," the Atlantic Union Committee believed, could "a union of democracies achieve a viable economy and sufficient defensive strength to assure peace."[37]

Similarly, NATO was at first perceived by many unionists as a half-way measure potentially injurious to more fundamental progress. Much stronger than an alliance, a union would have a single foreign policy, a more effective and efficient defense force, and a stronger economy. Mutual commitments could not weaken as time and conditions changed, and a union would gain strength as it prospered economically and added new democratic members. Although NATO was producing close cooperation, particularly military cooperation, among its members, it stopped well short of political federation. As a *New York Times* reporter commented during the Ottawa Conference, there was much support for democratic union in general, "but when the ministers leave the sunny uplands of the future and descend from generalities to immediate concrete problems, they are not in much agreement." Like world federalists, worried Atlantic unionists doubted that the great chasm separating nationalism from supranationalism could be leaped in a series of small steps.[38]

But despite such reservations, unionists were pleased by Western preoccupations with unity during the late 1940s and early 1950s. Given the pervasive interest of so many influential people in European unity, NATO, "Atlantic Community," and Atlantic federation, AUC leaders were convinced that they were on the cutting edge of history. Also, given mounting fears of war with the Soviet Union, there existed a sense of urgency that might move people beyond intermediate measures to the pooling of sovereignty deemed essential to economic recovery and an enduring peace.

After Kefauver introduced his resolution in July 1949, the Atlantic Union

Committee's strategy was to generate maximum publicity, educate public opinion regarding federal union, increase the membership of the committee's local chapters, gain the adherence of many prominent Americans, and then persuade Congress to request the president to invite the Atlantic democracies to a federalist convention. Some elements of this plan worked better than others. While the movement failed to generate much public enthusiasm or to swell its membership rolls anywhere near its targeted one million, it did appeal to a relatively large, prestigious elite who were influential enough to win impressive congressional support. Progress was promisingly steady as the nation experienced the darkest days of the cold war.

During its first two years, the committee enjoyed a good and lively press. Its clipping service reported that from the fall of 1949 to the fall of 1950, over 200,000 agate lines were devoted to federal union in the nation's newspapers, a total that rose to 300,000 the following year. Although most of this reportage was informational, there was significant editorial support as well. Endorsements of the resolution came from the *Baltimore Sun, Detroit News, Minneapolis Morning Tribune, Pittsburgh Post-Gazette, Louisville Courier-Journal, Augusta Chronicle, Brooklyn Eagle, Dallas Morning News,* and the *New York Herald-Tribune,* and both the *Washington Post* and the *Christian Science Monitor* offered much more than routine applause.[39] The *Post* argued that passage of the resolution would moderate the unwise military emphasis of American diplomacy and "show the world that the maintenance of peace is as much the American goal as preparedness for war," while the *Monitor* welcomed Atlantic union as "the most likely blend of realism and idealism to be hoped for" during these times of atomic cold war:

> The Atlantic Union people have a great deal of history and human nature on their side. The rule of law has normally grown from small units to larger ones where there were common ideals and interests. Moreover, in the world's experience, the great periods of peace have been those policed by some great power—as the Pax Romana and the Pax Britannica. The most immediate purpose of the Atlantic Union would be to establish a Pax Democratica.[40]

Even the cautious *New York Times* concluded that "sheer necessity" was forcing Western democracies toward what America's founders termed "a more perfect union." Now, "it is time to be done with doubt and apologies and get our courage back. This is what the growing union of the free ought to mean."[41]

Among nationally circulated magazines, the greatest assistance came from the Luce empire, perhaps due to Streit's conversion of *Fortune's* managing editor, Russell Davenport, in the late 1930s. Also, after the war, both Clare Boothe Luce and Henry Luce III were members of the AUC advisory board. *Life* insisted that Atlantic union be seriously considered, and *Time* devoted a cover story to Clarence Streit in March 1950. Meanwhile, *Fortune* suggested that union was essential for peacefully defending Western freedom and predicted that assurances of free trade, free enterprise, and lasting peace would fuel unprecedented economic growth. Atlantic union offered "the greatest political and economic opportunity in history, by comparison with which the opening of the North American continent was a modest beginning."[42]

Articles explaining and encouraging federal union appeared in other large circulation magazines, such as *Look* and the *Saturday Evening Post*, as well as in more specialized publications like *Kiwanis Magazine* and *Glamour*. Also, there was editorial support from the Left to balance Luce's more conservative views. *Commonweal*, the *New Leader*, and the *New Republic* all perceived Atlantic union as an effective means of protecting American security, and the *New Republic*'s editor, Michael Straight, further argued that Westerners needed such supranationalism to assure effective cooperation and inspire needed loyalty and sacrifice.[43]

This publicity found the public in a receptive state of mind. By 1950, most Americans believed that the Russians sought world domination, that they were winning the cold war, and that Soviet-American conflict was likely within the next five years. Americans thereby favored larger defense expenditures, development of the hydrogen bomb, civil defense, and universal military training. Losing confidence in the United Nations, they also strongly approved the North Atlantic Treaty.[44]

The extent to which they endorsed Atlantic union, however, is difficult to judge because so much depended on how the question was phrased. Pollster Elmo Roper, an officer in the AUC, thought he saw increased sentiment in favor of federal union. Since 1946 he had asked Americans if they believed that, among various alternatives, a "world government of democracies" was "the best" agency for peace. Sixteen percent responded affirmatively in 1946, 25 percent in 1948, 30 percent in 1949, and 48 percent in 1950. But in 1950 Roper had subtly altered his question: he asked if federal union was *one* of the best hopes for peace, and he did not list it in opposition to other "hopes," such as world government or the United Nations. Compounding the confusion, the Gallup Poll in 1950 asked whether the North Atlantic Treaty nations should seek "closer relations, or union," a single concept in Gallup's view. Sixty-four percent of the respondents thought this was a good idea, and 8 percent considered it "fair"; but meaningfulness was lost in a poll that lumped two possibilities into one.[45]

When Gallup focused on union itself, asking Americans if they favored a federal union comparable to the forty-eight states of the United States, 36 percent thought this a good idea, with another 8 percent judging it fair. The total of 44 percent was encouraging to unionists and seemed to represent substantial progress since late 1949 when a National Opinion Research survey found only 19 percent in support of a "single federal government." Yet the questions were so abstract. Were Americans actually prepared to submerge their nationality into a democratic, supranational federation?[46]

It was difficult for realistic unionists to answer that question positively, more difficult than it had been for world government advocates. Atlantic union was probably not fully understood by most Americans, despite its analogies to their own experience, but what most bothered leaders of the Atlantic Union Committee was the obvious lack of any popular mass movement on their behalf. Mothers were not putting "Union Now" bumper stickers on their baby carriages, nor were students neglecting their studies and delaying their marriages to labor for the cause. Worried Americans were not sending checks to Owen Roberts, and, far worse, few were joining the Atlantic Union Committee. By September 1951, there were 136 local chapters and four state branches, but total paid membership stood at only 8,158. While this represented a 250 percent increase in one year, the figures were unlikely to impress some ill-disposed senior senator from the state of Indiana, and letters from the committed were not going to overflow the White House mail room. The public opinion polls were useful, but they did not account for the Atlantic Union Committee's substantial progress in Congress in 1951. Popular emotions were never harnessed to Clarence Streit's plan as well as they had been to visions of world government.[47]

But what the AUC lacked in public support it more than made up for in the reputation of its leadership. College coeds were not pinning William Clayton's picture on the wall next to Cord Meyer's, but Clayton was much more likely to be invited to the White House for dinner. The Atlantic Union Committee began and remained an elitist organization, powerful enough to enjoy easy access to the executive branch and persuasive enough to win over nearly one-third of the House and Senate.

During the early 1950s, the committee continued to be vigorously led by Owen Roberts, William Clayton, and Elmo Roper, with Clarence Streit in the wings to keep everyone on the doctrinal straight and narrow. Many names were added to the advisory council—educators, clergymen, editors, former government administrators, and a disproportionately large number of businessmen. In its first year of activity, the council attracted the presidents of Rutgers, Radcliffe, Dartmouth, Brooklyn College, and the Universities of Michigan, Arkansas, Kansas, and Virginia. The Episcopal bishops of New York and Southern Ohio joined the AUC, as did the editor of the Baptist *Christian Herald*. Many newspaper and magazine editors, particularly from the South and Midwest, lent their support—a long list that included such diverse publications as the *Wisconsin State Journal*, the *Arkansas Farmer*, the *Chicago Defender*, and the *Minneapolis Star*. Among government administrators were a dozen men who had held federal cabinet posts at the assistant secretary level or higher, three governors and four former governors, and the wartime chief of naval operations, Admiral Ernest King. Businessmen—from presidents of small local companies to chief executive officers of the country's industrial giants—were soon listed by the hundreds.[48]

The committee also made several ad hoc attempts to organize appeals for Atlantic union by particular groups of distinguished Americans. For example, in August 1950 nine State Department alumni sent a letter to Senator

Tom Connally favoring a democratic union of unchallengeable political and economic power. Signatories included Joseph Grew, former undersecretary of state and ambassador to Japan, Paul Porter, who had headed America's economic mission to Greece, and William H. Standley, former ambassador to Russia. Twenty-two leading businessmen asked General Eisenhower for his reaction to the need for Atlantic democracies to pool their resources for defense, and nine high ranking military officers and veterans leaders advised Secretary of Defense George Marshall that it was no longer possible for individual sovereign states to maintain an adequate defense—the NATO partners needed single, unified departments of defense and foreign affairs.[49]

The major challenge for AUC's strategists was to orchestrate this elitist support to achieve maximum effect in Congress and the State Department. Timely speeches and press conferences were offered in New York and Washington; the joint appeals from leading businessmen, military officers, and diplomats were all publicized within the six months period prior to the reintroduction of the AUC resolution; and select delegations of Atlantic union advocates met personally with the secretary of state and the president. The committee hoped that such coordinated efforts, assisted by the public's fear of war and the West's quest for unity, would lead to the triumph of democratic federalism.

Shortly after Senator Kefauver introduced the AUC resolution in July 1949 the House Foreign Affairs Committee held hearings on "the development of the United Nations into a world federation." This was the United World Federalists' day in court, the climax of their four years of postwar activity, but the unionist movement was allowed a brief appearance and could witness with satisfaction the ultimate course of the deliberations. To perceptive observers, it was clear that the one-worlders had fought the good fight and lost.

In his own testimony before the House Foreign Affairs Committee, Senator Kefauver conceded that only a democratic world government could prevent wars, but a world state including the Soviet Union would be neither democratic nor successful. Atlantic union, he insisted, was the next logical step after the Marshall Plan and the North Atlantic Treaty, "the next in a series of moves through which democracy is seizing the initiative from the tyrants." Owen Roberts also emphasized both the impracticality and undesirability of world federalism in 1949—the Russians would not likely join a federation, and if they did, they would seek either to destroy or to dominate it. Americans would have to accept the reality of two worlds.[50]

Committee members moved toward similar conclusions as the hearings progressed. Although impressed by the sincerity and logic of UWF witnesses, the Committee refused to endorse their resolution. Indeed, many supporters of the resolution saw it as a means of driving the Russians out of the UN and thereby organizing the non-Communist nations in a grand coalition on behalf of containment. This was not quite what Atlantic unionists had in mind, but its rationale could be tied to the unionist cause. Even

Cord Meyer's fallback position (that if the Soviets refused to join a federation, other nations could proceed without her) pointed in the direction of Clarence Streit's "Union of the Free."

In February 1950 the Senate held its hearings on revisions of the United Nations Charter, and this time, Atlantic unionists were well represented. Speaking on behalf of the twenty-five cosponsors of the Atlantic union resolution, Senator Kefauver warned that by 1952 the Soviets would have enough atomic bombs to destroy many of the great cities of Western Europe, a development that could undermine the defensive value of the North Atlantic Treaty. At about the same time, the Marshall Plan was scheduled to terminate, and it was doubtful that the American economy could carry the burden of renewing such a massive aid program. Time was thus short if Americans were to move beyond piecemeal policies and adopt an effective, affordable "over-all plan for peace."[51]

A series of Atlantic union specialists then testified before the Senate committee—Owen Roberts on the political and jurisdictional aspects of the unionist proposal, William Clayton on economics, William Patterson on defense, and Harold Urey on atomic and scientific implications. Together, they tried to convince their audience that an atomically armed Soviet Union was successfully on the march, that communism could conquer the world either by military conquest or by forcing democratic economies to collapse under unbearable defense costs, and that only a democratic union could offer adequate protection at an acceptable price. In order to survive in the postwar era, Americans had to choose between universal government (probably impossible) or "an imbalance of political, ideological, economic and military power between the east and the west" (clearly achievable). The democracies could, if united, deter the Soviets, weaken their imperial power, restore Western economic prosperity, and attract the support of the uncommitted. Atlantic union would reduce military expenditures, dispel fear of war, and restore and strengthen the free enterprise system. "It would give a great new hope to the world that we are on the road to permanent world peace."[52]

The State Department's reaction to the Atlantic union resolution was unequivocally negative. While Deputy Undersecretary Dean Rusk agreed that closer associations within the Atlantic community were desirable, he cautioned against placing exaggerated faith in institutional changes to solve basic political, economic, and military problems. Furthermore, he had the same reservations about democratic union as he had about world federalism: he doubted that Americans fully understood the proposal or would accept its political and economic implications. More specifically, John D. Hickerson, assistant secretary of state for United Nations affairs, asked if Americans were prepared to cede power in such fields as foreign policy, control of armed forces, taxation, currency, immigration, and exploitation of the nation's natural resources. What effects would federal union have on agriculture, industry, and labor in the participating countries? Would Americans prove willing to accept a blend of political systems as well as minority status in a union parliament? Would negotiating a political federation increase or erode Western unity, and what would be the reaction of nations left out of the new association? In short, Hickerson considered the AUC proposal vague, essentially unendorsed by the American people, and likely to breed conflict among allies and jealousy among nations excluded from the Western federation.[53]

Kefauver was furious. "I regret the necessity of making this observation," he told his Senate colleagues, "but the State Department's lack of vision at this time is shocking and alarming to many of us. If there ever was a time when we were in urgent need of creative leadership, it is now." The West had lost vast territories to dictatorship, remained on the defensive in both Europe and Asia, and daily drifted closer toward major war. Yet recent congressional solutions, intended to make American foreign policy more positive, efficient, and coherent, have all been discouraged by the secretary of state. Regarding Atlantic union, senators were told that "the Department cannot support this resolution until we answer to its satisfaction a series of school-teacher questions with a few $64 questions mixed up with them." The State Department, Kefauver charged, had no interest in taking advice from the people or their representatives and greeted every proposal for peace with a request for time to consider and reject:

> My heaven, Mr. President, the one thing we do not need is time to consider. We need to utilize the brief time we have . . . to quit drifting and start moving. I am afraid the hydrogen bomb wears no wrist watch. It is not a question of the democracies doing too much too soon, as it is a question of the slow-moving democracies coming up again with too little, too late.[54]

The senator claimed that Atlantic unionists had effectively answered most of Hickerson's questions about their proposal. Their resolution only requested an exploratory conference that could be organized in a way to minimize the price of failure. Congress and the people would have an opportunity to ratify any agreement, and nations not originally included would later be able to join if they could participate democratically. As for public opinion, beginning the exploratory process would encourage the maturation of support, while simply waiting for a clear mandate would be both futile and dangerous:

> Mr. President, the State Department looks through its mirrored windows and sees the American people ready to enter entangling alliances, ready to make the hydrogen bomb, but it sees them unready even to explore whether they can win simply by forming an Atlantic Union.
>
> We who have been elected to the Senate know that it is not enough to consider what the people think at any given moment. We must also judge what they may be thinking later on—on second, third, or fourth thought, in light of events. We must have vision, or we go down to defeat. I appeal to the State Department to think in those terms.[55]

But during the early 1950s, the State Department never did change its mind. In May 1951 an AUC delegation lobbied Dean Acheson personally, but to no avail. The secretary remained opposed to the resolution and would suggest no modifications to make it useful or acceptable. In December the department reiterated its view that the calling of a convention, even an exploratory meeting, would be interpreted by other nations as an American commitment to create a federal union. Unofficial efforts to encourage unity would be tolerated, but until there was a clear public mandate for Atlantic union, the government wished to avoid even mentioning the subject to its allies. Essentially, Acheson had little use for the AUC. When John J. McCloy asked him what private citizens could do to develop a program for peace, the secretary suggested that the proper role for citizens groups was simply to support government policies and programs.[56]

John Foster Dulles was no more helpful. He had privately endorsed Federal Union in 1939 and had even helped draft a congressional resolution for federation, a proposal he once discussed with Jean Monnet. In the late 1940s Dulles contributed articles to Streit's magazine, *Freedom and Union,* wrote the introduction to the 1949 edition of *Union Now,* and publicly endorsed the AUC's objectives during his New York senatorial campaign. (His successful opponent, Herbert Lehman, also favored Atlantic union.) But despite those early flirtations, Secretary of State Dulles was almost as unencouraging as his predecessor. When Roberts and Streit met with him in February 1953 he warned that an American proposal for federation would disrupt more immediate objectives—the European Defense Community and broader efforts to unify the nations of Western Europe. He also considered a diluted AUC resolution in 1955 to be "untimely" and later told his assistant, Christian Herter, that he "did not want a bunch of amateurs muddling up the international situation." This sort of reasoning baffled Senator Kefauver, who wondered how someone like William Clayton could be a valued colleague one day and then a "muddler" on his first day of retirement.[57]

Blocked by the State Department, AUC leaders tried to convert President Truman. A large delegation visited the president in early 1950 to inform him of their objectives. Truman vaguely replied that "nothing but good" could result from their efforts but withheld any commitment of support. Later delegations also failed. The president publicly endorsed European union and urged democratic nations "to stick together and to build their strength together," but while in office he never endorsed the AUC's proposed exploratory convention. The issue did not arouse the president's interest; his relations with Senator Kefauver were never cordial; and the State Department was always there to smother any flickering enthusiasm in a blanket of caution. Letters to the president regarding Atlantic union were routinely referred to the department.[58]

Lacking encouragement from either Truman or Acheson and diverted by the outbreak of war in Korea, the Senate failed to act on the Atlantic union resolution. Undaunted, Kefauver reintroduced it in January 1951 and, in cooperation with allies in the House, constructed an impressive list of cosponsors and pledged voting support. By fall, he had twenty-eight collaborators in the Senate and 110 in the House, a diverse group that included cold warriors like Richard Nixon, champions of Atlantic Community like Christian Herter, and old-fashioned liberals like Senator Guy Gillette, an Iowa Democrat who condemned the militarism of Truman's early postwar diplomacy. Clayton believed he could count on House Speaker Sam Rayburn, and AUC leaders claimed majority support on the House Foreign Affairs Committee.[59]

It was a crucial moment for the Atlantic Union Committee. American fears of war with the Soviet Union were at their height, and the State Department was determined to forge a more unified Atlantic alliance. There was significant elitist support for Atlantic unity in Canada, Britain, and Western Europe. AUC membership and financial contributions were growing rapidly, and in November the organization held its first annual Congress of Delegates in Memphis. The seeds planted by Clarence Streit in the late 1930s now seemed about to produce a full harvest.

But the harvest never came: like the United World Federalists in 1949, the Atlantic Union Committee faltered just as it appeared to be on the brink of success. In both the House and Senate, the AUC resolution was denied hearings as more immediate issues crowded committee calendars—the rearmament of Western Europe, the Korean War, and major foreign policy hearings following Truman's dismissal of General Douglas MacArthur. The delay sapped the morale of unionist leaders, who concluded that they could not maneuver around the indifference or opposition of the State Department, and AUC members were also becoming apathetic as momentum was lost. Local chapters became largely inactive, and it was difficult to raise the committee's budget of $9,000 per month. Market researcher Elmo Roper complained that federal union was the hardest thing he had ever tried to sell, as respondents regarded the proposal as too visionary to warrant their time or money. Moreover, there was growing opposition from patriotic groups and the Hearst-McCormick press. By late 1953, Roper found that only 6 percent of the American people believed Atlantic union to be "the best" means of promoting world peace.[60]

What went wrong? As with the United World Federalists, there were many interrelated reasons for the unionists' decline. Organizational problems hindered the group from its founding. The sense of emergency that buoyed the AUC's hopes and attracted public and congressional support inevitably waned, and concurrently, nationalist criticism increased and further undermined congressional enthusiasm. The ideas of the Atlantic union movement were also being subjected to good, critical analysis, often difficult to rebut. And, finally, moderate and gradualist methods of achieving Western unity were being employed, a promising, tangible reality that lured Atlantic unionists away from their discouraging battle for uncompromised supranationalism. When unionists ultimately did win congressional approval for their resolution in 1959, it was, in Clarence Streit's judgment, an adulterated product.

Organizationally, the AUC's major problem was that it failed to become a mass movement. While the world government crusade was one of the most popular reform efforts of its time, Atlantic unionists never caught fire, never aroused the emotions of the young, the socially conscious, and the politically committed. Due partly to choice and partly to fate, the AUC remained narrowly elitist. Elitism certainly has its advantages in a society where some people are more equal than others. Aware that Nelson Rockefeller had once given Streit free office space in New York City, reminded that Henry Luce supported federal union in the widely read pages of *Time* and *Fortune*, and directly confronted by the likes of Owen Roberts, William Clayton, Robert Patterson, Joseph Grew, and the early John Foster Dulles, congressmen could hardly ignore the Atlantic union movement. But supranationalism was a radical idea to American leaders just getting used to internationalism, and politicians were understandably nervous about racing too far ahead of the voters. Unionists suffered from having such shallow grass roots.[61]

This problem was never satisfactorily addressed. Mesmerized by successful citizens committees of the past, AUC managers gloried in the quality of their adherents. They collected legions of retired establishment middleweights and allowed themselves to be led by men well advanced in years. (In 1950 Roberts was seventy-five years old, and Clayton seventy.) Also, the organization's hierarchy was heavily dominated by men either in, or closely identified with, American business. In vain did the group search for token Negro and labor board members, and by early 1951, it was forced to conclude that unfortunately it was perceived as a "Park Avenue organization."[62]

But AUC's precipitous decline was due to much more than the organization's immodest respect for good pedigrees. World government advocates had convincingly argued that their cause was the only effective answer to the atomic bomb—there would be one world or none. It was less obvious that federal union was the only effective answer to the Russians. There were many other responses, including military rearmament, a new intelligence agency, the Marshall Plan, NATO, and foreign aid. Also, partial federation lacked the simplicity, grandeur, and soaring idealism of world government—the unification of all humanity to save the planet from atomic destruction. Streit's disciples accepted a divided world and envisioned a massively armed Western megastate that would intimidate all rivals, hardly an ennobling prospect, despite its commitment to the defense of democracy.

Still, the public might have considered it necessary if the alternatives had been frightening enough. Americans did deeply fear war in the early 1950s, and anticommunism was a powerful sentiment. The problem for unionists was that, like concern about the bomb, preoccupying fear of the Soviets could not be sustained. Americans had other things to worry about and daily lives to lead. Moreover, the Russians themselves were uneasy about the American state of mind and sought to modify it. They asserted their readiness to help negotiate an end to the Korean War, warned of the horrors of atomic weapons, and encouraged a popular global peace movement. Concentrating on consolidating their postwar empire, the Soviets also avoided provocative actions that would increase cold war tensions.

Meanwhile, having rushed to the assistance of Greece and Turkey, financed the Marshall Plan, joined their first peacetime alliance since the late eighteenth century, sent troops to Korea, and commenced development of the hydrogen bomb, Americans were psychologically in need of a breather. Although frustrating, containment policies seemed to be redressing the balance of power and restoring stability to the shell-shocked postwar world. Weary of Korean casualty lists, foreign loans, and burdensome taxes, Americans were ready for the presidency of a General Eisenhower, not of another General Washington.

Under those circumstances, there was less sense of urgency about the Russian challenge. The cold war was still several years from its first substantial thaw, but at least Americans were seldom hearing that they were reliving the summer of 1939. American military strength had doubled from June 1950 to March 1951; Communist party membership in Western Europe was down 30 percent in Italy and France (compared to 1946); and Korea had been saved if not united. In April 1951 Secretary of Defense Marshall complained that Americans were letting down, losing their sense of urgency, and *Time* published a cartoon of both Congress and the public complacently snoozing under a tree. "Where was the clear and present danger?" the magazine asked.[63]

Americans were not asleep. They were anxious about Communism at home and abroad and aware that war with the Soviet Union remained a serious possibility. They continued to live under the dark shadow of the atomic bomb. But their brief feeling of panic was gone, a casualty of successful policies, continued Soviet-American peace, and human nature. Shouts of alarm, which shortly before expressed a popular mood, now seemed paranoiac, and Atlantic unionists who continued to muse about the demise of Western civilization and America's loss of the cold war were preaching to a shrunken congregation. Their proposals also seemed increasingly unnecessary and extreme. In July 1951 the AUC's executive director lamented the public's devotion to personal concerns, and a year later, he concluded that the deep fear that had contributed so much to the committee's success was lost. War with the Soviet Union no longer seemed imminent.[64]

Equally troublesome and even more bewildering to unionist cold warriors was a harsh political attack from conservative nationalists. Only a month after Senator Kefauver introduced the AUC resolution, a coalition of eighty-five patriotic organizations announced their intention to oppose Atlantic unionists as well as world federalists. Both groups, they feared, would reduce American armed forces to internal police units and sacrifice other essential aspects of national sovereignty, ambitions that appeared sinister as well as naive. A spokeswoman for the National Defense Committee of the Daughters of the American Revolution reasoned that "since these idealists would have us weaken our position, both in the matter of arms and national security, we cannot but believe that their attempt is Communist inspired, although they [unionists] may not be aware of the fact."[65]

In late 1951 the *Saturday Evening Post* editorialized that "defense doesn't require America to go socialistic." Alarmed by the NATO conference at Ottawa, the magazine feared a plan "to sell out American independence as a nation," a scheme to "socialize" the United States by international action. Under a cloud of secrecy, the nation was being nudged toward supranational government involving vast new boondoggles at the expense of the American taxpayer. Americans, the *Chicago Tribune* predicted, would ultimately pay all the costs of Western defense, would have to lump its economy with that of Europe, and watch helplessly as the predominance of European socialism spread to North America. The *Tribune* favored Atlantic federation only if other nations became states in the American Union.[66]

In vintage isolationist prose, John S. Knight wrote in the *Detroit Free Press* that supporting Europe's stumbling economies would drain the American treasury and exhaust its gold supplies. Distribution of American wealth and resources would lower her own living standards without effectively rescuing private enterprise in Europe, and elimination of passports and immigration restrictions would make the United States "a happy hunting ground for the crackpots of the world." "At the risk of appearing to be unenlightened," Knight concluded, "I am writing no checks and joining no committees for a federated world until someone can convince me that Uncle Sam won't be left holding the sack." With similar suspicion, the *Washington Times-Herald* warned against the supposedly noncommittal "exploratory" character of the Atlantic union resolution: "A man who intends to spend a quiet evening at home does not make a date with his girl friend, reserve a table at a night club, and climb into his dinner clothes."[67]

In his book *We Must Abolish the United States*, Joseph Kamp darkly reminded his readers that Clarence Streit had once been a Rhodes Scholar and that the first advocate of "Union Now," who wrote in 1780 that he would devote his life to the reunion of the British Empire, was Benedict Arnold. John T. Flynn also noted Streit's Rhodes connection and worried about the hundreds of rich, influential Easterners who promoted the Atlantic union cause. Even the cautious John Foster Dulles was not immune from Flynn's attack: "However tough and pragmatic this gentleman is when breaking a lance with a professional [legal] adversary, he can, when he puts his weapons aide, adjust his wings, spread them bravely and take off in the circumambient clouds of religion, philosophy, and politics; and can turn flipflops and nosedives in competition with the professors, theologians, social philosophers, and global architects on a most impressive scale." Americans had a new secretary of state who had once concluded that "the sovereign system is no longer tolerable."[68]

This nationalist criticism, which hardly facilitated the unionists' political progress in Washington during the early 1950s, mystified the group's conservative, militantly anti-Communist leadership. Some of them believed that the world federalists were suspect. California architect Edgar Bissantz wondered if searching investigations might disclose Communist penetration of the United World Federalists, and fellow AUC board member Stella Osborn reported to J. Edgar Hoover that federalists' opposition to unifying the democracies against Communist expansion seemed to verify "rumors of Communist infiltration." Believing herself immune from such charges, she described Russian leaders as "a cold-blooded group of murderers of nations and men" that needed to be decisively defeated. "There is only one way to deal with a rattlesnake," she insisted, "and that is to strike first, and at its head." Thus it must have been painful for her to be accused by Congressman Clare Hoffman of "climbing into bed with the Reds." Similarly, Hoffman insisted that he needed no advice from Owen Roberts, "who would haul down the Stars and Stripes and run up the international rag."[69]

Actually, much like the United World Federalists, the Atlantic unionists were nationalists as well as supranationalists, a characteristic that did much to undermine their intellectual credibility. Clarence Streit's original voting formula for federal union placed the United States in a commanding position politically, and even more equitable arrangements would have permitted the United States to exert enormous influence upon her democratic allies. Writing in *Freedom and Union*, William L. White, roving editor for *Reader's Digest* and editor of his father's *Emporia Gazette*, argued that union would enable the United States to police the troublesome European states that Americans were pledged to defend, to assure that Europeans contributed their fair share to Western defense costs, and to see that Americans received something (European goods) in return for financial aid and heretofore unrequited exports. Americans, he said, were "tired of dashing off to die for Gallant Little Globia, of fighting the Korean War in Splendid Isolation, and of always getting a whipping in this matter of foreign trade. Let's think of ourselves for a change. Let the Eagle Scream!"[70]

Most unionists were less effusive, but no less clear in indicating how Americans could benefit from a democratic federation. William Clayton repeatedly maintained that a North Atlantic common market was essential to European and American economic prosperity, and AUC literature emphasized that money saved from armaments and foreign aid, combined with expanded European and colonial markets, would create jobs and thereby prevent an otherwise inevitable postwar depression. A transatlantic union would offer a peaceful, secure environment for capital investment and thus render European socialism irrelevant. Neutralism would be discouraged, and European policies regarding Korea, China, and other non-European nations could be coordinated with American objectives. Also, Germany could be harnessed to those purposes in a manner that would prevent her from again becoming a political and economic danger to the West. These were satisfying visions: in an American-dominated democratic federation, which in turn would dominate the world, the United States could retain at minimum cost her extraordinary early postwar status.[71] Livingston Hartley predicted:

> The United States . . . cannot expect to maintain indefinitely the favorable position in the world we now enjoy in relative power, influence and security. This danger can be avoided by an expansion of the American system of federal union beyond the United States. In the past we expanded this system from the Atlantic to the Pacific and then stopped. The apparent shape of things to come emphasizes the need to bring about somehow a further expansion of this system.[72]

Relatedly, there was an exclusiveness about the Atlantic unionist proposal that was only partly a practical effort to restrict membership to the most experienced democracies. Such a union was a partnership of the nations (except Russia) that had dominated world politics for three hundred years and were reluctant to yield their preeminence. American unionists were filled with gloom about the decline of Western civilization, including the future of the white race. Writing to Michael Straight, William Clayton lamented the world's archaic political and economic structure but found hope in a union "confined to people of the white race and with the same ideals of human liberty."[73] With less confidence, Stella Osborn warned of the Yellow Peril, the "grim dread of half a century":

> The numerical superiority of the yellow people has always been recognized as overwhelming. What saved us was their failure to realize their strength and their inability to organize. Stalin has now awakened them. He has given them the most efficient organization in history. They are on the march. They are marching against us.[74]

Such attitudes naturally aroused suspicions at home and abroad. Former unionist Harris Wofford, Jr., doubted that 300 million white Atlantic democrats could assure peace by excluding the rest of the planet's two billion people. Those awakened multitudes would not welcome being relegated to second-class status until they became sufficiently educated and successfully democratic:

> Psychologically, union of the imperialist white countries who, with the U.S.A., hold most of the world's wealth, might assure defeat for the democratic idea in Asia and the whole colonial world. Instead of a "torch of

freedom," nuclear union might be only the match which would light the anti-Western tinder built up by years of exploitation and subjugation, by Oriental Exclusion Acts and Negro lynchings in the South. Communists everywhere would pour fuel on the fire.[75]

Aware that they were promoting a relatively exclusive private club, unionists considered admitting the Philippines and tried to inspire interest among Australians, but they had no more success in the Pacific than with their local quest for liberal blacks and leaders of organized labor.[76]

How could unionists exclude 77 percent of the earth's population, including several countries with long experience in parliamentary government (Austria and Italy) and many with modern constitutions who were working toward democracy (India, Mexico, and Japan)? What would happen to associations of nations transcending different political systems—the Pan American system, the British Commonwealth, the French Union, and the United Nations? What would happen to existing colonies? Would they be retained under a new collective colonial regime or be set adrift, excluded from the Western federation? Behind these questions lay doubts and reservations difficult to address.

One of the fundamental intellectual problems for unionists arose from their desire to argue on the one hand that the nation-state was obsolete and, on the other, that a new North Atlantic nation-state ought to be created. Denying the immediate practicability of universalism, they were left to defend a narrow particularism that excluded most of the world's people and promised to overpower the hostile Soviets. But would not the world's peoples rebel? And how, in the atomic age, could even a powerful Western superstate achieve unchallengeable superiority?

In criticizing the AUC, world federalists predicted that an exclusive federation of democracies would not end the global struggle for power, would not ease tensions between East and West, would not control weapons of mass destruction, and would not prevent an arms race that would ultimately lead to disaster. Challenged by an amalgamation of hostile powers seeking global domination, the Soviets would accelerate their own military preparations and ally with other nations also denied admittance into the western Union Club. "The unbalance of power is a precarious treasure," some of the atomic scientists warned, "which might slip from our hands with a new device made elsewhere. To counter this, we should be impelled to embark on a scheme designed to maintain the unbalance . . . an atomic arms race."[77] Furthermore, how could a union devoted to overwhelming military superiority assure the survival of democracy? Would not an unlimited arms race "lead to increasing regimentation and the sacrifice of living standards to military needs and industrial dispersal." Scientists feared that civilian control of atomic energy would have to be abandoned and that "military expediency would everywhere outweigh democratic principle." Why would a democratic federation be spared the terrible problems that Streit believed were characteristic of any nation-state?[78]

Like world government advocates, Streit was guilty of inordinate vagueness in responding to such criticisms. How could his complicated plan be implemented in time to counter Soviet expansionism? Would arguments over the nature of the federation, including its "Made in America" design, divide rather than unite the Western allies? Were balances or unbalances of power meaningful in the atomic era? Would Europeans accept permanent partnership with an American Goliath, and would the rest of the world tolerate Western exclusiveness? Would other partial federations be formed, and why would their interrelationships be essentially different from those of traditional nation-states?

But beyond vagueness, which was somewhat understandable (the Founding Fathers had no blueprint when they gathered in Philadelphia), Streit and his followers were also incorrigible idealists. This was ironic, since they believed themselves to be far more realistic than the Cord Meyers and Alan Cranstons. Unionists accepted the cold war and designed a plan to survive it while moving beyond it toward world government. Yet, theoretically, Atlantic unionists were also utopians who allowed their faith in democracy to blind them to the harsh realities of international politics.

Not only did they believe that, by virtue of its overwhelming power, their proposed megastate would be immune from arms races, brushfire wars, harsh internal discipline, and other imperatives of a competitive balance of power system, but also they assumed that democratic institutions would save federal unions from the traditional perils of nation-states. Unionists said almost nothing about political conflict within the union: somehow the democratic process would settle all disputes, including the strong possibility of American domination, without resort to secession or civil war. Externally, this powerful behemoth would not threaten other states simply because it was democratic. "Free peoples," Senator Kefauver stated categorically, "do not make aggressive war." Committed to law and order and placing the highest value on the life, dignity, and the happiness of each individual, democracies were supposedly incapable of using raw force to achieve their national objectives.[79]

Such comforting assumptions had captivated Americans since Woodrow Wilson popularized his vision of a liberal democratic world order during and after World War I. Events in the twentieth century had given the arguments plausibility as autocratic and totalitarian regimes, most of which held their military in high regard, violently challenged the international status quo. Yet to leap to Kefauver's conclusion required considerable ignorance of Greek and English history, America's policies south of the border (including the Mexican War), and the efforts of all democratic nations to maximize their security and freedom of action. Cord Meyer realized this when he faced his Japanese fellows in that lonely island in the Pacific, and most proponents of world government did not believe that democracies could avoid traditional nation-state behavior. Unionists, however, were unconvinced: William Clayton told Cord Meyer that while he liked the young man's book (its style and most of its argumentation), he dissented from any implication that American foreign policy was as bad or as aggressive as Russia's.[80]

This was only one example of unionist utopianism. Unable to restrain his enthusiasm, Clarence Streit made claims for his plan that severely pushed the limits of public credibility. In his judgment, Western democracies could easily create common supranational institutions, and the resulting federation would assure peaceful relations among its members and provide unprecedented postwar prosperity. It would ease the burdens of defense (thus maximizing domestic freedoms), yet force the retreat of the Russian empire. Then, while posing no threat to any other responsible state, the union would draw more democratic peoples into a new world government that would guarantee perpetual peace. Promoting such views, even the severely practical William Clayton began to sound like the tooth fairy.

Unionists were promising so much at so little cost. Private investment would replace foreign aid; Americans could spend $4 billion less for defense while increasing their military power by 30 percent; taxes could be reduced and Western peoples freed from the heavy hand of government. Yet despite such economies, collective Western power would be so great as not only to contain the Soviet empire but to force it to recede. Without higher taxes, debts, inflation, sacrifices of domestic freedom, or resort to violence, the Western democracies could win the cold war. Even the calling of a conference to discuss federal union would have a sobering effect on Communist leaders.

As Americans grew weary of the duration, inconclusiveness, and expense of the cold war, it was a popular time for promising more for less. Senator Joseph McCarthy offered the nation renewed security simply from eliminating Communists in government. John Foster Dulles was promising to "roll back" the iron curtain by pouring more funds into Radio Free Europe. By relying more on atomic weapons and less on expensive conventional warfare, Eisenhower gave Americans "more bang for the buck." China could have been "saved," Republicans argued, had a few more rifles been sent to Chiang Kai-shek. Frustrated by what President Kennedy would later describe as "the long twilight struggle" between East and West, Americans were receptive to easy solutions.

But the problem with Atlantic union was that it demanded such a high emotional and institutional price: Americans would have to sacrifice their traditional national sovereignty. Less fearful of war with the Soviet Union, accustomed to coexisting with atomic weapons, unclear as to how Atlantic federation could be established, and unconvinced that Clarence Streit had discovered the holy grail, interested Americans resisted a hazardous leap into Western supranationalism. Peace advocates were suspicious of Streit's appeal for an unbalance of power, and cold warriors, many of whom were extremely protective of American sovereignty, focused on more immediate and more achievable measures, some of which seemed substantially to increase Western unity in any case.

Just as potential support for world government was tapped by more moderate appeals for United Nations reform and functional cooperation, democratic federalism lost ground to proposals for European unity, development of NATO, and the creation of new agencies of Western international collaboration. European unity promised to energize economic recovery, coordinate defense policies, and safely integrate Germany into the North Atlantic orbit. NATO could theoretically be reformed to include improved consultation, more unified command structures, more complementary defense policies, and (under Article Two) a broadening of responsibilities into economic as well as military activities. Similarly, outside NATO, new agencies might be established to consider common problems, especially economic relationships between the United States and Europe's evolving common market.

As unionists lost hope for the immediate creation of their supranational federation, these gradualist measures that seemed headed in the right direction held much appeal. Perhaps the Atlantic community could make incremental progress toward the institutions ultimately required for its prosperity and security. Time might expire, but movement toward the federalist goal appeared preferable to faltering demands for Union Now.

However, as Clarence Streit feared, the price of gradualism was alienation of the faithful and abandonment of truly supranationalist objectives. During the 1950s, AUC membership continued to dwindle until their annual conventions had to be abandoned for lack of a quorum. The organization's proposed congressional resolutions were diluted, and even then the Atlantic Union Committee began to disguise its advocacy to avoid frightening potential supporters. Finally, in 1959, shortly after the death of John Foster Dulles, a resolution was passed asking Congress to name delegates to a convention of democracies to consider methods of strengthening Atlantic unity. But any mention of federal union was carefully avoided, for, according to an AUC official, "If anyone had made a real case for the fact that this resolution was the pride and joy of the Atlantic Union Committee, it would never have passed the Senate, and it might not even have passed the House."[81]

When delegates were appointed to the convention, held in Paris in 1962, Clarence Streit was purposely ignored, a bitter blow to someone who had dedicated twenty-five years of his life to democratic federalism. Wistfully, he recalled the moment when the idea had come to him:

> It was like Paul on the road to Damascus. It was as if one were in a strange room in the dark, stumbling over the furniture, groping for a way out, and suddenly a finger touches an electric switch, the light flicks on, and everything can be seen clearly. I went for a walk—and a thought came to me—"Now I can die in peace."[82]

In those early days Streit believed he was fulfilling his life's purpose, but by the 1960s he must have realized that he had failed. In common fear of the Soviets and encouraged by powerful postwar American statesmen, the

Atlantic democracies had achieved an extraordinary degree of unity, but they had stopped well short of supranational federation. History never did quite catch up to Union Now.

Not that the federal union movement expired without accomplishment. Streit's original plan aroused the interest of many influential people, including Franklin Roosevelt, and probably inspired Winston Churchill's proposal for Anglo-French union in 1940. In many ways, Streit was the founder of the modern American world government movement, as his supranationalist ideas converted and inspired hundreds of concerned citizens who later transferred their allegiance to the world federalists. The prestigious Atlantic Union Committee lobbied energetically for the passage of the NATO treaty and helped popularize Walter Lippmann's notion of Atlantic community and the vital need for Europeans and Americans to coordinate their political, economic, and military policies during the most threatening days of the cold war. In collaboration with like-minded Europeans, Atlantic unionists suggested joint meetings of NATO parliamentarians (members of various national legislatures) and founded the Declaration of Atlantic Union group and the Atlantic Convention of 1962. During this more moderate, gradualist phase, the committee was even able to gain the publicly expressed support of Harry Truman, George Marshall, Adlai Stevenson, Eugene Rostow, Edward Teller, and Henry Kissinger.[83]

The 1959 convention resolution was maneuvered through Congress by Elmo Roper, who had assumed the presidency of the AUC after Roberts's death in 1955. Roper's task was complicated and was designed to gain maximum advantage from a briefly favorable set of political circumstances. One of the committee's traditional supporters, Christian Herter, had succeeded Dulles as secretary of state. There was mounting public concern about the condition of the NATO alliance, especially in response to Russian nuclear armament, Khrushchev's Berlin ultimatum, and the collapse of the Paris summit conference. Eisenhower, Nixon, and Nelson Rockefeller were sympathetic to the Atlantic convention project, and on the Senate Foreign Relations Committee, Frank Church committed his time to steering the resolution past powerful opponents. "The beautiful thing about this resolution," he noted, "is the fact that it does not mention federation and yet it can serve as the vehicle for obtaining a federation. By passing the resolution, we may be able to get what we need, but because it does not say so, we stand a chance of passing it."[84]

But probably the most important reason for the resolution's success, aside from the State Department's unprecedented benevolence, was the assistance given by Senate Majority Leader Lyndon Johnson. Driven by strong presidential ambitions, Johnson needed to improve his reputation as an expert in foreign affairs, wanted to forge links with the European-oriented Eastern establishment, and undoubtedly welcomed the opportunity to capture the loyalty of one of the nation's major pollsters. Roper managed Johnson skillfully, and the Atlantic Convention resolution cleared the Senate Foreign Relations Committee by just a one-vote majority. After Senate passage, the House also approved the measure. House Speaker Sam Rayburn was a Johnson ally and had been attentively lobbied by Clayton, Roper, and even Washington socialite Perle Mesta, a member of the AUC council.[85]

The convention proved to be a disappointment to unionist stalwarts. Meeting in January 1962, delegates from the NATO democracies advocated a Permanent High Council that could recommend, and sometimes adopt, policies regarding issues of common interest, a High Court of Justice to settle disputes arising from NATO treaty obligations, a consultative assembly of NATO parliamentarians, and an Atlantic Economic Community to facilitate freer trading relations. The Declaration of Paris, which included these recommendations, demanded "the creation of a true Atlantic Community within the next decade," a community that would receive "a measure of delegated sovereignty" from its member states.[86]

For committed federalists, these were vague, moderate proposals that would do little more than consolidate the incremental progress of the previous decade. The press took little notice; governments failed to act; and soon Charles de Gaulle revived French unilateralism. On his way home from Paris, Walden Moore vented his poetic wrath against the moderation of delegates like Herter, Roper, Clayton, and Adolph Schmidt:

> As we wax hot in faction,
> In battle we wax cold;
> Men fight not as they once fought
> In braver days of old.
>
> Was none who would be foremost
> to lead such dire attack;
> While those behind cried "Forward!"
> Those in front cried "Back!"[87]

But the moderates were also realists—governments too were waxing cold.

The Atlantic Union Committee soon disbanded, giving way to yet another elitist citizens group, the Atlantic Council, which was so cautious that it attracted the active participation of Dean Acheson. Federal Union, Incorporated, continued to exist, and Clarence Streit still published *Freedom and Union*. But unionist political ranks were thin. It was difficult enough in the 1960s to salvage the NATO alliance, let alone transform it into a supranational federation. A "true Atlantic Community" seemed a distant destination, much too far to become one of the immediate concerns of a people preoccupied with poverty programs, civil rights, and Vietnam.

Supranationalism had not succumbed, however. Indeed, it was about to experience a vigorous revival. American interests in poverty, social justice, environmental safety, sustained economic growth, and world peace all inspired renewed doubts about the viability of the nation-state. World and Atlantic federalism had failed, but the functionalism that seemed so successful in Europe offered an attractive alternative. Perhaps one could progress toward a network of global institutions in small ways on many fronts; perhaps there were rope bridges that could be thrown across the crevasse that Norman Cousins once said had to be leapt in a single mighty effort. Cousins now thought so, as did many others who had once been active in the federalist movement.

Part Three

Global Managers:
The Functionalist Movement,
1968–1985

VII.

THE IMPERATIVES OF
INTERDEPENDENCE

> There is a question in the air, more sensed
> than seen, like the invisible approach of a
> distant storm, a question that I would
> hesitate to ask aloud did I not believe it
> existed unvoiced in the minds of many: "Is
> there hope for man?"
>
> —Robert Heilbroner, *An Inquiry into the
> Human Prospect*, 1974

> We are living now in the first stages of a
> planetary crisis. An adequate response
> eventually requires a new pattern of
> organization and coordination that needs to
> encompass the entire planet.
>
> —Richard Falk, *This Endangered Planet*,
> 1971

On a fine, sunny morning in late March 1967, the 974-foot supertanker *Torrey Canyon* was smoothly sailing about eighteen miles west of Land's End off the coast of Cornwall. En route from Kuwait with a cargo of thirty-six million gallons of crude oil, the ship planned to dock at Milford Haven, Wales, by the end of the day. With visibility of about eight miles, the tanker moved confidently at seventeen knots, a speed that required at least one mile to bring the vessel to a full stop. Suddenly, about 9:30 A.M., it hit at full force the notorious Seven Sisters reef, a jagged ledge of underwater rocks that sliced a gash of 650 feet along the ship's side. The oil instantly began to ooze from the cracked hull and moved "slowly and imperceptively like a big disease" toward beautiful Cornish beaches, 120 miles of coastline in a region dependent on fishing and tourism for its economic survival. The area was also a haven for seabirds, shellfish, and other types of marine life.

The English offered a gallant response. While the Royal Air Force dramatically bombed the *Torrey Canyon* from several hundred feet, a small fleet of patrol vessels dumped detergent into the sea to break up the oil. Two

thousand soldiers literally scoured the shorelines, and women and children cleaned birds and attacked the incoming slicks with small pails and
shovels. Yet the battle seemed hopeless. The black goo kept coming, and
the detergents caused as much destruction of wildlife as the oil itself. One
hundred thousand birds were killed; dead crabs and fish piled the shore;
and starfish simply came apart in the middle. Meanwhile, once lovely
white Cornish beaches were coated with oil patches sprayed with detergent, an unpleasant combination resembling dried blood.

The cleanup cost the British government $2 million, money that would be
difficult to recover through lawsuits. The ship had been American owned,
under Liberian registry, chartered to a British company, and manned
entirely by an Italian crew. Moreover, it had run aground outside British
territorial waters. No one was clearly responsible for this environmental
disaster, and further incidents were inevitable, as tankers were built twice
or even four times as large as the *Torrey Canyon*. The bombed, half-sub-
merged ship thus sat on the rocks as a monument to the anarchy of the
high seas and as, in *Newsweek*'s words, "a horrifying symbol of man's awful
ability to befoul the world that harbors him." According to Professor
Richard Falk of Princeton, this first great oil spill was "the Hiroshima of the
ecological age."[1]

Oil spills off Cornwall, Santa Barbara, and the Gulf coast were spectacular, but they were hardly the only dramatic examples of the fragility of
man's environment. Pollution of water and air had become increasingly
serious problems with advancing industrialization, problems that by the
early 1970s raised questions of human survival. How much poisonous
waste could man's environment absorb before losing its capacity to sustain
life? No one could answer with certainly, but many experts predicted a
grim future.

Throughout the world, fresh, clean water was becoming difficult to find.
In America, the Mississippi River carried more sludge than mud, the west
branch of the Potomac contained corrosive amounts of sulfuric acid, and
the Cuyahoga River in Cleveland held so many pollutants that it actually
caught fire. Industrial wastes, agricultural fertilizers, and untreated urban
sewage poured into the nation's waterways, fouling drinking water, killing
fish, and depriving lakes of needed oxygen. Conditions in other developed
nations were equally bad. By the time the Rhine reached Holland it was an
open sewer; the romantic Volga was badly polluted, as was the Seine; and
in London tour boat operators joked about how long their passengers could
survive if they fell into the Thames.[2]

Occasionally, disaster struck. In the 1950s in villages around Minamata
on the island of Kyushu in Japan, over two hundred people were poisoned
by contaminated fish. As the death toll mounted, scientists discovered that
the fatal illness was due to mercury poisoning sustained from eating crabs
and fish that had absorbed methyl mercury from factory wastes dumped
into Minamata Bay. By the late 1960s, when the cause of the Japanese
deaths was proven beyond doubt, unsafe levels of mercury were found in

Great Lakes fish and even in canned ocean tuna. Responsive action was taken by various national governments, but mercury was only one of many toxic substances emptied into the world's waters.[3]

Inevitably, most pollution from either inland waterways or airborne dust found its way into the ocean. Scientists estimated that five thousand tons of mercury and ten million tons of oil flowed into the sea each year, along with unknown quantities of radioactive wastes, untreated sewage, and junk. Twenty-five hundred feet beneath the sea, fifty miles off the coast of San Diego, Admiral R. J. Galanson peered from the Navy's deep submersible craft to gain man's first view of that particular part of the vast ocean floor. The first thing he noticed was an empty beer can. In 1970, while sailing his frail Egyptian reed boat across the Atlantic, Thor Hyerdahl found it difficult to escape blobs of solidified oil along with plastic bottles and other human refuse. DDT was discovered in distant Antarctica, and Jacques Cousteau reported declining sea life even on remote reefs off Madagascar. "The oceans are dying," he lamented. "The pollution is general."[4]

Air pollution also seemed much more severe by the late 1960s. In Los Angeles, despite years of reform, school children were frequently excused from outdoor exercise, and nearby forests wilted in the whisky colored haze. Apollo 10 astronauts could recognize the city as a dark smudge from twenty-five thousand miles in space. Other cities were similarly noticeable by airline pilots from distances of seventy miles as the nation's industries collectively spewed 172 million tons of smoke and fumes into the air each year. In addition, the weight of American automobile pollutants was reportedly equivalent to that of a line of cars bumper to bumper from New York to Chicago. Again, however, the problem was global, not national. In Tokyo, traffic policemen took hourly "oxygen breaks," while in Venice heavily polluted air slowly dissolved the city's ancient architecture.[5]

Problems associated with water and air pollution were not limited to ugly sights, bad smells, inconvenienced school children, or even poisoned consumers of mercury-laced fish. Many environmentalists feared that ultimately at stake was the very survival of life on earth. Pollution could destroy the organisms that naturally cleanse human water supplies or could drastically reduce the ocean plant life that produces so much of the world's oxygen. Scientists debated two doomsday scenarios involving worsening air pollution: either large amounts of gases and solid particles carried high into the atmosphere would block enough sunlight to cool the earth's temperatures, or excessive amounts of carbon dioxide, like a large pane of glass, would allow sunlight to pass through while trapping the earth's heat. This "greenhouse effect" might significantly increase the earth's temperatures. Also, the planet's ozone layer could be damaged by man's careless actions. Supersonic transports, or even the modest aerosol spray can, could diminish the ozone vitally required to shield life from ultraviolet radiation.[6]

World population growth was another issue in the early 1970s that

produced anxiety about mankind's future. Indeed, Stanford biologist Paul
Ehrlich spoke for many when he maintained that rampant population
growth provided the fundamental explanation for the general deterioration
of planetary welfare. By his calculations, about one-half of the world's
people were hungry, a situation that would surely worsen as additional
millions were annually added to the earth's population. Enormous pressure would be placed on food supplies, resources, and the environment's
waste disposal capacity. Even simple breathing could become a problem as
consumption of oxygen increased while natural production declined due to
the destruction of forests and ocean plants. Ehrlich was convinced that the
earth's life-support systems would break down if mankind's growing numbers continued to force additional industrial and agricultural production.[7]

Other writers played variations on the same basic theme. In his book
World without Borders, Lester Brown warned that doubling the earth's population every thirty-five years was instrumental in widening the gap between rich and poor. Poor nations, whose populations grew at a much
faster rate, would suffer severe problems of unemployment, urban crowding, and famine, problems that would cause desperate peoples to violently
challenge the wealth and privilege of their more fortunate planetary neighbors. In contrast, Richard Falk argued that while increased population did
put pressure on food, resources, environmental quality, psychic health,
and the ability of poor nations to cope with mass misery, the most dangerous growth in numbers occurred in the wealthier nations. It was the
richer peoples who consumed so many resources and who placed such
demands on the earth's fragile environment.[8]

Peaceful relations between rich and poor, the continued availability of
resources, and a healthy world trading system were all widely perceived as
crucial to the planet's general welfare. Brown observed that the world
economy had become increasingly interdependent: most nations relied
heavily on relatively easy access to new technologies, energy supplies, raw
materials, and markets. But while he tended to be optimistic about the
overall effects of such mutual dependence, others were not so sure. Joseph
Nye and Stanley Hoffmann both emphasized that degrees of dependence
were often unequal among nations and that interdependence could as
easily lead to conflict as cooperation. Even more darkly, Robert Heilbroner
feared violent struggles over scarce resources and efforts by poor nations to
use modern weapons of mass destruction to force redistribution of wealth.[9]

Fears also arose in the 1970s that an integrated world economy could be
seriously disrupted by the roguish behavior of only a few nation-states. The
sudden rise of oil prices was a good example, but there were many other
potential problems—higher tariffs, irresponsible banking practices, inadequate assistance to poorer nations, or nationalistic attacks on multinational
corporations. As the international economy experienced its worst recession
since World War II, concern mounted that the world shared a common fate
in a complex, interdependent economy that lay beyond collective management or control. This could easily result in collective disaster.[10]

The remaining fear regarding the fate of the earth in the early 1970s centered on nuclear weapons. This fear had always existed since the bombing of Hiroshima in 1945, but it had waxed and waned during the postwar period and had varied in its political focus. While Americans initially worried mostly about a devastating atomic exchange with the Soviet Union, concerns in the late 1950s turned to the more subtle dangers of radioactive fallout from the mere testing of nuclear weapons. As early as 1953, scientists in the eastern United States noticed significant increases in radiation levels as heavy rains brought down contaminated debris from tests in Nevada, and subsequent investigations confirmed higher radioactivity in air, water, and soil in all areas normally downwind from the exploding bombs. While that was disturbing enough, the public soon learned about strontium-90, a radioactive isotope that, as Barry Commoner wrote, "moves through the environment in concert with calcium, a chemically similar element." Traveling through the food chain via plants, cows, and milk, the isotope could settle in the bones of humans thereby increasing the risk of cancer. American children were apparently being invisibly poisoned from the air![11]

For scientists like Commoner, it was an early lesson in ecology. Human actions in one remote area had unpredicted and certainly unintended results somewhere else due to complex interactions of air, plants, animals, and people. Arctic Eskimos and Laplanders suffered from the fallout, and for some inexplicable reason, the worst recorded strontium-90 levels in milk were in Milan, Italy. Awareness of those problems triggered global protest and helps explain the success of the Test Ban Treaty of 1963. That agreement was a failure in halting nuclear testing, but it did eliminate most explosions in the atmosphere.[12]

Heightened cold war tensions during the Kennedy years returned fears more to the possible wartime use of nuclear weapons. Kennedy massively increased the American defense budget and publicly promoted the construction of public and private fallout shelters throughout the country. Thereafter, until the late 1970s, intensity of public concern about nuclear arms diminished, but the issue was always naggingly present. Weapons of mass destruction still posed the gravest, most immediate threat to millions of human beings, perhaps to life itself. Furthermore, fortunes were being spent by the major powers on expensive armaments at a time of increasing scarcity of world resources and increasing inequality of international wealth and income. As with nuclear tests, mere preparations for war could contribute to the destruction of the environment and the general worsening of the human condition.[13]

This conclusion illustrates an essential argument that many reformers were making in the 1970s, namely that nearly all of the serious problems adversely affecting the fate of the earth were related and mutually reinforcing. Population growth placed intense pressure on food supplies, natural resources, and effective waste disposal. Using more fertilizer to grow more food produced additional pollution and encouraged even more population growth. Higher industrial production, which offered surplus wealth to assist the poor, consumed huge quantities of raw materials and worsened pollution. Using nuclear power to conserve other energy resources and reduce air pollution brought new hazards of radioactive accidents and disposal of dangerous by-products. The interrelated world economy required the economic development of most nation-states, but such progress could impose significant strains on traditional trading patterns for raw materials and finished products. Economic inequalities and resource scarcity increased the chances of war, yet preparations for war wasted resources and perpetuated inequalities. The world seemed full of trade-offs, vicious circles, and dead ends. It would be extremely difficult to escape the many traps that men had tragically set for themselves.

It is hard to account for this sudden awareness of the interrelatedness of things. Perhaps the computer had much to do with it, since that tool was encouraging people to appreciate, measure, and study complex relationships. Experience was also instructive. Problems such as strontium-90 or the effects of DDT on plant and bird life alerted scientists to the elaborate interdependence of ecological systems. Commoner's basic thesis was that "every living thing is dependent on many others, either indirectly through the physical or chemical features of the environment or directly for food or a sheltering place." Moreover, the neo-romantic intellectual rebellion of the 1960s may have encouraged a more holistic view of life—a healthy suspicion of the traditional scientist's infinite fragmentation of knowledge into easily examined bits and pieces and his questionable assumption that the whole is nothing more than the sum of its parts.[14]

In any case, the most influential pioneering effort to systematically interrelate various major threats to human welfare was the Club of Rome study, *Limits to Growth.* An informal international association of scientists, educators, industrialists, and civil servants, the Club of Rome was established in 1968 after a meeting hosted by Aurelio Peccei, an Italian businessman. About seventy members from twenty-five nations were asked to consider such global problems as population growth, poverty, the environment, urban sprawl, inflation, loss of faith in institutions, alienation of youth, and the rejection of traditional values. The group assumed that most of those problems were complex and interrelated and therefore well beyond the capacity of existing institutions to understand or engage.[15]

Limits to Growth was the club's first report on "the present and future predicament of man." Financed by a grant from the Volkswagen Foundation, a Massachusetts Institute of Technology team led by Dennis Meadows examined five basic factors that significantly influence global economic development: population, food production, availability of natural resources, industrial production, and pollution. An elaborate computer model was constructed to demonstrate the interaction of those factors based upon certain assumptions about the probable extent of population growth, potential improvements in agricultural productivity, known supplies of nonrenewable resources, rates of future industrial production, and likely thresholds of environmental disaster.[16]

Published in 1972, the study reminded its readers that both population and industrial production were increasing at very rapid rates. World population, which stood at about 600 million in 1650 and reached only 1.7 billion by 1900, was expected to be about six billion by the year 2000. Meanwhile, industrial growth was increasing at about 7 percent annually. These two trends would make enormous long-term demands on cultivatable land, fresh water, nonrenewable resources such as metals and fuel, and the resiliency of an already deteriorating environment. In fact, increases in resource use and pollution were already exceeding the growth rate of population.[17]

Seeking to interrelate these various factors with as much sophistication as possible, the Meadows report reached sobering conclusions: limits to growth would be reached, and the world's economic system would collapse, well before 2100. Even considering several important mitigating circumstances, the team found the result would be essentially the same. Doubling predicted supplies of resources would not prevent collapse due to pollution and lack of food. Strict pollution controls would dramatically increase the costs of industrial production and would still not prevent massive food shortages. Diverting capital into agricultural production would cripple industrial development. Even a best case, composed of nuclear power, recycling, doubling of resources, extensive pollution abatement, and pervasive birth control, would fail to rescue the economic system from collapse by the end of the twenty-first century.[18]

Despite the study's methodological problems and its emphasis on preliminary conclusions, *Limits to Growth* was translated into a dozen languages and sold over three million copies. The Club of Rome membership was prestigious, and the book's conclusions gave apparent scientific legitimacy to what many interested readers were already beginning to suspect. Present trends could not continue: there were limits to the earth's capacity to support additional people, especially people committed to rapid industrial growth. While the Meadows study did not claim to make precise predictions, it convincingly described the global economic system's disturbing behavioral tendencies. The future looked unprecedentedly bleak.[19]

This popular idea that various major threats to human welfare were reinforcing and cumulative produced in the late 1960s and early 1970s a strong sense of urgency that at times bordered on despair. Robert Heilbroner wrote an entire book dedicated to answering the question, "Is there hope for man?" He concluded that there wasn't. C. P. Snow sadly related that in his travels in America and elsewhere he had encountered vast uneasiness about the future. "We feel," he said, "as though we are in a motorbus driven very fast by a probably malevolent and certainly anonymous driver; we can't stop, all we can do is show a stiff upper lip and pretend to smile at the passing countryside." While acknowledging that despair was a sin that paralyzed needed effort, he nonetheless admitted that "I have been nearer to despair this year [1968] than ever in my life." Physicist George Wald described American youth as "a generation in search of survival"; President Richard Nixon warned that the world faced "the prospect of ecological disaster"; and UN Secretary-General U Thant feared that time was running out in mankind's effort to assume control of its destiny:

> I do not wish to seem overdramatic, but I can only conclude . . . that the Members of the United Nations have perhaps ten years left in which to subordinate their ancient quarrels and launch a global partnership to curb the arms race, to improve the human environment, to defuse the population explosion, and to supply the required momentum to development efforts. If such a global partnership is not forged within the next decade, then I very much fear that the problems I have mentioned will have reached such staggering proportions that they will be beyond our capacity to control.[20]

The American public's mood during this period defies precise description, but there is much indirect evidence of increased anxiety. A writer in *Public Opinion Quarterly* commented in 1973 that ecological issues had "burst into American consciousness" with "unprecedented speed and urgency" as alarm about the environment "sprang from nowhere to major proportions in a few short years." George Gallup discovered in 1969 that Americans judged pollution to have the highest priority for increased government spending, and a Harris poll in 1971 ranked environmental problems second among issues demanding congressional attention. Concern about resource supplies rose dramatically with the energy crisis of the early 1970s, and fear of nuclear war increased once again as Soviet-American détente failed to meet optimistic expectations. Hollywood pandered to the decade's mood of public gloom with a flurry of disaster films depicting helpless individuals caught by either the hostile forces of nature or by uncontrolled technology. Movies were released about earthquakes, man-eating sharks, falling airplanes, sinking ships, runaway trains, and malfunctioning nuclear reactors. Even major politicians reflected the pessimism: while Henry Kissinger strolled through the gardens of Versailles philosophizing about Western man's collapse of self-confidence, President Jimmy Carter appeared on national television to complain about the American people's pervasive malaise.[21]

Why that malaise in the 1970s? Environmental problems were certainly not new to Americans; population growth was a familiar issue; nuclear weapons had been menacing humanity since 1945; and the world economy had long been becoming more integrated and interdependent. Why had these problems come to have such a powerful collective impact that young couples hesitated to raise families and old religions swelled their ranks by predicting impending doom?

Events were important in conveying a sense of planetary crisis. The *Torrey Canyon*, Santa Barbara, urban smog alerts, massive electrical power failures, wildlife killed by DDT, sterile lakes and rivers—all suggested that the traditional pursuit of massive economic growth carried a large, often hidden cost in environmental degradation. The Arab oil boycott dramatically demonstrated the vulnerability of American prosperity to the vagaries of international politics, while defeat in Vietnam raised questions about America's ability to promote her interests successfully in a dangerous, nuclear world. Meanwhile, the flight of Apollo 11 to the moon inspired deeper concerns for the earth as a whole. From cold, hostile space, the earth seemed a small, fragile planet in desperate need of human protection. It became commonplace to refer, as did Buckminster Fuller, to "spaceship earth," a tiny craft with delicate life-support systems, finite resources, and limited room for passengers. Enhanced realization that the earth was more "the city of man" than wide open frontier was both sobering and humbling.[22]

Events such as these were intrinsically significant, but they gained added force from the general context within which they took place. Pittsburgh was badly polluted in the nineteenth century, and Los Angeles was gasping for air in the early 1940s. Americans had already tasted defeat in Korea. Concern about availability of resources began in the 1890s, and long before the spaceship, the airplane had drawn attention to the smallness of the planet. In the late 1960s and early 1970s, however, there were various reasons why such experiences were perceived as part of a disturbing pattern demanding immediate and fundamental response. Of considerable influence was the state of the American economy. The United States enjoyed a mature industrial economy that had performed exceptionally well since the beginning of World War II. Having achieved large-scale mass production, good public education, basic welfare programs, and much private affluence, Americans were positioned to concern themselves with public sector issues concerning the quality of life. A wealthy nation could afford to devote additional resources to parks and wilderness, cleaner air and water, and more costly methods of production and development. Furthermore, many Americans were now questioning the wisdom of unrestrained growth and the pursuit of private profit. Having attained comfortable wealth, they began to doubt that more was necessarily better or that it made sense to live in private comfort amidst public decadence.

The nation's economic growth also made Americans particularly sensitive to problems of pollution and dwindling resources. The United States was the world's largest producer of both industrial and agricultural products and therefore a prolific generator of severe environmental problems, problems duly noted and publicized by the nation's unusually large scientific establishment. Also, accounting for nearly one-half of the world's consumption of raw materials, Americans became worried when future supplies seemed doubtful. The oil embargo sent shock waves through the nation's entire economic system.[23]

The impact of that embargo revealed another major characteristic of American life in the late 1960s and the early 1970s: the obvious decline in the country's international power. After losing the Vietnam War, the

United States was disengaging from the Asian mainland, relinquishing the Panama Canal, and adapting to increased Soviet military capabilities in nearly all types of warfare. Europe and Japan had completely recovered from the war, were more independent politically, and were challenging the United States in world markets. In international economic matters generally, the United States carried less weight, and politically and culturally, the American example seemed less enviable after Vietnam and the domestic turmoils of the 1960s. Nearly everywhere, American prestige and influence diminished.

Americans were becoming aware that they were less in control of their own destiny, that the fate of the United States, and indeed the fate of the earth, were being determined by peoples and governments far from American shores. Somehow, Arab hostility to Israel led to long lines at American gas stations, and OPEC price increases helped push the Western world into severe inflation. Brazilian deforestation posed a threat to the earth's oxygen supply. Indians and South Africans were reputedly developing atomic weapons. All of these developments were beyond the reach of American power, and realization of that harsh reality inspired a depressing sense of deepening vulnerability.

Finally, the American political climate during this period was receptive to gloomy prognostications and emotional appeals for fundamental change. Energized by the American population's unusually high proportion of young people in the 1960s, reform movements had challenged conventional attitudes regarding diplomacy, race relations, sexual morality, patriotism, the work ethic, and economic justice. Included in those rebellions was broad, basic criticism of industrial civilization and scientific modes of thought, of the unfortunate side-effects of new technologies, and of the petty tyrannies of specialized knowledge and expertise. Prepared to believe the worst about American industrial society, those critics heaped particular scorn on the supposedly mindless materialism of the wealthier classes. What was the point, they asked, of growth for the sake of growth, the endless conquest of nature, and commitments to additional production and profits at the expense of increased leisure and to the neglect of distributive justice?

Political activists who had battled over civil rights, poverty programs, and Asian wars were ready for new issues related to their previous concerns, and established elites were still off-balance from the attacks of militant reformers and the debacle of Vietnam. Thus there were many Americans prepared to believe that unrestricted industrial growth and unguided technology were endangering the environment, that hopeless efforts to deny international interdependence could lead to economic disaster and war, and that major military conflict could destroy human life. With conservative elements still on the defensive, those issues rose in popularity to dominate the reformist agenda of the 1970s. Reformers were convinced that they faced a series of urgent crises, that time was of the essence, and that fundamental change was required to alter patterns of behavior perhaps lethally hazardous to human welfare.[24]

Much like the world federalists, reformers in the 1970s believed technology lay at the heart of mankind's most serious problems. Advancing technology produced the many new chemicals that polluted lakes and rivers, the cars and airplanes that endangered the atmosphere, the tankers and oil rigs that threatened the seas, and the nuclear weapons that could in seconds ruin the planet. Technology was enabling man to encroach on the last remaining commons beneath the sea and in outer space. And technology held people together in tightening bonds of interdependence. As Lord Ritchie-Calder observed: "Today ours is a global civilization; . . . it is the whole world. Its planet has shrunk to a neighborhood round which a man-made satellite can patrol sixteen times a day, riding the gravitational fences of man's family estate. It is a community so interrelated that our mistakes are exaggerated on a world scale.[25]

The atomic scientists in the mid-1940s had cautioned Americans that effective control of man's scientific achievements could hardly be taken for granted, and within a decade, scientists like Barry Commoner were issuing similar warnings about the state of the environment. Within another fifteen years, the warnings took hold, and Commoner rose to elder statesmen of a strong political movement determined to harness runaway technologies to the public welfare.

Commoner was born in 1917 in Brooklyn of Russian immigrant parents. Although a street-wise member of a local city gang, he was also fascinated by nature and devoted spare hours to collecting specimens from the neighborhood's Prospect Park. He studied biology in high school, earned a zoology degree from Columbia in 1937, and a Ph.D. from Harvard in 1940. After naval service in World War II, he became an associate editor for *Science Weekly* and in 1947 joined the Botany Department at Washington University where he became a popular lecturer and an accomplished researcher, specializing in plant viruses. A traditional believer in the obligation of scientists to inform the public about the effects of science and technology on man's environment, he persistently investigated the probable ill-effects of strontium-90 from nuclear fallout in the United States and helped lobby successfully for the Nuclear Test Ban Treaty of 1963.[26]

He subsequently turned his attention to various other environmental hazards as he became convinced that man's habitat had to be studied holistically, with an appreciation of the interrelationships of many natural phenomena. In time, he also became convinced that environmental degradation was due less to population growth or to industrialization itself than to particular adverse technologies of production. At fault had been the extensive manufacture of synthetic fibers, plastics, detergents, pesticides, chemical fertilizers, smog producing automobile engines, and other products that displaced earlier, less dangerous technologies. "The present system of production," he concluded, "is self-destructive; the present course of human civilization is suicidal." Modern, technology-based society contained "an insidious fraud," a "blindly accumulated debt to nature" that would have to be repaid.[27]

Another successful pioneer in the effort to warn Americans of the dangers as well as the blessings of modern technology was Rachel Carson. Like Commoner, Carson was a nature lover from early childhood, a period pleasantly passed in suburban Pennsylvania. In 1929 she received a science degree from Pennsylvania College for Women in Pittsburgh, and, in 1932, an M.A. in zoology from Johns Hopkins. She taught for a while, worked at the Marine Biological Laboratory at Woods Hole, Massachusetts, and then in the late 1930s became an aquatic biologist for the United States Bureau of Fisheries. While at the bureau, she pursued her other childhood interest, popular writing. Her studies of marine life along the Atlantic coast earned her promotion to editor-in-chief of publications for the Department of Interior's Fish and Wildlife Service. In 1951 she published *The Sea around Us*, a work that elegantly bridged the gap between science and the humanities, between esoteric knowledge and popular understanding. Excerpted in the *New Yorker*, it went through nine printings and was widely distributed by the Book-of-the-Month Club. Then, in the early 1960s, she wrote the book that would make her, according to the *New York Times*, "one of the most influential women of her time." That was *Silent Spring*, a study that Justice William O. Douglas described as "the most important chronicle of this century for the human race."[28]

Her target was chemical pesticides, products that had hitherto been considered miraculously beneficial to mankind. DDT, for example, won fame during World War II as an effective counter to malaria and other insect-borne diseases, and it proved equally popular as a potent weapon against agricultural pests. Its discoverer won a Nobel Prize. Yet subsequent investigations revealed that DDT had devastating effects on bird life and ominous possibilities for animals and humans. Other pesticides were even more dangerous, and their massive use led Carson to ask whether anyone could believe it possible "to lay down such a barrage of poisons on the surface of the earth without making it unfit for all life." She concluded that "along with the possibility of the extinction of mankind by nuclear war, the central problem of our age has become the contamination of man's total environment with substances of incredible potential for harm. . . ."[29]

Margaret Mead similarly warned that "not war, but a plethora of man-made things . . . is threatening to strangle us, suffocate us, bury us, in the debris and by-products of our technologically inventive and irresponsible age." E. B. White lamented that he was "pessimistic about the human race because it is too ingenious for its own good," and Professor Richard Falk agreed that it is the technological nature of contemporary society "that gives the planetary crisis its apocalyptic character." Mankind was doing so many "good things" too well—keeping babies and children healthy, extending life expectancy, increasing food production with chemical fertilizers and pesticides, improving living standards for millions through unlimited mass production. In this productive process, wrote White, "our approach to nature is to beat it into submission." Nature was to be endlessly conquered, exploited, and improved for man's material gain.[30]

This approach to nature was deeply rooted in man's historical experience. Long vanished was a mentality that perceived humans as an integral part of nature and that identified the forces of nature with gods who had to be pleased and placated. Scientific man, rational man, saw himself detached from nature and superior to it. Dealing with it was less a matter of coexistence than manipulation and control. In Lewis Mumford's view, modern science is composed of "empirical knowledge based on an ability to formulate and manipulate symbolic abstractions of quantity, number, relationship, structure—an ability that disentangles the mind from the often impenetrable and indescribable confusions of concrete existence." Relatedly, "inquiry into the immediate nature of the 'physical world' takes precedence over that into the nature of life and the environment of life." The ultimate consequence of such a mechanical world picture is "an environment like our present one: fit only for machines to live in."[31]

Blending these attitudes toward nature with Protestantism and liberal capitalism, American culture valued hard work, competitiveness, individualism, acquisitiveness, and national economic development. Man's possibilities seemed as infinite as the earth's resources, and progress was essentially defined as utilizing new technologies to produce improved working conditions and higher standards of living. As Robert Heilbroner noted, Americans (and Westerners generally) have been driven by their Promethean spirit, marshaling nervous will and intellectual daring to subjugate nature and "create societes designed to free man from his animal bondage."[32]

In contrast, reformers championed new "ecological values" that emphasized harmony, cooperation, respect for nature, more leisure, reduced consumerism, and limits to growth. Paul Ehrlich called for "new men," a new stage of cultural evolution, a new consciousness that reunited men and nature. The authors of *Limits to Growth* demanded a basic change of values and goals at the individual, national, and world levels—"a Copernican revolution of the mind." Heilbroner suggested that Prometheus be replaced by Atlas as a model of human aspirations. Mankind needed endless perseverance, a patient determination "to preserve humanity at any cost, forever." And Barry Commoner concluded:

> The lesson of the environmental crisis is clear. If we are to survive, ecological considerations must guide economic and political ones. And if we are to take the course of ecological wisdom, we must accept at last the even greater wisdom of placing our faith . . . in the desire that is shared everywhere in the world—for harmony with the environment and for peace among the peoples who live in it.[33]

There were reformers who believed that the problems seriously threatening human welfare could be solved by such enlightened popular attitudes
and resulting changes in national policies. Enormous hopes were placed in
public education, personal conversion, and political action. Confidence was
expressed in the influence of the counterculture, increased public
awareness of planetary dangers, and the apparent responsiveness of most
politicians. Furthermore, as the world's largest economic and military
power, the United States itself could do much to improve the environment,
conserve resources, promote economic justice, and moderate the arms
race.

Yet, there was considerable awareness that no single nation, not even the
United States, could single-handedly rescue humankind from its many
dangers. As Commoner realized, the world's peoples were linked through
their interconnected needs to a common fate. Few of mankind's major
problems lent themselves to purely national solutions. Global cooperation
was required, what Ambassador George Kennan termed "an international
effort more urgent in its timing, bolder and more comprehensive in its
conception and more vigorous in its execution than anything created or
planned to date." Many reformers described the various ways in which
nations had become interdependent and how difficult it was to deal with
such problems as pollution, mining of the seas, trade, arms sales, resource
allocation, and population control on a unilateral, bilateral, or even regional
basis. Mankind was experiencing a common vulnerability, Barbara Ward
observed, and there had to be instruments of worldwide order and welfare
or all could "tumble into annihilation." This would be a difficult task, she
concluded, but not impossible.[34]

Concerned mainly with environmental issues, Kennan advocated international collaboration that would include the collection and dissemination
of information regarding common problems, the coordination of research,
and the establishment of global standards of environmental protection.
Also required were rules governing all human activities on the high seas, in
outer space, and in Antarctica, places not yet subject to any sovereign
government. To implement all this, Kennan suggested a new institutional
entity whose basic concern would be mankind generally, along with man's
"animal and vegetable companions." This would have to be a ruggedly
independent agency that would determine what is desirable from a conservationist standpoint, thereby offering a point of departure for subsequent negotiations and accommodations. It would review the activities of
governments and other international organizations, inform them regarding
basic needs, and coordinate the setting and enforcement of rules and
standards. Established and financially supported by the major powers, the
new agency would be staffed by true international civil servants "bound by
no national or political mandate," and in time it might evolve from advisory
status to become a genuine authority with powers of enforcement.[35]

Similarly, Lester Brown argued in his book, *World without Borders*, that
only broadly based international cooperation could peacefully apportion

the earth's finite resources, narrow the margins between rich and poor, control population growth, feed the hungry, educate the illiterate, and ease the tensions of the cold war. International agencies could administer foreign aid programs, facilitate free trade, regulate multinational corporations, encourage family planning, foster a common global language, regulate mining of the seas, and promote the peaceful settlement of disputes. According to Brown's popular vision, men could create "a world in which conflict and competition will be replaced with cooperation and a sense of community."[36]

Such appeals, as common as rain in the early 1970s, were analogous to support in the 1940s for the United Nations. Advocates of a new, cooperative world order again placed great faith in UN conferences to publicize common problems, UN treaties to register agreement on cooperative solutions, and UN specialized agencies to execute collective intentions. While reformers believed the United Nations needed to be improved constitutionally, they basically assumed that the organization could function well if most nations, particularly the most powerful nations, so desired. In essence, these writers were adhering to an adage as old as the San Francisco conference of 1945: the United Nations would work if people wanted it to work.

But was that necessarily so? Once more, as among world federalists and Atlantic unionists after World War II, there were those who insisted that mere cooperation among sovereign nation-states could not succeed. With regard to questions of war and peace, these arguments had changed very little, and now they were expanded to cover newer issues of economic coordination and environmental protection. Just as a general international preference for peace would not prevent war, vague desires for mutual economic assistance and cleaner air and water would not assure prosperity or a healthy planet. Far more fundamental reform of public attitudes and political institutions was surely required.

The most cogent defense of this renewed supranationalism came from Richard Falk, Albert G. Milbank Professor of International Law and Practice at Princeton. Falk had written much about law and morality in international politics and, despite his genteel surroundings at Princeton, was a severe critic of American policies in Vietnam. He was a somewhat radical freethinker within a traditionally conservative field of study at an established university, a man fully aware of both the failings of existing institutions and their powerful resistance to change. In many ways, he was what John Kennedy believed himself to be, an idealist without illusions.

In his 1971 book, *This Endangered Planet*, Falk accepted the urgent need to alter human behavior in order to preserve the earth's habitability—man, he predicted, could face extinction within several decades. He was pleased that public awareness of this reality was growing and that national governments seemed increasingly willing to cooperate. Yet he had little faith that those governments could adequately cope with global problems or that the United Nations could successfully manage more than the simplist, most apolitical tasks. Progress in delivering the mail, battling smallpox, feeding hungry children, or saving the blue whale would not assure lasting peace or avert an ecological crisis.[37] In Falk's judgment, national governments remained unwilling to subordinate their own immediate concerns to larger, more long-term planetary interests. Only weak instruments existed even to identify those interests, and meanwhile, national survival in the traditional state system seemed to demand competition and conflict rather than coordination and cooperation. Preparing for war was still the major preoccupation of the great powers, and all nations were devoted to maximizing their own economic growth, political stability, and international prestige. Furthermore, since there were so many inequalities both within and among nations, elites were far more interested in maintaining their own and their country's privileges than in making sacrifices for the common good.[38]

Like the early federalists, Falk had a dark view of human nature. "Men are by and large animated by selfish motives of greed and fear," he wrote, "and social and political patterns reflect this outcome." Moreover, such motives have normally been accompanied by "callousness toward the suffering and destruction of others." The world had become accustomed to witnessing mass suffering "without displaying any deep compassion for the victims of war or natural catastrophe," an indifference that easily extended to man's suicidal destruction of the environment. Thus, until man's greed and fear could be aroused and positively directed by some clear and present danger, there would be little progress toward effective international cooperation. And even if fearful people became wiser and more generous and statesmen more enlightened in their definitions of the national interest, common action for the good of mankind would be difficult. Again, the problem lay in the competitive international system within which self-denial on the part of one or a few nations could have the perverse effect of rewarding the most unscrupulously selfish.[39]

This discouraging observation was elaborated in one of the environmentalist movement's most influential articles, Garrett Hardin's "The Tragedy of the Commons." A professor of biology at the University of California at Santa Barbara, Hardin used persuasive historical examples to prove his pessimistic conclusion, "tragic" in the sense of "the remorseless working of things." Hardin asked his readers to imagine a pasture open to all. On that pasture, individual herdsmen have an interest in raising as many cattle as possible, a system that works well until the resources of the pasture are inevitably destroyed through overgrazing. Then all the herdsmen suffer. The tragedy is that "each man is locked into a system that compels him to increase his herd without limit—in a world that is limited. Ruin is the destination toward which all men rush, each pursuing his own best interest in a society that believes in the freedom of the commons. Freedom in a commons brings ruin to all." One did not need, of course, to rummage through history for examples of this phenomenon. It was still evident, according to Hardin, in the pressures of cattlemen on federal lands, the overfishing of the seas, the crowding of national parks, and the pollution of the earth's air and water.[40]

To make matters worse, appeals to individual conscience, sacrifice, and self-denial were useless, in Hardin's view. Indeed, "to make such an appeal is to set up a selective system that works toward the elimination of conscience from the race." People vary in their responsiveness, and since that is true, the least sensitive are the most rewarded. The most sensitive are caught in a double bind—irresponsible behavior produces guilt, while responsible actions lead to feelings of being duped by the more clever. Appeals to conscience become tools of those who wish to preserve or extend their own inordinate shares of the commons, those who wish to get something for nothing. The solution to this problem, Hardin insisted, was "mutual coercion, mutually agreed upon by the majority of the people affected." Abstinence or temperance had to be imposed on all for the good of all. If the commons is to remain public, which in the case of air and water is virtually unavoidable, then everyone's use of the commons would have to be regulated. The alternative was collective ruin.[41]

Many reformers concurred in Hardin's judgment. Just as restrictive pollution laws adopted in one particular American state could cause its industries to move to less regulated jurisdictions, national environmental protection could raise costs in ways that would favor imports and drive domestic industries to foreign shores. Refusal to sell arms to nations preparing for conflict with their neighbors would reward sellers less concerned about global instability and violence. Similar self-restraint in fishing, energy consumption, and ocean mining would also favor the unrestrained. Clearly, global problems would require global solutions.

Within this context, Falk advocated "stronger cooperative patterns of behavior and more embracing forms of organization." Assuming that sovereign states could not resolve the planetary crisis, he sought a new model of world order that would provide "unified guidance for the benefit of all men." A political leap, similar to that demanded by the world federalists, was required to carry mankind beyond mere international collaboration:

> The essential modification of the world system as it operates today would involve the elimination of the national boundary as the basic organizing idea for purposes of security, wealth, and loyalty. If the boundaries between sovereign states could become as inconsequential as the boundaries between Connecticut and Massachusetts, Hunan and Hupeh, Rajasthan and Uttar Pradesh, then the new era will have emerged.[42]

Yet Falk was not a world federalist. While he advocated "government planning and enforcement on a planetary scale," he did not desire extensive centralization of power and authority. He wrote not of world government but of "managing" resources and human behavior. He perceived an ethical imperative for centralized management in the ideal of mankind's essential unity; a political imperative in the prohibitive costs of modern war; and an ecological imperative in the need for common standards of behavior. But much like the Atlantic unionists, Falk maintained that such centralization would actually lead to a reduction of bureaucratic interference in people's affairs. In a less competitive, less hostile environment, national governments could be less powerful both internationally and domestically.[43]

While Falk offered no blueprint of his future world order, he was outlining a new managerial style of world politics within an institutional context of functional supranationalism. He envisioned that most of the world's peoples, pushed forward by fear and pulled along by hope, would realize that cooperation was necessary for human welfare. Then, in pursuit of the common objectives of arms limitation, population control, alleviation of world poverty, limitation of industrial growth, and protection of the environment, various routes could be taken toward the level of supranationalism required to achieve those objectives.

He noted structural elements of the existing system that, if expanded sufficiently in scope, could fundamentally transform the international order. Ideally, the United Nations would extend its authority, especially over such remaining areas of the commons as the oceans and outer space, a process that would be easier if there were modifications in both the great power veto in the Security Council and the one nation-one vote principle in the General Assembly. Specialized, functional agencies staffed by international civil servants might gain authority and prestige by at least beginning to labor on major global problems. Frequent meetings of government officials and of private transnational groups (such as scientists and businessmen) could encourage shared perceptions, awareness of man's basic unity, and coordinated responses to common concerns. Regionalism might dilute loyalties to the nation-state and facilitate the meeting of ecological dangers. World-oriented reform at the national level, along with apparently contradictory movements for subnational autonomy, could also help demythologize national governments and encourage functional cooperation.[44] The resulting "central guidance mechanism," a composite of these various elements, would need to have "the overall ability to evolve and maintain a dominant structure of planetary cooperation to take the place of existing international structures whose origins and functions concentrate upon the competitive drives of sovereign states." Although some kind of world government might eventually be desirable, the immediate objective would be a web of international, transnational, and supranational associations and institutions that would both attract peoples' ultimate loyalty and reverse the world's steep slide toward self-destruction.[45]

How was all this to be accomplished? Education was certainly necessary. People, especially national elites, had to understand the seriousness of their predicament. Yet Falk emphasized that the "rhetoric of apocalypse" would probably not alter basic patterns of behavior. People rarely move from below a volcano or from a hazardous earthquake zone. No one could confidently predict the future, and such conjecture combined with uncertainty regarding appropriate remedies bred confused immobility. But if dire warnings were insufficient in themselves to promote fundamental reform, the educational process could be invaluably assisted by a series of disastrous events. The resulting sense of crisis, along with a useful sense of direction, could offer just the right compound of fear and hope essential to progress.[46]

Reform, however, must not come too slowly. As a standard governmental defense of the status quo, gradualism could easily become an excuse for excessive caution and moderation. Also, the standard federalist reliance on reason could hardly be relied upon, since those in favored or privileged positions threatened by reform would not relinquish power except under coercive pressure. Falk called for well-organized domestic and transnational political movements that, strengthened by events, would advocate fundamental change. Such change would have to be system-wide and, if conditions became desperate, might have to be stimulated by violence and other illegal means. As a political realist, Falk did not underestimate the system's inertia.[47]

Yet his hopes did soar. In his ideal future, the world's peoples would become increasingly aware of their predicaments, would reach a consensus on the proper direction of political change, and would move decisively toward "a new world community that eliminates war and poverty and works to achieve harmony between man and nature." There would emerge a new prevailing philosophy of ecological humanism, new global institutions to manage global problems, and "a new political man" devoted in his own enlightened self-interest to the welfare of the commons. It did sound idealistic, but Falk repeated the rhetorical question posed by the world federalists. Who were the utopians? Were they the defenders of a status quo recklessly allowing humanity's boat to go over the falls, or were they the uncompromising advocates of a basically different course?[48]

And who could say what, under the pressure of events, was politically possible? Falk reminded his readers that with past movements such as abolitionism, Zionism, and anticolonialism, the sum of many separate individual efforts suddenly erupted into irresistible political forces. This was the major promise of functional supranationalism. New technologies of communications and industrial production, the widely recognized importance of military, economic, and ecological problems on a global scale, and the efforts of various groups to solve those problems as well as profit from the world's interdependence would lead to a network of activities and loyalties transcending the nation-state. "Federalism à la carte," one writer described it.[49]

A reformed United Nations could assume extensive jurisdiction over the oceans and outer space, a task that through royalties and licensing fees could give the organization an independent source of revenue. International agencies could facilitate international banking and commerce, charter multinational corporations, administer development programs for poorer nations, monitor the environment, and at least coordinate the en-

forcement of agency regulations. International agreements could be negotiated regarding limits to industrial growth, availability of resources,
disposal of wastes, arms control, fishing quotas, and appropriate population levels. Pragmatically, gradually, and almost painlessly, the world
would progress toward redemptive unity.

It was an appealing vision centered on the ancient ideal of human beings
living in harmony with one another and with nature. It promised rational
solutions based on human needs rather than competitive advantage. It
posited a more smoothly functioning world economy less burdened by
disruptive nationalisms. And it held out the hope that expanding supranational management of global interdependence would substantially reduce
the risks of war and ecological disaster.

So once again during a time of pervasive fear about mankind's future, the
case for supranationalism was effectively and eloquently made. In response
to many alarming events that seemed to demand immediate response, the
environmentalist movement gathered momentum, proponents of a more
integrated world economy earned a respectful hearing, and the search for
ways to avoid a nuclear war was passionately resumed. Again it became
commonplace to argue that the nation-state was obsolete and that an
alternative political order was possible if frightened people were given the
right sense of direction. For the third time since the end of World War II,
the international system seemed vulnerable to proposals for fundamental
reform. If the world could not be centrally governed, perhaps it could at
least be properly managed.

VIII.

PROGRESS AND SECOND THOUGHTS

> Never has there been such widespread recognition by the world's intellectual leadership of the necessity for cooperation and planning on a truly global basis, beyond country, beyond region, especially beyond social system. And never have we seen such an impressive array of ongoing negotiations aimed at the cooperative management of global problems.
>
> —Richard N. Gardner, *Foreign Affairs*, April 1974

> The fragmentation of man is one of the great pervasive facts of contemporary human affairs. It forms part of one of our many pervasive great paradoxes: the more global our science and technology, the more tribal our politics; the more we see of the planets, the less we see of each other. The more it becomes apparent that man cannot decently survive with his separateness, the more separate he becomes.
>
> —Harold Isaacs, *Wilson Quarterly*, Autumn 1976

On April 22, 1970, about the time of the vernal equinox, millions of Americans paused to demonstrate their concern for life on earth. In New York City, Fifth Avenue was closed for two hours while Mayor John Lindsay, after receiving a daisy from a young Girl Scout, led a large crowd to the official ceremonies in front of the Public Library. In Cleveland, university students gathered tons of litter and staged a reenactment of Moses Cleaveland's original landing along the Cuyahoga River. Concluding that the area was too filthy for the building of a settlement, Moses rowed away. In Letcher County, Kentucky, twelve hundred protesters buried a casket filled with trash; at San Jose State College in California students interred a brand new car; and, in Denver, Citizens Concerned about Radiation Pollution (CARP) awarded the Environmental Rapist of the Year Award to the Atomic Energy Commission. Meanwhile, at the University of Wisconsin, students held a dawn "earth service" of Sanskrit incantations.[1]

Less exotically, in ten thousand public schools and on fifteen hundred college campuses, young people studied and debated environmental issues—the national debate topic for 1970–71 was "How Can Our Physical Environment Best Be Controlled and Developed?" Several state governors created new environment departments, and Massachusetts passed a constitutional amendment establishing an Environmental Bill of Rights. Many large corporations, even in the oil and paper industries, denounced pollution, and the public generally indicated a willingness to help pay for a cleanup of the nation's air and water. A delighted Senator Gaylord Nelson concluded that "Earth Day may be a turning point in American history. It may be the birth date of a new American ethic that rejects the frontier philosophy that the continent was put here for our plunder, and accepts the idea that even urbanized, affluent, mobile societies are interdependent with the fragile, life-sustaining systems of the air, the water, the land."[2]

Nelson had become interested during the previous fall in applying the tactics of the Vietnam War protest to issues of environmental protection. Speaking on many university campuses, he helped mobilize support for a national teach-in to dramatize the many dangers to planetary welfare. A small group of organizers calling themselves Environment Near Death (END) was established in Washington under the direction of Dennis Hayes, an "intense, ascetic activist" who had been president of the student body at Stanford. By April, their plans had evolved well beyond anyone's expectations as over four thousand environmental groups coordinated their efforts to publicize a wide range of problems from littered highways and excessive noise to more fundamental problems of auto exhaust, pesticides, population growth, and world hunger. *Time* reported that "dismay over the decaying state of the environment is fast replacing peace as the gut issue among the nation's young." Environmentalism was an immensely popular cause that nearly everyone could abstractly support, a common cause that was especially welcome after the political divisiveness of the late 1960s. In his own Earth Day address to a Washington audience, Hayes thus seemed to be justifiably optimistic: "We are building a movement with a broad base, a movement which transcends traditional political boundaries. It is a movement that values people more than profit. It will be a difficult fight. Earth Day is the beginning."[3]

It was one thing, however, to sponsor a national day of protest, a day dominated by "folk-rock music and moral exhortation," and quite another to coordinate a thoughtful national movement effectively devoted to political and economic change. Mother Earth Day, as *Science* magazine noted, was filled with excitement, indignation, and dedication, but what would come next? How could popular support be mobilized politically?[4]

There were many organizations prepared to meet the challenge. Ideas and information came from the American Association for the Advancement of Science, the Institute for Policy Studies, the John Muir Institute for Environmental Studies, Barry Commoner's Committee on Environmental Information, and other organizations, including the well-financed Sierra Club, the Audubon Society, the militantly political Friends of the Earth, the Wilderness Society, Environmental Action, the League of Conservation Voters, Planned Parenthood, and Zero Population Growth, Inc. Also, the Environmental Defense Fund, founded in 1967 by lawyer Victor Yannacone, had matured into an effective legal instrument wielded by a coalition of sixty lawyers and seven hundred scientists. Yannacone's motto was "Sue the bastards," and his organization became accomplished at promoting environmental protection in the courts. In the early 1970s it forced the banning of DDT in several states, delayed the Alaska pipeline, and defeated the infamous U.S. Army Corps of Engineers over several canal and dam projects.[5]

Between 1970 and 1971, membership in the five largest environmental organizations increased by 400,000 to produce a total following of over 1.5 million Americans. Earth Week was widely observed in 1972, and public support for government spending on pollution control remained high. Student demonstrations continued, including a mock trial in New York, "The People vs. Technology," that included the participation of Louis Nizer and several of the original atomic scientists. Californians by a three-to-one margin favored Proposition 9, which would have banned new coastal oil drilling, slowed development of nuclear power plants, prohibited DDT, eliminated lead additives in gasoline, and levied severe fines on polluters. Universities established courses and degrees in ecology, the Boy Scouts launched Project SOAR (Save Our American Resources), and more sedentary Americans could purchase new board games called "Smog" and "Dirty Water." Meanwhile, some environmentalists embraced direct action: in Kane County near Chicago, a mysterious man nicknamed "The Fox" plugged the sewers of polluting companies and dumped buckets of river muck and dead fish on the carpeted floors of company reception offices. To make matters worse, he described himself in messages as a card-carrying Republican.[6]

While environmentalism remained a disparate cause resistant to well-focused coordination, it was obvious in the early 1970s that the movement was strongly advancing along a broad front. Nervous politicians had little choice but to join the discontented or silently await a major change in the political climate. Even before Earth Day, President Richard Nixon had established, under the terms of the National Environmental Policy Act of 1969, an advisory Council on Environmental Quality and delivered a prescribed "state of the environment" report to Congress. In that report he requested Congress to establish national standards for air and water purity, to appropriate $4 billion for municipal sewage plants, and to require gradual reductions of harmful automobile exhaust emissions. Encouraged by Interior Secretary Walter J. Hickel, the president had also increased penalties for oil drillers and shippers guilty of accidents or willful negligence. After April 22, he was even more active, creating the Environmental Protection Agency to coordinate a vigorous federal attack on pollution and thus rescuing the states from risky unilateral action. In early 1971 he substantially increased the agency's budget and broadened its powers. Although cooperation between president and Congress was minimal, environmentalists had accomplished much by the end of Nixon's first term. Pollution standards were raised, and a potentially strong agency was in place to enforce them.[7]

But while such progress was gratifying to Americans concerned about their own national problems, environmentalists were being constantly reminded that the United States alone could not rescue mankind from fatally fouling its own nest. It seemed obvious, as George Kennan observed, that the ecology of the planet was not arranged in isolated national compartments, and the simple truth that everyone was living in the same neighborhood soon attained the status of conventional wisdom.[8] Less clear, however, was the kind of political action demanded by that truth. Predictably, there were many appeals for international cooperation, requests that all nations voluntarily put their own houses in order and agree on common standards for the neighborhood. Frightened by local crises and nurtured by popular values devoted less to competition and growth, public opinion would ideally lead one nation after another toward needed reform at home and enlightened collaboration abroad.

But many reformers doubted that voluntary cooperation would be adequate. *Fortune* magazine recalled the tragedy of the commons: "Unless some sort of international machinery is constructed, nations will be in the position of river towns, no one of which has a political incentive to build a sewer-treatment plant unless the others do so." Paul Ehrlich and Lester Brown saw no alternative to some relinquishment of sovereignty by national governments, the gradual denationalization of the nation-state, while Richard Gardner envisioned many institutions of "limited jurisdiction and selected membership to deal with specific problems," institutions that would execute "an end run around national sovereignty, eroding it piece by piece." And George Kennan similarly hoped that new cooperative international organizations, "as powers were accumulated and authority delegated," would assume the enforcement functions appropriate to a "single commanding International Authority." All of these writers shared the view that there had to be eventual reform of the nation-state system.[9]

There were still some dogged champions of world government. What was left of the old United World Federalists argued that effective global administration necessitated a world state. Their frequent president, *Saturday Review* editor Norman Cousins, had not retreated an inch from the strong opinions he had voiced shortly after Hiroshima:

> The price of his [mankind's] survival is the management of his planet. The
> fully sovereign state is incapable of dealing with the poisoning of the en-

vironment. Worse than that, the national governments are an important part of the problem. They create anarchy on the very level where responsible centers and interrelationships are most needed. The management of the planet, whether we are talking about the need to prevent war or the need to prevent ultimate damage to the conditions of life, requires a world government. This will be the test of man's vision and greatness.[10]

Most reformers, however, were not prepared to go that far. Richard Falk rejected traditional notions of world government as both unachievable and dangerous. Rich, dominant governments could hardly be expected to negotiate away their prerogatives, and effective world government in a divided world would require totalitarian methods. Brown and Ehrlich agreed that world government was not likely to be created in the near future, and Gardner expressed no hope for "ambitious central institutions of universal membership and general jurisdiction." There existed no consensus on basic values, he noted, nor was there any willingness to entrust vital interests to community judgment. "One need only picture a world constitutional convention including Messrs. Nixon, Brezhnev, Mao, Brandt, Pompidou, Castro, Perón, and Qaddafi. What rules or procedures for world government could they agree upon?"[11]

Functionalism seemed the most promising response to global environmental problems. If national governments by themselves were incapable of solving those problems and if world government was impossible to create, then perhaps cooperative arrangements evolving toward supranational status offered the wisest strategy. Each step would be so modest and gradual that it would arouse minimal suspicion or fear, and eventually a complex network of specialized agencies would acquire supranational authority backed by extensive popular support. The Europeans had made impressive progress of this sort in the Coal and Steel Community and the Common Market; surely, in response to problems of even more vital importance, the world (or much of it) could follow that instructive example.[12]

This functional supranationalism never enjoyed the status of a popular political movement similar to world federalism. The functionalist case was complicated and promised only long-term, gradualist solutions to problems that were also long-term and gradualist in nature. Americans in the late 1940s feared the loss of their atomic monopoly and suspected imminent war with the Soviet Union, but environmental issues in the 1970s constituted what Stewart Udall termed a "quiet crisis," a slow slide toward some eventual, unknown disaster. Consequently, although later proponents of supranationalism could count on much goodwill from the powerful environmentalist lobby in America, they could not mobilize public support behind some immediate response to a credible threat of impending doom. They tended to attract supporters who were comfortable with ideas, were concerned about the distant future, and were prepared to move slowly toward undramatic, pragmatic objectives.

Internationally, the late 1960s and early 1970s were devoted mostly to encouraging greater awareness of environmental problems. The International Council of Scientific Unions funded studies of pollution control in hopes of facilitating a global warning system to detect significant hazards. An international symposium on conservation was held in Paris in 1970, a meeting that drew over one thousand participants from fifty nations. The United Nations sponsored a conference on the oceans in 1970 and another on urban environmental problems in 1971. Also, various Western European nations beginning to address their own national problems came to realize that unilateral efforts were inadequate and would have to mesh with more ambitious international or supranational activities.[13]

As early as 1968 the Swedes had proposed a comprehensive United Nations Conference on the Human Environment, but initially global reactions were tepid. Industrialized nations believed they could deal with their own problems, while developing countries feared that the conference would divert attention from their overriding concern for economic growth. But relatively quickly ecology had become a globally popular cause, "a new political substitute for the word motherhood," according to California politician Jesse Unruh. As a result, a conference was scheduled for Stockholm in June 1972, and elaborate efforts were made to devise an agenda that would be both manageable and politically acceptable to most participants. Barbara Ward was requested to prepare the official background report for the conference, and a twenty-seven nation preparatory committee suggested topics for discussion and concrete proposals for international action.[14]

The fate of the conference illustrated both the high degree of concern for environmental problems and the enormous obstacles to solving them. One hundred thirteen nations assembled in Stockholm and were able to reach agreement on a Declaration on the Human Environment specifying new principles of behavior and responsibility and on a program of global monitoring and assessment that would generate objective scientific information to help guide the political decisions of national governments. Canadian industrialist Maurice Strong, who served as secretary-general for the conference, termed these results "nothing short of remarkable," while U Thant hoped that mankind's common interest in survival would lead most nations down the functional path toward significant institutional reform: "Perhaps it is the collective menaces, arising from the world's scientific and technological strides and from their mass consequences, which will bind together nations, enhance peaceful cooperation, and surmount, in the face of physical danger, the political obstacles to mankind's unity."[15]

Yet given the agenda of the conference, which included the identification and control of environmental hazards, the careful management of economic growth in both developed and underdeveloped nations, and the establishment of new institutions to help accomplish those objectives, the results of Stockholm were disappointing. Difficulties emerged early in the planning stage, bedeviled the conference itself, and left participants and observers much wiser regarding the intractability of the problems they faced. Environmental dangers were acknowledged, as was the need for an effective response, but severe disagreements over the nature of that response thwarted institutional change. Many people might favor international collaboration in the abstract, even consider it vitally necessary, but then would come the hard questions of what sort of collaboration for what purposes and at what costs to whom.[16]

Some conflicts arose between East and West. The Soviets, who had already insisted that any new environmental institutions would have to be "international and not supranational in character," led several Eastern European states out of the conference because of its exclusion of East Germany. Obviously, despite Richard Nixon's optimism, détente had major limits, and to the extent that collaboration with the Soviets was possible, it could operate "only through cooperative actions of sovereign states." The Russians would agree to nothing more than joint research on a case-by-case basis.[17]

Friction also developed between rich and poor nations. The poor believed that pollution was largely a problem for developed nations and were concerned lest international controls throttle Third World economic growth. In trying to penetrate competitive world markets, developing nations had little use for expensive measures of environmental protection. To the contrary, they were often prepared to assist industries escape from expensive regulation elsewhere. "Why not?" asked Brazil's planning minister. "We have a lot left to pollute." The preparatory committee prevented a boycott of the conference by developing nations by endorsing economic growth for poor societies and suggesting that "since the less industrialized countries have by and large put lighter burdens on their environment resources than the industrialized countries and may therefore be able to afford less stringent environmental standards, this could give them a competitive advantage in the establishment of certain new industries. . . ."[18]

Finally, most environmental issues raised complex political problems for both national and international politics. Barry Commoner argued that "the solution to the environmental crisis is not to be found in new kinds of automobile mufflers or in legal constraints on waste emissions, but in the radical reorganization of national economies and international commerce along lines that make ecological sense." For example, noting the heavy environmental costs of synthetic rubber production, he advocated a return to natural sources. But such a course would destroy the synthetic rubber industry and its associated employment, leave Western military establishments dependent on foreign control of a vital raw material, and probably encourage rubber-producing countries such as Malaysia to manufacture their own finished products as well. Regretfully, Commoner concluded that ecology was a "subversive science" because it involved a zero-sum game: "if the environment wins, someone loses."[19]

The Stockholm conference avoided that problem by limiting itself in

advance to what was "feasible"—vague declarations of principle or commitments to further research. Largely left beneath that placid surface were
what Commoner called "the long-standing, unresolved conflicts that trouble the world." Little attention was devoted to reducing the growth rates of
the industrial giants, to the trade-offs of limited growth and unemployment, to the distribution of world production and wealth, or to the irrational demands and dangers of military preparedness. It was hardly clear
how UN conferences could handle dangerous issues like these or how
nations could leave such matters to functional cooperation, especially of a
supranational variety. In Commoner's judgment, peace among men would
have to precede peace with nature.[20]

Mankind's disunity was symbolized by the Stockholm conference itself—
"Woodstockholm," *Time* called it. As official representatives clashed,
dodged, and patched, one observer noted that "each delegation consists of
an environment minister with a scientist behind him telling him what to
say and a diplomat telling him not to say it." Concurrently in the same city
a semiofficial environmental forum met for the benefit of various scientific,
conservationist, and other nongovernmental groups and individuals. Furthermore, Stockholm was filled with interested bystanders—oil company
public relations men, pollution control salesmen, and a whole tent city of
concerned students located at a nearby abandoned airport. There was a
representative from Hog Farm (an American commune), an organic foods
enthusiast, a contingent of save-the-whale demonstrators, and Chief Roll-
ing Thunder, a Shoshoni medicine man chanting helpful incantations.
Apparently, environmentalism meant all things to all people.[21]

There was minimal progress after Stockholm. The UN General Assembly
established a Governing Council for Environmental Programs to coordinate
activities both within and outside the United Nations, and international
agreement was reached in London regarding the dumping of toxic substances into the oceans. But the council was so dominated by developing
nations that it established its secretariat in Nairobi, and no international
agreements for pollution control provided for effective enforcement. The
environmentalist movement at the international level was clearly stalled.
The ill-timed Stockholm conference had come too late to arouse public
opinion (already accomplished), but too early to find nations receptive to
decisive action. Probably this inertia could be overcome only by some great
crisis.[22]

The domestic movement was also losing momentum by 1973. For a time,
it seemed to unify nearly everyone behind an irreproachable appeal for a
cleaner, safer environment. After a period of unusual political strife, the
New Republic observed, all Americans could once again march in the same
parade. But once the implications of environmentalism became better understood, there was far less unanimity. Cleaning the air and the water were
wonderful goals in the abstract, but as Barry Commoner had asked in
another context, who would pay the costs? As the environment won, who
would lose?[23]

The political Left in America was unhappy because the movement directed attention and resources away from what were considered to be more important matters. On Earth Day, black militants interrupted an environmental teach-in at the University of Michigan to warn the audience not to be diverted from continuing battles for racial equality. Vietnam War protesters were worried that their long struggle would be drained of vital energy, and liberals feared that environmentalism would swallow all of their traditional concerns for education, urban reconstruction, and the war against poverty. The Left was not impressed by Sierra Club conservationists whose definitions of the "quality of life" never seemed to include a rat-free apartment and three square meals a day, nor were political cynics reassured by the appointment of Laurance Rockefeller as chairman of President Nixon's Citizens' Advisory Committee on Environmental Quality.[24]

Meanwhile, conservatives also became alarmed at many aspects of the environmentalist movement. Countering attacks on capitalism, growth, and technology, they argued that pollution was a product of all economic systems, that growth was necessary to maintain employment and to pay for social services, and that technology was required to help solve environmental problems. Flaming manifestos, prophesies of doom, and a search for scapegoats were no substitutes for facing the choices implied in most policies of environmental protection. While writers in *Fortune* magazine were prepared to admit that innovations were necessary to reduce fragmentation of governmental authority, to offer incentives to polluters to reform their behavior, and to heighten everyone's awareness of interrelated ecological problems, they ridiculed the notion that modern man was "going to snuggle back into the bosom of nature" and warned against devastating condemnations of society that could sap the morale essential to reform.[25]

Further to the Right, there were the familiar complaints that reformers threatened the nation's sovereignty and the American way of life. The DAR feared that "subversive elements plan to make American children live in an environment that is good for them." A bitter attack on the environmentalist movement by Melvin Grayson and Thomas Shepard, entitled *The Disaster Lobby*, condemned "save-the-world do-gooders" and "self-anointed saviors of humanity" joined by "millions of sincere, dedicated but hopelessly ill-equipped rank-and-file Americans who, . . . alarmed by what they heard, embraced the most fatuous causes of their own." Compounding the problem, the authors concluded, were "the nuts and the almost nuts":

> From the dimly-lit rooms of back-street boarding houses, from the depths of the stacks in college libraries, from the park benches and skid-row bars and the all-night movie palaces, there emerged . . . "the lunatic fringe"—the hot-eyed men and women with bulging briefcases under their arms and tales of horror on their lips who, in normal times, remain hidden, but who, when the times grow fey, come out to peddle their manic wares.

Newspapers from Alabama to Alaska noted also that Earth Day had been scheduled on Lenin's birthday.[26]

But aside from ideological assaults from Left and Right, there were many other reasons why the movement faltered. Critics accused environmentalists of ignoring the past, distorting the present, and foreclosing the future. Also, a series of events, culminating in the deepest economic recession since the 1930s, produced apathy, or even hostility, toward many environmental objectives.

For many reformers, the past did not exist except as an assumed time of pristine cleanliness prior to a relatively recent plunge toward environmental disaster. Few recalled the thick, dark air of nineteenth-century Pittsburgh, the belching stacks and piercing screams of old steam engines, or the hopelessly overtaxed sewage systems of American cities that had sometimes doubled their size in two or three decades. Pollution problems were as old as human beings themselves, and not all of those problems had become progressively worse over time. To deny that was to exaggerate the ill effects of technology and economic growth and to expose reformers to charges of excessive devotion to prophesies of doom.[27]

Similarly, recent events did not invariably suggest despair. Food production was increasing dramatically throughout the world, and population growth was diminishing among peoples who became more urban, educated, and prosperous. Many raw materials could be produced synthetically or be replaced by adequate substitutes. In some dramatic instances, such as the purification of the Thames, pollution had been substantially reduced, and steady progress had been made in the United States in lowering sulfur dioxide and carbon monoxide levels in the air and curbing industrial pollution of the nation's waterways. Deadly serious environmental problems remained, but a relentless preoccupation with crises, it was argued, strained credibility and failed to provide a favorable context for rational decision making.[28]

Habitually cataclysmic visions of the future exacerbated these problems. Confident predictions about demography, climatic changes, ozone deterioration, oxygen supplies, and the resiliency of polluted seas were based on imperfect knowledge and understanding, and foretelling the future on the basis of worst-case extrapolations from present trends seemed naive. The scale of the earth is so vast (hardly a small spaceship), and nature herself had provided ice ages, enormous volcanic eruptions, and many other natural disasters that had sometimes eliminated whole species. Were human beings' activities, critics inquired, really so crucial to the fate of the earth? Also, could not technology be relied upon to help solve, as well as help cause, environmental problems? Food might be produced synthetically, water pollution might be attacked by various micro-organisms, more energy might be taken from the wind and the sun, and all types of human transportation might be made more clean and efficient. The possibilities seemed endless, and reformers who suggested otherwise were accused of political irresponsibility. Here again was the classic tale of the child who cried wolf—even the Club of Rome's computers were accused of such self-defeating behavior.[29]

The environmentalist movement had done a magnificent job in gaining people's attention, but its blanket indictment of technology and economic growth and its obsession with potential disasters eventually proved to be costly in terms of intellectual persuasiveness and political acceptability. Moving beyond initial feelings of panic, many people realized that environmental problems could not be attributed simply to capitalistic greed and that many difficulties were side effects of highly desirable objectives such as reducing infant mortality, increasing agricultural production, or improving global standards of living. Consequently, there could never be an environmental code similar to a criminal code, full of absolute prohibitions. As University of Michigan law professor Joseph Sox observed: "We don't want to say never fill a marsh, cut a tree, or dam a river. We are always looking for some subtle balance between industry and nature, between high-density and low-density uses, between preservation and development."[30]

This sort of balance was particularly difficult to strike during an economic recession. Hard times led people to concentrate on personal problems, and youthful concerns about America's opulent materialism gave way to more mundane worries about finding a job. The deep recession of the mid-1970s refocused attention on traditional priorities of economic growth, and governments had less money to spend on tasks unrelated to the encouragement of production. Furthermore, there was considerable hesitancy to impose new government regulations that might alienate manufacturers or lessen their competitiveness in international markets. In 1975 President Gerald Ford recommended a five-year moratorium on 1977 automobile emission standards and an eight-year moratorium on clean air standards.[31]

Events generally had not been kind to the environmentalist movement. The disintegration of the Nixon presidency, an energy crisis, and baffling problems of both inflation and recession diverted attention from environmental problems and led many American industrialists, workers, and politicians to conclude that environmental issues, while significant, had to yield to more pressing demands of political and economic reconstruction.

The tenth anniversary of Earth Day was celebrated in April 1980. Again, there were speeches, concerts, cleanups, tree plantings, solar power demonstrations, and organic picnics. In Washington, there was choral music at the Jefferson Memorial, and at dawn atop Cadillac Mountain along the Maine coast, bagpipers played "Amazing Grace." Activists were able to look back at the previous decade with considerable satisfaction: much legislation had been passed, the EPA had been established, and the public remained concerned about environmental issues. Lake Erie was reviving, the Potomac was safe for swimming, and even the Cuyahoga River was less flammable. America's air was noticeably cleaner, and industrial pollution of waterways was down by one-half. Ironically, one of the major problems had now become what to do with the noxious chemicals that had once been casually dumped into the nearest sewer or stream.[32]

But momentum was lost as a more conservative administration presided over yet another economic recession and worried about the nation's ability to compete in an increasingly jungle-like world economy. Symbolically, the Environmental Protection Agency was staggering under serious charges of corruption and incompetence. Nationally and internationally, environmentalism had proven to be expendable, highly vulnerable to the imperatives of economic growth. Unless prosperity could once again make environmental protection a luxury most developed nations could afford or until new disasters offered political leaders little choice, there seemed to be no way fundamentally to address the global tragedy of the commons.

In happier, simpler times, George Wildman Ball had enjoyed a comfortable, middle-class childhood in the American Midwest. His grandfather had emigrated from the island of Jersey to a small town in Iowa where he opened a hay and feed business that gradually evolved into a general store. Ball's father worked in the family enterprise until, at the age of nineteen, a traveling salesman offered him a modest job with Standard Oil in Marshalltown, Iowa. Soon a promotion moved him to Des Moines where George was born in 1909. Until the age of twelve, he attended public schools there and contentedly matured within a family of avid readers who enthusiastically shared and debated their views on literature, history, and politics. Collective visits to the local library were a weekly ritual.

In 1922 the Ball family moved to the wealthy community of Evanston, near Chicago. There George attended high school and then Northwestern University where he earned an honors degree in literature. At Northwestern, he was influenced by the provocative social critic Bernard De Voto and by the more scholarly Garrett Mattingly. Ball was president of the poetry society and editor of a new literary magazine, *MS*. Continuing to read widely and deeply, he developed a particular fondness for Voltaire, especially his devotion to reason and his fundamental optimism. "I felt myself a citizen of the Age of Reason," Ball recalled, and optimism was in his judgment "the only respectable working hypothesis for a self-respecting man."[33]

As the Great Depression closed in, Ball entered Northwestern Law School where his excellent academic record enabled him in 1933 to find a government service position in Franklin Roosevelt's expanding New Deal. Ball initially worked for the Farm Security Administration, subsequently moving along with Henry Morgenthau to the Treasury Department. Those were exciting years in Washington, but by the late 1930s Ball wished to enter the more practical and lucrative world of private law. Returning to Chicago, he devoted himself to tax cases and corporate reorganization.

International politics also interested him as German and Italian expansion pushed Europe toward world war. An early interventionist, he regularly attended the Friday lunches of the Chicago Council on Foreign Relations and, with his young law partner, Adlai Stevenson, supported William Alan White's Committee to Defend America by Aiding the Allies. When the United States entered the war, Ball resumed his public career as counsel for the Lend-Lease Administration and later as director of the

Strategic Bombing Survey. Again, it was an exhilarating time to be in Washington as America moved boldly on stage as the world's most powerful nation.[34] By the end of the war, Ball was a seasoned political veteran. His government service had produced many useful associations. In Lend-Lease he had worked with Philip Graham, Joseph Rauh, and Eugene Rostow; in Europe he was assisted by John Kenneth Galbraith, Paul Nitze, and Adlai Stevenson. Wise in the ways of Washington bureaucratic politics, Ball was a moderate liberal domestically and a staunch advocate of deep American involvement in international political and economic affairs. In short, he was well positioned to become one of those influential corporate lawyer-lobbyist-public servants who would dominate American domestic and international politics for the next thirty years.

In a sense, his first major foreign client was Jean Monnet, whom Ball represented in Washington as lawyer for the French Supply Council in 1946. The wealthy inheritor of a successful French brandy enterprise that marketed its products throughout the world, the cosmopolitan Monnet had served as Deputy Secretary-General of the League of Nations and had forged close interwar relations with many American international lawyers and bankers, including Robert Lovett, John J. McCloy, and John Foster Dulles. Traditionally impatient with atavistic European nationalism, Monnet had worked on common European monetary problems in the 1920s, suggested French political union with Britain during the dark days of 1940, and then became a champion of European unity after the war. He was involved in joint Anglo-French preparations for the Marshall Plan, in establishing the Organization for European Economic Cooperation, and in creating the European Coal and Steel Community which he hoped would evolve toward economic and political union.

Ball sympathized with those objectives. Critical of economic nationalism, he had encouraged the use of Lend-Lease as a lever to promote freer postwar trading relationships, and he would later help establish a citizens committee to resist protectionist pressures in the United States. Ball helped prepare the Schuman Plan, was retained as an adviser to the European Coal and Steel Community, and shared Monnet's vision of a more unified Europe (including Britain) closely associated with the United States. This was the essence of President John F. Kennedy's "Grand Design" that George Ball championed as undersecretary of state.[35]

Ball's dream of a cooperative, closely-knit Atlantic community, an objective pursued by many members of the transatlantic economic elite, led him into membership in the prestigious Bilderberg group. The idea for regular, informal meetings of political and economic leaders from both sides of the Atlantic originated with a Polish adventurer, Joseph Retinger, whom Ball later described as a romantic mixture of Casanova, Cellini, and Tom Paine. Friend of André Gide and Joseph Conrad, economic advisor to Plutarco Calles in Mexico, and a freedom fighter in Poland during World War II, Retinger emerged from the war physically weakened but with undiminished intellectual energy. In the early 1950s, concerned about deteriorating American-European relations, he took his conference proposal to Paul van Zeeland, prime minister of Belgium, Paul Rykens, chairman of the board of Unilever, and Prince Bernhard of the Netherlands. While the prince organized the European contingent, the Americans were coordinated by Burroughs Corporation president John S. Coleman and by George Ball. These efforts culminated in the first general session, held in 1954 at the hotel Bilderberg as Oosterbeek, Holland. Thereafter, at least once each year, about eighty European and American leaders have met to exchange views on issues significantly affecting Atlantic relations.[36]

After serving the Kennedy and Johnson administrations as undersecretary of state for economic affairs and then as second in command to Secretary of State Dean Rusk, Ball turned in 1965 to a new career in investment banking. Remaining a forceful critic of narrow economic nationalism, he now became convinced that the multinational corporation offered the most efficient means of utilizing the world's finite stock of resources, a necessary precaution if mankind were to "avoid a Darwinian debacle on a global scale." The political boundaries of nation-states, he concluded, had become "too narrow and constrictive to define the scope and activities of modern business":

> The urgent need of modern man [is] to use the world's resources in the most efficient manner. That can be achieved only when all the factors necessary for the production and use of goods—capital, labor, raw materials and plant facilities—are freely mobilized and deployed according to the most efficient pattern—and that in turn will be possible only when national boundaries no longer play a critical role in defining economic horizons.[37]

In Ball's judgment, commerce was much in advance of politics. Instant communications, rapid transport, and modern managerial techniques enabled large corporations to obtain raw materials, utilize labor, and find markets anywhere in the world. All the factors of production could move with considerable freedom. Yet archaic nation-states tried to limit that freedom, especially when multinational corporations were perceived as instruments of another nation's political and economic self-interests. The answer to that problem, argued Ball, was not to regulate closely or to nationalize a corporation's local subsidiaries but rather to make the multinationals truly multinational. World corporations would "become quite literally citizens of the world." An International Companies Law, administered by a supranational body, would provide legal incorporation, supervise corporate behavior, enforce regulations regarding antimonopoly law and expropriation, and limit the restrictions nations could impose on the multinationals. Ball denied that he was advocating world government, but it was nonetheless necessary to create "new world instrumentalities . . . to close the gap between the archaic political structure of the world and the visions of commerce which vault beyond confining national boundaries to exploit the full promise of the world economy."[38]

As a young literature student at Northwestern, George Ball had considered himself a citizen of the world. In the late 1940s and early 1950s he had with Jean Monnet promoted European unification and a closely associated Atlantic community. Then, in the 1960s and 1970s, he suggested that the world's peoples needed to "modernize" their political structures, "to evolve units larger than nation-states and better suited to the present day." He became an active member of World Federalists, USA, the major organizational remnant of the 1940s world government movement, and he would join the Trilateral Commission, a group dedicated to functional cooperation among the world's economically developed nations. The son of a Standard Oil vice-president, lawyer and banker to foreign governments and multinational corporations, at home in Paris and London, as well as in Washington and Chicago, Ball was part of a new transnational elite that felt frustrated and unduly restricted by the traditional nation-state system. For Ball, the global economy had outgrown its old institutional clothing, and he firmly believed that this awkward adolescent promised enormous benefits for the good of all mankind. It simply needed the freedom to mature.[39]

Richard Barnet and Ronald Müller wrote a book about the new "world managers" such as George Ball. "The men who run the global corporations," the authors observed, "are the first in history with the organization, technology, money, and ideology to make a credible try at managing the world as an integrated unit." They certainly have had the will to do so. The president of the IBM World Trade Corporation noted that "for business, the boundaries that separate one nation from another are no more than the equator. They are merely convenient demarcations of ethnic, linguistic, and cultural entities. They do not define business requirements or consumer trends." Bank of America president A. W. Clausen boasted that only the world managers have freed themselves from the bonds of nationalism: "The expansion of our consciousness to the global level offers mankind perhaps the last chance to build a world order that is less coercive than that offered by the nation-state." "In the forties Wendell Wilkie spoke about one world," concluded IBM's Jacques Maisonrouge; "in the seventies we are inexorably pushed toward it."[40]

As George Ball suggested, the multinational corporations have been interested in world planning, in globally integrating the factors of production in ways to maximize efficiency as measured by profit. In a world increasingly aware of its limited resources, this quest for efficiency has had considerable appeal, and the broad perspectives of the global managers have provided hope of ameliorating other problems affecting mankind such as environmental pollution and international military conflict. Multinational corporations have been defended as instruments of world economic development, as powerful agents for the internationalization of human society, and as champions of an economic interdependence conducive to cooperation. IBM's company slogan is "world peace through world trade."[41]

The nation-state is perceived as an impediment to such progress. William I. Spencer, president of First National City Corporation, lamented that "the political boundaries of nation-states are too narrow and constricted to define the scope and sweep of modern business," while Maisonrouge insisted that the rationality of international business was frequently defeated by dangerous myths of national prejudice and fear. "The world's political structures are completely obsolete," he concluded. "They have not changed in at least a hundred years and are woefully out of tune with technological progress." Or, as business consultant Peter Drucker more dramatically advised, "We need to defang the nationalist monster."[42]

In Barnet's view, world managers "think and talk of themselves as a revolutionary class." As a new elite aspiring to considerable power, they have sought legitimacy. They have wished to convince their global audience that their authority is both inevitable and reasonable, that they can provide what people so desperately need—the managerial skills to create a cooperative world of greater productivity and economic growth. To deliver on such grand promises, they have argued that most of all they need freedom from nationalistic interference. A new global economy requires sound global management.[43]

Multinational businesses were not something new under the sun in the 1960s. The ancient Phoenicians traded throughout the known world, carrying their technology, manufacturing, and culture to much of the Mediterranean, and the East India Company came to preside over most of the Indian subcontinent. Many American firms had established global markets by 1900, and giant corporations from various nations negotiated cartel arrangements between the two world wars. But modern multinationals flourished after World War II thanks to improvements in communication and transportation and the global dismantling of restrictions on the movement of goods and capital among developed national economies. From 1953 to 1965, the volume of international trade among those nations nearly tripled. Increasingly, individual countries became mere parts of intricate webs of trading relations, technology transfers, and capital investment. Interpenetration and interdependence were common throughout the world, offering vast economic opportunities to the multinationals and leaving nation-states feeling much less in control of their own destinies.[44]

Nations had become accustomed to formulating their own economic policies, whether guided by mercantilism, liberal free trade, or Keynesianism. Moreover, since the late nineteenth century, and especially since World War II, governments had assumed growing responsibilities for social welfare and domestic economic management. Thus they have been vulnerable to powerful multinationals that could control the flow of considerable capital, move in and out of various national currencies, relocate plants to escape unpleasant regulation, hire creative accountants to avoid taxation, and pressure labor to accept lower, competitive wage levels. Nations have also complained about corporate bribes and favors, unfair competition with local industries, research and marketing decisions that do not necessarily benefit host countries, and economic or political actions imposed on multinationals by home governments wishing to make the companies instruments of national policy.[45]

In self-defense, national governments could become more nationalistic. They could force corporations to reveal information about their activities, require minimum levels of exports and reinvestment of profits, review mergers and takeovers by foreign companies, and suggest that multinationals assume greater responsibility for local services. Labor organizations and national industries might seek tariff protection, and as a last resort, governments might consider expropriation, with or without compensation. To various degrees, nations have resorted to these remedies during the postwar period.

Theoretically, nations or individuals interested in policing the behavior of multinational corporations could also seek international or supranational solutions. Logically persuasive arguments were made that the multinationals needed to be made accountable to some public authority that matched their geographical reach. As Harvard professor Raymond Vernon noted: "In the best of all possible Panglossian worlds, the writ of every government would extend as far as the interests that might affect it." Global economic enterprises seemed to necessitate global government, or at least effective functional institutions:

> The basic asymmetry between multinational enterprises and national governments may be tolerable up to a point, but beyond that point there is a need to reestablish balance. When this occurs, the response is bound to have some of the elements of the world corporation concept: accountability to some body, charged with weighing the activities of the multinational enterprise against a set of social yardsticks that are multinational in scope.[46]

Hence, both the defenders and critics of multinational corporations came to advocate supranational institutions, albeit for quite different reasons. Seeking protection against national interference in their global activities, the multinationals have generally sought truly supranational status. Instead of relying on their home governments for defense, a course both unreliable and provocative, the multinationals have advocated international agreements regarding such things as trademarks, double taxation, and property protection, as well as a supranational body that would incorporate companies and encourage codes of fair conduct to assure respect for local laws, the training of local workers, and minimum levels of investment in local economics. Ideally, in their view, multinationals would not be directly responsible to any particular national government. Carl Gerstacker, chairman of Dow Chemical, once said: "I have long dreamed of buying an island owned by no nation and of establishing the World Headquarters of the Dow Company on the truly neutral ground of such an island, beholden to no nation or society." Apparently, Gerstacker seriously considered acquiring such neutral ground—on Minerva atoll near the Fiji Islands.[47]

Critics of the multinationals, on the other hand, have sought interna-

tional or supranational means to discipline, not liberate, the great corporations. Fearing that the economic benefits of economic integration will be
unevenly distributed, that an unfettered transnational elite will create a
new feudalism, that corporate planners will produce the wrong kind of
growth (threatening to the environment and insensitive to the particular
needs of local societies), and that the multinationals will not be concerned
about problems of hunger, unemployment, and inequality, critics have
proposed various measures of control. Professor Joseph Nye warned that
unilateral policies could be self-defeating unless there were international
rules and mechanisms for coordination, and Raymond Vernon spoke for
many critics in appealing for "a set of common rules that shape and limit
the application of domestic law, as well as ongoing institutions to administer the rules."[48]

There was some progress. Among developed nations, the Organization
for Economic Cooperation and Development helped create a model bilateral tax treaty, developed consulting mechanisms for disputes over anti-
trust laws, and adopted a voluntary code of fair practices for multinationals
regarding tax information, labor relations, and anticompetitive behavior.
Six Latin American states attempted in the Andean Pact to coordinate their
relations with the multinationals, and the developing countries in the UN
agreed to common expectations regarding just treatment by the industrialized economies. Meanwhile, a UN Center on Transnational Corporations was established in 1975 to provide information and advice to
developing nations.[49]

Yet none of these efforts has been effective in forcing the multinationals
into greater accountability. Appeals for supranationalism from both defenders and critics of the corporations were vague and without much
popular support, even among people knowledgeable about such a complicated subject. There were deep suspicions of men such as George Ball who
argued that supranationalism was in the interest of the corporations themselves. Thus, while an ambivalent Richard Barnet could suggest that public
authority had to be "shared at the supranational, national, state, local, and
neighborhood levels," he also feared that "the corporate prospect of a world
without borders offers something more distressing than uncertainty. It is a
vision without ultimate hope for mankind." The safer route, however, of
combining national action with coordinated international measures under
existing institutions would not produce impressive results.[50]

Far more threatening to the multinationals have been the actual and
potential actions of individual national governments that have feared loss of
sovereignty or have been pressured by injured domestic interests. But
while most writers have agreed that national power could bring the multinational corporation to its knees, they have also noted the caution demonstrated by nations who feel protective toward their own companies or who
do not wish to discourage investment from abroad. It remains unclear
whether individual nations in practice can effectively tame the multinationals or whether such uncoordinated flailing would make much sense in

an interdependent world economy. Barnet and Müller attempted to resolve that dilemma by insisting that "*both* a global vision and radical decentralization and diffusion of political power now appear to be requirements of a stable and just human order." In the interest of human survival, they concluded, people will need to reject the values of the multinationals' "Global Shopping Center"—competitive individualism on behalf of infinite accumulation. Democratized local and national power is needed to resist the corporate global planners, but local and national decisions must be made with the larger, common concerns of mankind in mind. This theoretical marriage of parochialism and world-mindedness is appealing, but other observers have been much less sanguine about local altruism or the ability of local interests to deal effectively with corporate power and other modern economic problems.[51]

An important writer who shared those doubts was Columbia political science professor Zbigniew Brzezinski, a student of Soviet and American diplomacy and author of *Between Two Ages: America's Role in the Technocratic Era* (1970). In that book, he argued that "the paradox of our time is that humanity is becoming simultaneously more unified and more fragmental." Modern weaponry, instant communications, swift transportation, and new transnational associations were all making the nation-state obsolete, and, consequently, a new pattern of international politics was emerging: "The world," he wrote, "is ceasing to be an arena in which relatively self-contained 'sovereign' and homogeneous nations interact, collaborate, clash, or make war." The immediate effects of such changes have been frustration and disorder as national governments have been unable to meet their traditional obligations and as their authority and prestige have correspondingly eroded. Feeling less in control of their own fate due to national weakness amid rapid and fundamental change, people have sought assistance and comfort closer to home where they at least have some sense of cultural identity. As political sociologist Daniel Bell observed: "In a world marked by greater economic interdependence, yet also by a growing desire of people to participate at the local level in the decisions that affect their lives, the national state has become too small for the big problems in life, and too big for the small problems."[52]

Yet, according to Brzezinski, chaos and fragmentation would not dominate the future. "A global human consciousness is for the first time beginning to manifest itself" among new transnational elites of businessmen, scholars, professionals, and public officials whose ties cut across national boundaries. "Their perspectives are not confined by national traditions, and their interests are more functional than national." This new consciousness "still lacks identity, cohesion, and focus," and the "majority of humanity still neither shares nor is prepared to support it." But while the old national framework has been disintegrating, a new world unity has sought its own consensus and structure.[53]

Brzezinski recommended "a community of developed nations" be created that could mitigate traditional conflicts and center the world's attention on more basic problems of economic development. Initially, a community composed of Western Europe, North America, and Japan would be established, an association that would find institutional expression in regularized meetings of political and economic leaders assisted by a permanent organization that would supervise the study of common political, economic, and technological problems. Those meetings would discuss political relations both within and outside the community, encourage educational and scientific collaboration, shape a new monetary structure to replace the antiquated arrangements of the 1940s, and promote a "truly international structure of production and financing" that would remove restrictions on multinational manufacturing, banking, and trade. Ideally, such a community would expand and gain enough public support to become a useful instrument for addressing global issues of environmental protection, economic development, and peace.[54] Brzezinski conceded that a community of developed nations was a less ambitious goal than world government, but his objective seemed more attainable and promised evolution toward global cooperation. A functional approach "emphasizing ecology rather than ideology" would "encourage the spread of a more personalized, rational humanist world outlook that would gradually replace the institutionalized religious, ideological, and intensely national perspectives that have dominated modern history." Once again, the world would be managed in ways appropriate to economic and technological realities.[55]

About the time Brzezinski's book appeared, a series of shocks disturbed the once stable economic world order dominated by the United States and her major cold war allies. By the early 1970s, due to the postwar recovery of Europe and Japan, the escalating costs of maintaining America's vast international commitments, and the problems arising from considerable economic mismanagement during the Vietnam War, the United States was suffering from inflation, sluggish economic growth, and severe balance of payments deficits. In this exposed position, Americans then faced the Arab oil boycott, the rise of OPEC, and generally increased militancy from the Third World. The great economic boom of the 1960s now seemed endangered, and nations once again considered more nationalistic policies to maintain their weakened competitive positions. In 1971 President Nixon unveiled his New Economic Policy which suspended the convertibility of dollars into gold and other reserves, thereby devaluing the American currency. Moreover, he and Treasury Secretary John Connally imposed surcharges on imports and in other ways pressured foreign industrial nations to ease their restrictions on American products. Traditional monetary and trading arrangements were now in disarray, and a general Nixon-Kissinger preference for unilateral decision making left old allies feeling unconsulted and abused, an especially troubling situation in light of increasing Soviet military strength.[56]

By 1972–73, there were therefore many good reasons for improved cooperation among non-Communist, economically developed nations. The old postwar international economic order was flying apart; the United States could no longer preside (at some sacrifice) over that order; Third World exporters of natural resources were threatening to alter terms of trade traditionally favorable to the West; and the Soviet Union appeared to be increasingly powerful and ambitious. Furthermore, the renewed nationalism among developed nations that threatened their economic order and stability also challenged the multinational corporations which needed an open world economy to realize their extravagant expectations. The West's collective economic future seemed cloudier than at any other time since the end of World War II.

In response, one of the West's most powerful bankers, Chase Manhattan's David Rockefeller, joined with Zbigniew Brzezinski in early 1972 to propose a new Trilateral Commission to receptive audiences in Western Europe (including the Bilderberg group), North America, and Japan. With assistance from the Brookings Institute and the Kettering Foundation, the commission was formally founded by July 1973, with Brzezinski as director and with a membership roster that resembled a social register of Western political and industrial leaders. Concerned that most people continued to live in a "mental universe which no longer exists—a world of separate nations," the Trilateral Commission wished to nurture the collective management desirable and necessary for an interdependent world. Among advanced market economies, there would ideally evolve closely coordinated policies toward trade, monetary policy, energy, and pollution abatement. Through "frequent and intimate consultation," Western leaders would, in Professor Richard Ullman's words, "abstain from measures conducive to short-run, one-sided advantage" at the cost of long-term general community interest. Similarly, these leaders would develop common policies regarding defense, nuclear proliferation, and the needs and demands of developing nations.[57]

In theory, a "community" of democratic, economically developed nations would be created and maintained through a process of "piecemeal functionalism." Within a context of similar values and parallel economic and security interests, Western elites would apply their technical expertise to problems of trade, finance, communications, ecology, economic development, and world peace. There were no blueprints for world government or Atlantic union, but the very *process* of routine consultation and cooperation would supposedly create a community of shared perspectives and a willingness to transcend the immediate demands of narrow nationalism. Thus, similar to Barnet's enlightened parochialism, trilateralism was essentially a new state of mind.[58]

Perhaps for that reason, results have been unimpressive. There have been many meetings and reports, both devoted to a great variety of topics from the governability of democracies to the world energy crisis. Many members of the commission were appointed to the loftiest ranks of the Carter and Reagan administrations—indeed, the list included such influential men as Secretary of State Cyrus Vance, National Security Adviser

Zbigniew Brzezinski, and Defense Secretary Casper Weinberger. But although these elitist meetings and weighty presidential appointments fueled conspiracy theories from both ends of the political spectrum, it was difficult to demonstrate much commission influence beyond Carter's interest in human rights, economic summitry, and the law of the seas, and Reagan's general commitment to free trade. Much like Bilderberg, commission meetings probably promoted smoother personal relations among national leaders, but progress toward a new transnational or supranational community was minimal.

Within the United States, the Trilateral Commission was under constant fire, particularly from liberals or radicals who perceived it mainly as an instrument "to safeguard the interests of Western capitalism," especially American capitalism, in an increasingly chaotic world. Global management was designed, they charged, to avoid trade wars, to bargain collectively with OPEC and other suppliers of raw materials, to smother Third World nationalism in moderate reform, and generally to strengthen and rationalize the world economy in the interests of multinational corporations. A new international ruling class supposedly sought to utilize world resources for the maximization of profit, and to accomplish this they wished to promote dependence rather than genuine interdependence. Trilateralism, the indictment concluded, was a conspiratorial effort to perpetuate existing power relationships for the primary benefit of a transnational corporate elite.[59]

The commission was, of course, a consciously elitist organization that was far more interested in influencing government policy than in seeking broad public support, and resulting public suspicion from Left and Right, from organized labor, and from other foes of the multinationals did the commission's cause no good. Brzezinski could rapturously describe the new breed of transnational technocrats liberated from atavistic nationalist sentiments, but to most Americans these superbureaucrats were invisible and were hardly perceived as being concerned with the average person's day-to-day problems. There is little evidence that a "global consciousness" was shared by many Americans, even at the governmental level.

Partially because of this, the United States did not become a champion of the new community Brzezinski and David Rockefeller had in mind. In fact, the industrial nations in general demonstrated little willingness to reform the monetary system, coordinate energy policies, further unclog the channels of international trade, address the issue of Third World poverty, or harmonize their great power diplomacy. Hard times produced hard bargaining positions, and the conservative political resurgence brought a deeper sense of political and economic nationalism. The Reagan administration, for example, adopted a more unilateral approach to diplomatic and security matters, avoided collective policies regarding environmental protection and law of the seas, and emphasized the primacy of the American economy and its leadership role in encouraging general economic recovery. When told that allies objected to high American interest rates, White House Chief of Staff Donald Regan typically responded: "Tell em, 'We upped our rates. Up yours.' "[60]

Relatedly, insofar as the commission was designed to enhance Western, or American, industrial power in the world, other nations were naturally suspicious. For example, a prominent Chilean economist viewed appeals for a more highly integrated global economic and political system as a thinly disguised plan for perpetuating the subordination of less developed countries. Even international institutions established to regulate multinational corporations could easily become means by which Western nations would dominate the process of regulation, probably to Third World disadvantage. Similarly, Japan and the Common Market countries were uneasy about conceding economic advantages for the greater good of some vaguely defined "community." American self-interest was always lurking in the background, and the great American multinationals were not universally popular. Even security issues were increasingly difficult to resolve as political-economic perceptions and interests continued to diverge.[61]

Generally, trilateralism has suffered the traditional fate of ambitious twentieth-century internationalism—modest success until forced to deal with issues that matter. Inspired by tough economic times, nationalism has rallied to defend economies threatened to some extent by the very forces the trilateralists have so deeply admired. This defense has been awkward and weak, but there have recently been many pressures for stronger efforts. If international cooperation is ineffective and suspect and if supranational institutions appear beyond reach, then failure to act nationally could leave the economic field to the strongest players. Yet national economic sovereignty is largely an illusion, as there are severe limits to the ability of any government to chart its own economic course. What remains, then, is a dilemma thus far unresolved, the question of how the new global economy can be managed without the world's peoples losing control of the managers. There is a natural reluctance to embrace George Ball's international laissez faire, and little public confidence is inspired by periodic meetings of trilateral elites. Consequently, there is a sense of drift as nations address their own economic problems with ancient remedies and hope that somehow they can avoid becoming victims of events over which no one has much control.[62]

A similar sense of events beyond anyone's control led to functionalism's most impressive accomplishment during the 1970s, a new Law of the Seas Treaty. For three centuries following Hugo Grotius's skillful legal defense of the far-flung interests of the Dutch East India Company, freedom of the seas was a sacred principle of international law. Save for a modest territorial sea near national coastlines, the oceans were free to all who wished to navigate or fish. Also, nations accepted the concept of common ownership: "The sea," wrote Grotius, "since it is incapable of being seized as the air, cannot have been attached to the possessions of any particular nation." With the oceans so vast, fish so plentiful, and powerful trading nations so interested in unhindered navigation, those traditional laws and customs generally remained in force until after World War II when advanced technology and expanded international commerce made the seas more crowded, polluted, exploited, and potentially valuable. The great oceans, covering about 70 percent of the earth's surface, were then increasingly the subject of international tension and conflict.[63]

There were many ways in which the oceans were being drawn into the normally anarchic state of international politics. Responding to the discovery of oil just off the American coast and to the development of new technologies that brought this seemingly scarce resource within man's reach, President Harry Truman in 1945 claimed for the United States exclusive ownership of all resources on its continental shelf. In response, other nations made similar claims or, more commonly, assumed exclusive fishing rights in nearby waters threatened by efficient new technologies that increased the world's total harvest from sixteen million tons in 1950 to sixty-nine million in 1974. Peru and Ecuador forced American ships out of their proclaimed two-hundred-mile fishing zones, while Iceland and Britain nearly came to blows over disputed grounds. Meanwhile, dramatic increases in merchant tonnage created environmental problems that led some nations, such as Canada, to impose pollution controls well beyond their traditional three mile limits. Indeed, many nations now sought to extend their territorial seas, a development that had serious implications for access to resources and freedom of navigation. By 1974, about 35 percent of ocean space was claimed by individual nation-states, a major blow to traditional assumptions that the oceans were mankind's last great commons.[64]

Beyond the actual or anticipated jurisdiction of coastal nations, however, there was another potential problem due to the discovery on the seabed of vast quantities of nodules rich in manganese, nickel, copper, and cobalt, minerals that new technologies would soon be able to exploit. For nations concerned about dwindling supplies of raw materials at home and abroad, seabed mining promised renewed abundance and self-sufficiency, at least for those already sufficiently wealthy and technologically advanced. It seemed time to stake claims as governments parceled out small seas and mining companies sought legitimate title either from national governments or no government in particular. One British-American corporation claimed 270 square miles in the Red Sea simply by publishing a public notice in the London *Daily Express*.[65]

Thus, rather suddenly, nations found themselves caught in a maze of overlapping, often conflicting interests for which traditional law of the sea was woefully inadequate. Consequently, there were many appeals for fashioning "a new public order for the oceans," for "global administration" that would exercise "sovereignty" over the two-thirds of the earth beyond national jurisdiction. "Time is short," warned a writer in *Foreign Affairs*, "if anarchy and chaos are not to acquire squatter's rights on our last common," and Lord Ritchie-Calder feared that in the absence of international collaboration the world would witness "the biggest smash and grab since the European powers at the Berlin Conference in 1885 carved up black Africa."[66]

In response to these concerns, Malta's UN ambassador, Arvid Pardo, requested the General Assembly in 1967 to reserve the mineral wealth of the seabed beyond "present national jurisdiction" for the benefit of mankind in general. The ambassador was interested in various maritime problems, such as fishing rights, pollution, and the militarization of the ocean floor, but he worried most about the ultimate fate of what he called "the last great frontier for natural resources." For Pardo, those resources were a "common heritage of mankind" that should benefit the poor as well as the wealthy, and, to ensure that result, he advocated a new treaty to safeguard the extranational character of the seabed and an international or supranational agency to implement and enforce the terms of the treaty. Sympathetically, the General Assembly soon established a Seabed Committee and in 1970 adopted, without dissent, a declaration of principles based on Pardo's recommendations. The seabed was to be considered the common property of all and would ideally be utilized for "the benefit of mankind as a whole, irrespective of the geographical location of states, whether land-locked or coastal, and taking into particular consideration the interests and needs of the developing countries." The assembly also decided to sponsor a conference that would comprehensively review seabed issues along with all other problems regarding the law of the sea. That conference, the first of many, convened officially in Caracas in June 1974.[67]

These meetings were supported by the United States government which had long been worried that "jurisdictional creep" would endanger American freedom of navigation and close large sections of the ocean to American scientific research and economic development. Moreover, in the new, untried field of deep sea mining, an international agency could legitimize claims, guarantee peaceful, orderly development, and prevent irresponsible practices injurious to the environment. As early as 1966, President Lyndon Johnson had said: "Under no circumstances must we ever allow the prospects of rich harvest and mineral wealth to create a new form of colonial competition among the maritime nations. We must be careful to avoid a race to grab and hold the lands under the high seas. We must ensure that the deep seas and the ocean bottoms are, and remain, the legacy of all human beings." Richard Nixon acknowledged a "world interest" to be served by the negotiations, while Henry Kissinger noted that "We are at one of those rare moments when mankind has come together to devise means of preventing future conflict and shaping its destiny rather than to solve a crisis that has occurred or to deal with the aftermath of war." And the chief American delegate to the conference, Elliot Richardson, enthusiastically announced: "Rarely has any generation had so clear a choice between order and anarchy." "We, as part of the world community," he later observed, "are strengthened by the strenghtening of the rule of law. A successful outcome of the Law of the Sea Conference . . . would extend the rule of law . . . over two-thirds of the earth's surface. In so doing, it would give powerful encouragement to the determined pursuit of other rational accommodations among the ever more complex issues forced upon the world by the imperious realities of its inescapable interdependence."[68]

These sentiments were cheered from the sidelines by reformers generally committed to functional internationalism or supranationalism. A study prepared for the Club of Rome considered the "common heritage" principle to be one of the most heartening of recent developments and hoped it would have other applications such as administering the resources of outer space. In his study of "future worlds," Richard Falk agreed that the oceans would have to be "beneficially managed to serve global community interests, including equitable distribution and preservation of the life chances of future generations." And, even more eagerly, Lester Brown predicted that "Should an international oceanic regime come into being, organized along the lines now being considered, it would have a profound impact on the way the global community is organized, greatly strengthening the case for international sovereignty and collective approaches to meeting mankind's needs." In his judgment, the UN would establish sovereignty over the oceans, and revenues from licensing governments or private companies wishing to mine the seabed would provide the UN an independent source of income and offer a precedent for the supranational taxing of multinational corporations. Proceeds could then be largely used to assist the economic development of poorer nations.[69]

Veterans of world federalism also endorsed the UN's efforts. The national organization of federalists extended its blessing, as did its president, Norman Cousins, in his new magazine, *World*. And from the old battlefields of the late 1940s came Robert Hutchins and Elisabeth Mann Borgese, participants in the University of Chicago project to draft a constitution for world government. As president of the Center for the Study of Democratic Institutions in Santa Barbara, Hutchins agreed to mobilize intellectual resources in the United States and abroad largely through a series of *Pacem in Maribus* conferences sponsored by the center. Borgese organized those conferences, reported on their progress, and even joined the Malta delegation to assist Pardo in the United Nations. She was convinced that the Chicago group's insistence on linking order and justice was being vindicated and that the Law of the Sea Conference now provided a means to apply the Chicagoans' constitutional theories to practical problems. Like Brown, she also believed that the results of the conference would fundamentally transform the United Nations and that concurrently the world's peoples would be won to the cause of functional supranationalism. "The world," she concluded, "will never be the same again."[70]

The Law of the Sea negotiations during the 1970s appeared to justify Borgese's optimism. In a series of plenary meetings of nearly two thousand delegates from 160 countries, combined with skillful committee sessions where agreements were reached by consensus among various powerful nations and coalitions of nations, a surprising number of issues were settled to the general satisfaction of most participants. Negotiations, normally informal and private, produced a package of arrangements that reflected years of hard bargaining and elaborate compromise. There was agreement on accepting international standards on pollution for maritime shipping, on the right of nations to regulate pollution in their own territorial waters, on a clear definition of the continental shelf (necessary for the assignment of various commercial privileges), on freedom of navigation through straits, commercial zones, and territorial seas, and on arbitration of disputes by an International Tribunal for the Law of the Sea. But, most dramatically, the treaty contained many innovative and precedent-establishing provisions governing deep-sea mining. An International Seabed Authority was created to grant leases to private companies and to conduct its own mining operations through its subsidiary, the Enterprise. The Enterprise would be able to choose from mining sites discovered by private companies, would impose royalties on private ventures, and would have guaranteed access to private technology. The Authority would have the power to establish maximum production levels (to protect land based producers) and to regulate the mining process to prevent unacceptable environmental damage. It would also "have the power to establish its own rules and regulations, subject to the approval of participating countries; to mete out (subject to appeal) penalties to offenders against them or against the prescriptions of the treaty; and to try disputes in its own courts."[71]

This unique world organization would thus have considerable administrative authority, would enjoy its own sources of financial support, and would have the potential to evolve into a prototype of world government. According to one of the conference's international lawyers:

> The Authority is a very interesting experiment in supranational or international government, a move toward something many idealists have talked about. It will supervise a large area and its resources, and in that it is like a government. It differs from the United Nations in that it will deal with things that are real—commodities and sales. It may reflect the present situation of the world; unquestionably, it's another example of how small the world has become.

Much less enthusiastically, a hostile former American delegate to the conference criticized the treaty's governmental ambitions and the precedents being established for handling other global problems. Richard Darman advised American rejection of the agreements in order to defend threatened principles of free enterprise, decentralization, diversity, and pluralism.[72]

As Darman's comments would suggest, the Law of the Sea Treaty drew heavy criticism from many Americans, particularly among conservatives in the new Reagan administration. Despite various compromises regarding production limits, technology transfers, ease of private leasing, and voting procedures in the Seabed Council and Assembly, compromises designed to circumscribe the supranational powers of the Authority, American leaders remained nervous. Ideologically, the seabed provisions seemed to promote, as negotiator James Malone described it, "a form of global collectivism" dedicated to "the redistribution of the world's wealth through a complex system of manipulative central economic planning and bureaucratic coercion." The treaty, he complained, assumed that every nation shared ownership in the oceans and was therefore entitled automatically to profit from the efforts of those who "produce wealth from what would otherwise be economically valueless." Moreover, political bodies beyond American influence or control could discriminate against private ventures, limit production, compel sharing of technological information, and "impose unconscionable financial and regulatory burdens on American industry and government." For months, new American delegates, sporting neckties embellished with portraits of Adam Smith, tried fruitlessly to modify a treaty they believed to be fundamentally flawed. Finally, in July 1982, President Reagan officially announced that he would refuse to sign. He allegedly told his cabinet: "We're policed and patrolled on land and there is so much regulation that I kind of thought that when you go out on the high seas you can do as you want."[73]

Altered perceptions of American self-interest were also involved. When the whole negotiating process began in the late 1950s and on into the next decade, American leaders were deeply concerned that continued anarchy on the high seas would erode navigational rights and lead to conflict over fishing privileges and rival mining claims. In 1975 Henry Kissinger warned that failure to negotiate a treaty would lead to "unrestrained military and commercial rivalry and mounting political turmoil." By the 1980s, however, the consequences of failure seemed far less serious. Agreements on issues other than the seabed conformed generally to current practice, and traditional international law could still be invoked to discourage ambitious territorial claims. As for deep sea mining, several nations were proceeding on their own and could hope to negotiate a mini-treaty among themselves to avoid conflict. Thus the United States, which had lost control of the Law of the Sea negotiations, could feel relatively safe in rejecting those parts of the treaty perceived as deleterious to its ideological and commercial interests.[74]

There were additional reasons for American caution. Powerful mining interests were opposed to the treaty, and the Senate was becoming increasingly suspicious. There is much truth in Darman's observation that, since the long negotiations had not commanded the attention of either the public or Congress, a Senate ratification debate was likely to be contentious. Once again, the elitism of functional supranationalism left proponents vulnerable to political assault. It was not immediately obvious to most Americans why substantial concessions should be made to Third World economic development or why American freedom of action should be limited by some unpredictable supranational authority.[75]

So, after many years of negotiations that were partly initiated and consistently encouraged by the United States, the American government refused to accept the Law of the Sea Treaty. Opinions differ regarding the consequences, but it is clear that internationalism had been tightly contained within its customary boundaries: the most daring functional experiment since the Common Market was not permitted to see the light of day. Large, albeit very long-term, profits seemed at stake and perhaps national security interests as well, but most revealing during the early 1980s was the depth of American nationalism as it recoiled before the specter of supranational global management. The necessity of functionalism in an increasingly interdependent world may have been obvious to reformers, but for most American political leaders the material and ideological costs seemed to outweigh the promised benefits. In a period of nationalist resurgence, the United States was determined to go it alone.

This heightened nationalism led in the early 1980s to renewed interest in the question that had preoccupied the world federalists after World War II—the maintenance of peace in a nuclear age. With the Reagan administration dramatically increasing the defense budget, developing major new offensive and defensive weapons systems, considering survivable and winnable nuclear conflicts, and generally pursuing a vigorously unilateral and anti-Soviet foreign policy, many people took to the streets to demonstrate their support for disarmament and peace. Such demonstrations began in Western Europe to protest the installation of Pershing II and cruise missiles, but fear of an escalating arms race involving retaliatory systems increasingly difficult to control spread beyond Europe and North America to encompass much of the world. The peace movement, latent since Vietnam, again became a powerful political force.[76]

In contrast to the late 1940s, most of the American movement's activities had little to do with supranationalism. Instead, demonstrators concentrated on defeating the MX missile proposal, opposing the strategic defense system, reducing the military budget, and freezing the size of Soviet-American arsenals in hopes of encouraging gradual reductions. Indeed, most efforts were devoted to a renewed campaign of fear designed to resensitize people to the reality of the nuclear threat. Once more there were articles, television programs, and motion pictures about the consequences of a nuclear exchange, and again American scientists played a major instructional role. Popularizers such as Carl Sagan were especially effective in describing the terrible devastation likely to endanger the entire planet, particularly the effects of what he called a "nuclear winter," the probable cooling of the world's climate caused by huge clouds of dust thrown into the atmosphere by the explosion of thousands of megaton weapons. Humankind could thereby meet the same fate as the dinosaurs, which, some suggested, were condemned to extinction by a great dust cloud caused by a meteor colliding with the earth. (Every generation seems to have a dinosaur theory that corresponds to current fears.)[77]

This fear, it was again assumed, was the beginning of wisdom. Aware that their very existence depended on the unfailing rationality and restraint of great powers armed with hair-triggered nuclear weapons systems, people protested their vulnerability, organized themselves for political action, and demanded a safer, saner world. Hope was especially high for influencing American foreign policy (seen as especially villainous by many reformers), but there were expectations that an aroused world public opinion would inspire caution in all the world's major leaders. Who could deny the need to reduce the threat of accidental nuclear war or to control weapons systems that would destroy both attacker and intended victim?

Paradoxically, however, the peace movement neglected international politics. It was far better at awakening consciousness and suggesting specific proposals for disarmament than at coming to terms with traditional great power conflict and explaining how substantial arms reduction could occur in a politically divided world. It was left in part to the supranationalists to fill this theoretical gap between the ends and means of the peace movement, to contribute traditional insights about the burdens of sovereignty within an inherently dangerous nation-state system. Two major cases for fundamental reform of international politics were advanced, and, examined together, they provide an excellent summation of the recent state of supranationalist thought.

Jonathan Schell's *The Fate of the Earth* first appeared in the *New Yorker* in February 1982, and then in book form became a national best seller. Schell was troubled that "hundreds of millions of people acknowledge the presence of an immediate unremitting threat to their existence and to the world they live in but do nothing about it." With fifty thousand warheads in the world threatening to end history, to annihilate man, "only recently have there been signs, in Europe and the United States, that public opinion has been stirring awake." While conceding that such denial may in part have been a healthy refusal to accept "immersion in death," he nonetheless believed that ignorance and escapism were of far greater explanatory importance.[78]

His initial task, therefore, was to describe the probable fate of the earth in the event of Soviet-American nuclear war. In chilling detail, he explained how such a conflict would totally disrupt modern societies and suddenly extinguish the lives of millions of people, but his greater concern was the bomb's effects on the habitability of the earth. In his judgment, the planet's delicate ecosystem would face a triple threat—delayed radioactive fallout that would work its way into the cells of most living things; partial destruction of the ozone layer, which would expose animal, bird, and plant life to harmful ultraviolet light; and huge clouds of suspended dust that would dangerously cool the world's temperature. Best equipped to survive all those disasters, according to Schell, are the insects and the grasses; with luck, they could inherit the earth. Human beings, socially interdependent and physically vulnerable, would be among the first species to succumb. While Schell could not prove this grisly analysis (only deadly experience could do that), uncertainty offered no comfort: "Our ignorance," he admonished, "should dispose us to wonder, our wonder should make us humble, our humility should inspire us to reverence and caution, and our reverence and caution should lead us to withdraw the threat we now pose to the earth and ourselves."[79]

He doubted that humankind had squarely faced the possibility of extinction, for extinction was much different from individual death. Death could have meaning and dignity; extinction could not. Death ends life, while extinction "locks up in the nothingness before life all the people who have not yet been born." People can experience death, at least the death of others, but extinction will leave none to remember. It is difficult to contemplate extinction in any meaningful way, and, perversely, the nuclear stalemate discouraged any serious effort:

> Once Hiroshima and Nagasaki had been pushed out of mind, the nuclear peril grew in such a way that while it relentlessly came to threaten the existence of everything, it physically touched nothing, and thus left people free not to think about it if they so chose. Like a kindhearted executioner, the bomb permitted its prospective victims to go on living seemingly ordinary lives up to the day that the execution should suddenly and without warning be carried out.

According to Schell, people have resigned themselves to "live on the edge of extinction": intellectually aware of mortal danger, they have nonetheless tried to live as if life were essentially safe. Consequently, life has proceeded with "a faltering and hesitant step," leaving mankind emotionally strained, morally crippled, and politically apathetic. After decades of denying reality, people have hardly begun to design an appropriate strategy for survival. They still live on borrowed time.[80]

A basic choice had to be made. People could deny the peril and continue to prepare for a suicidal conflict that sometime, somehow is bound to happen, or they could "dismantle the weapons and arrange the political affairs of the earth so that the weapons will not be built again." Disarmament *and* fundamental political change—both were required, in Schell's opinion. Weapons would have to be controlled, but since the scientific knowledge required to make them is so widely held, the potential for renewed armament would always remain. Because the nuclear threat "is global and everlasting, our solution must at least aim at being global and everlasting. And the only kind of solution that holds out this promise is a global political one." Within the nation-state system, governments feel compelled to defend their interests with weapons that threaten the planet, a reality that forces humankind to choose between "extinction or a global political revolution."[81]

In a later article, Schell placed much greater emphasis on arms reduction as an immediate objective. Pursuing the logic of deterrence, he argued that nuclear weapons had eliminated war among the major powers as a means to advance national interests. Traditional international anarchy had thus been replaced by order of sorts—stalemate rooted in fear of mutual destruction. War, at least as a rational activity, had been abolished. What remained was the task of dismantling weapons systems that could destroy all human life, a task that seemed theoretically possible because deterrence could just as easily rest on the ability to make nuclear weapons as upon the weapons themselves.

In the short term, in Schell's view, the great powers needed to accept the status quo established by World War II, arrangements that adequately protected the conventional security of both the United States and the Soviet Union. Neither nation would intervene militarily in their rival's sphere of influence. That accomplished, the two powers could then fashion a system of deterrence that would not through impatience, miscalculation, or accident threaten total annihilation. Conventional armaments and antinuclear weapons would be permitted, but both would be severely restricted to maintain their essentially defensive character. All this would not guarantee peace, even nuclear peace, but at least the lead time between crises and doom would be lengthened to a point where saner considerations might prevail. Also, the breathing space acquired from a step back from the brink could be used to discourage nuclear proliferation, construct rudimentary systems of collective security, and "address the radical and sweeping measures of global political renovation which alone can fully deliver us from the evil [of nuclear war]."[82]

When Schell wrote of "global political renovation," he did not have the federalists' world state in mind, although he acknowledged that they had a strong case:

> The consensus, among so many of those who have thought deeply about the nuclear predicament, that nuclear weapons cannot be abolished unless world government is established seems to find support in traditional political theory: in the distinction between the so-called state of nature, in which men live in anarchy and resolve their disputes among themselves, with war serving as the final arbiter, and the so-called civil state, in which men live under a government and submit their disputes to its final arbitration.

But, like so many other critics of world government, Schell worried about granting enormous power to some central, supranational authority. Such a regime would not necessarily be lawful and nonviolent, and unbalanced power on a global scale could have devastating effects on cultural diversity and individual liberty. In Schell's opinion, however, humankind did not have to choose between anarchy and world government: deterrence had imposed some order on international politics, and functionalism could complete the task as much as possible.[83]

Functionalism was vital because Schell did not believe that his "nuclear-weapon-free world of stalemated sovereign states" could be permanent, or even long-lasting. Ideally, nations would gradually deal with the many problems of interdependence—ecological issues, the global economy, the law of the sea, and, ultimately, with the stage thus properly set, the peaceful arbitration of international disputes. The end result would be effective supranationalism in many crucially important areas, but supranationalism checked and balanced by local power. In time, a much safer world would enjoy peace, order, and good government without sacrificing an inordinate amount of freedom. Cord Meyer would have been impressed.[84]

Like Schell, Richard Falk deeply distrusted traditional international politics. Within that system, he noted in *This Endangered Planet*, nations need *superior* power in order to compete economically and politically with other states for the earth's limited wealth, "and the pursuit of such superiority combined with the drive to avoid a situation of inferiority leads to continuous pressure on any apparent circumstance of equilibrium in international affairs." Postwar palliatives never dealt with war-making capabilities, the sovereign authority of national leaders, or the social, economic, and political causes of war. More fundamental change was required, not slow, gradual reform of a system inherently flawed.[85] Also, like Schell, Falk was not a champion of world government. Such peace plans appealed to reason, but they were apolitical in the sense that "the continued pressures of competitive activity made it unthinkable that governments, especially dominant and rich ones, would negotiate away their capabilities and prerogatives." Furthermore, a world state could hardly eliminate civil conflict rooted in alleged injustice, and efforts to do so would probably lead to totalitarianism. Logically persuasive, the case for world government underestimated the reluctance of national leaders and their constituencies to relinquish power and failed to come to terms with the objective causes of violent conflict within any national or supranational society.[86]

Falk looked forward to a process of adaptive change that would build the centers of value, action, and control required for a radical modification of the world-order system. He called for generous economic development programs to reduce disparities of wealth and for more vigorous subnational and transnational movements to diminish disparities of national power. He encouraged functional efforts to increase the role of global institutions demanded by environmental problems, the burdensome costs of armaments, and the simple "ethical imperative implicit in the unity of man." And he wished to nurture a deepening sense of community by educating the world's peoples to their common fate and enhancing their participation in decisions of global importance. Falk strongly emphasized the need to identify with "the long and widespread affirmation that all men are part of a single human family, that a oneness lies buried beneath the manifold diversities and dissensions of the present fractionated world, and that a latent oneness alone can give life and fire to a new political program of transformation."[87]

Basically, Falk dissented from Schell's emphasis on international politics and functional institution building in favor of a broader, more organic process of change that ties the search for peace closely to a quest for social justice and participatory democracy. Relatedly, instead of relying mostly on reason and logic to persuade governmental elites to embrace new policies, he rested most of his hopes on a universal culture that, given favorable opportunities, would peacefully or violently impose its will on nation-states. In some ways, Falk has recalled Reinhold Niebuhr's admonition that global institutions must follow, not precede, the existence of a world community within which most of humankind share common values and aspirations. Or, as Warren Wager wrote in *The City of Man*, a book warmly praised by Falk:

> The only movement with the moral dynamic to attract great numbers of men of intellect throughout the world will be a movement that seeks more than peace . . . and more than world federation. It will be a movement for the unification of mankind in a free and organic world civilization. It will be a movement . . . of a panethnic culture quite different from any present national culture, at once more complex and more inspiring, more highly integrated and more free.[88]

For Wager, a University of New Mexico history professor, it was impossible to achieve world order through the actions of national governments which were corrupt, immoral, degenerate structures quite willing to allow respectable reformers to forward harmless resolutions in favor of disarmament and peace. The world required an intellectual-cultural revolution from the bottom up, a universal demand for cooperation rooted in the brotherhood of man. From the most cosmopolitan and generous elements of the world's religions and philosophies would emerge a synthesis conducive to subsequent consensus in politics and economics. Cultural unity, an ecological approach to human beings' place in nature, and an appreciation of other elements of global interdependence could push humankind beyond the self-defeating limits of competitive nationalism.[89]

For Falk, the precise nature of future world order was unclear, but he believed that he knew how to get there. The transition would not be powered by appeals to reason or pleas for peace, by federalist constitutions or UN resolutions, by enlightened governmental elites or the routine duties of global managers. Political action for peace and justice would have to be promoted by peoples throughout the world who are aware of their cultural unity and their common planetary fate.

Neither Schell nor Falk has been able to look over his shoulder at multitudes of followers. Much like environmentalism, the peace movement has aroused millions to the present danger and inspired them to contribute time and money to the cause. But there has been far greater attention to specific disarmament issues such as the nuclear freeze than to more fundamental questions of world order. The case for such an order is complicated; ultimate solutions, not entirely pleasant, seem distant; and political advocacy is beyond the familiar competence of the average citizen. Meanwhile, Wager's "common culture" appears to be overwhelmed by renewed particularism and sectarianism throughout the world. With Schell, most people are concerned about "the fate of the earth," and, with Falk, they recognize that they live precariously on an "endangered planet." But arguments for supranationalism, however intellectually compelling, neither fire popular emotions nor convince national elites to abandon their leaking ships. Like the world federalists, more recent proponents of world order have been forced to labor outside the range of common political imagination and beyond the boundaries of acceptable political debate.

Thus once again by the early 1980s, American supranationalism's familiar cycle of boom and bust had repeated itself. Functionalism was largely a product of the 1970s, a time when deepening suspicions of centralized power blended with broad concerns about the environment, the faltering world economy, anarchy on the high seas, and renewed threats of nuclear war. Functionalism, for those who could comprehend it, seemed a promising solution to those problems, all of which could be partially attributed to the perpetuation of sovereign states in an increasingly interdependent world. The process of reform promised to be relatively painless. Pushed along by the global solidarity of peoples sharing common aspirations and confronting common dangers, functionalism would gradually produce transnational bureaucracies powerful enough to manage world problems but sufficiently weak to preclude serious threats to individual liberty. The vision was understandably appealing.

Like world federalism and Atlantic unionism, functional supranationalism was grounded in fear. The 1970s swarmed with prophets of doom who warned that the rivers and lakes were dying, that the air was corrosively polluted, that international economic relations were spinning out of control, that the oceans would soon be a setting for imperial conflict, and that the world teetered on the brink of nuclear holocaust. Fear was cultivated by reformers who sought to gain mass support, or at least lend a sense of urgency to their cause, and, reeling from Vietnam, OPEC price manipulations, bewildering stagflation, a series of environmental disasters, and a continuing arms race, Americans were prepared to be gloomy.

As in the past, supranationalists presented logical, well-reasoned argument. While they sometimes exaggerated dangers to the planet and became mystical about the unity of humankind, they made a good case for the extent of national interdependence and the unfortunate consequences of many individual, corporate, and national actions that occurred beyond the reach of common government. These were rational reformers concerned with practical problems, people generally content to address each issue on its own terms rather than flog some legalistic or institutional panacea. With the European Common Market as their model, they wanted to establish special commissions or agencies to which national governments would delegate just enough authority to get the job done. Ideally, such agencies would gain increasing recognition and loyalty from a grateful public and establish precedents for even more ambitious endeavors. Furthermore, in charge of these successful experiments would be a growing body of transnational civil servants progressively less identified with any particular nation-state.

The reformers' case was considerably strengthened by two scientific developments: space travel and the new, interdisciplinary field of ecology.

Space exploration, even more than long-distance air travel a quarter century before, provided a fresh perspective from which to view the earth as a whole: seen from hundreds of thousands of miles, this planet seemed to reside at a single address. Ecology reinforced that view by stressing the complicated interrelatedness of living things within a common fragile environment. According to this politically useful model, humankind at least lived in the same neighborhood, sharing services and facing the need to cooperate in order to live well and safely together.

By emphasizing man's interdependence and by offering reasoned responses to the period's deepening anxiety, functional supranationalism won substantial support among the attentive public, those who read and thought about world affairs. Countless books, articles, institutional studies, and conference reports agreed that for many reasons the nation-state was unable adequately to promote and defend the most fundamental interests of its citizens. Public concern focused on environmental issues, leaving various elites to consider world economic integration, the law of the seas, and international peace. But, in combination, American support for functionalist ideas was impressive.

Once again, concern for the welfare of the planet included narrow national self-interest. Global environmental controls could help equalize the burdens of regulation, punish unscrupulous competitors, and discourage developing countries from following the well-travelled Western path of uninhibited industrial growth. (Conservation has traditionally been advocated by the comfortable, already established upper class.) Supranational economc agencies could be used by great corporations to escape national interference, by industrialized nations to ensure steady flows of raw materials at "reasonable prices," and by export interests to gain access to new world markets. A new law of the seas was initially perceived by the United States as required to maintain freedom of commercial and military navigation and to preserve the ocean commons for exploitation by capital rich and technologically advanced American industry. And, almost by definition, peace favors those nations that benefit most from the status quo. Law and order, at home and abroad, is a conservative principle.

But while the nationalism of supranationalism was much in evidence, larger concerns predominated. The Club of Rome study, despite its flawed methodology, communicated the basic truth that the earth could not support unlimited population growth and economic development. With large cities gasping for air, forests yellowing from acid rain, and great tankers crashing into reefs, pollution was an obvious problem. National governments were clearly losing effective control over their domestic economies, and great power military establishments could instantly destroy most life on earth. Consequently, many Americans read, wrote, demonstrated, lobbied, and donated money to the cause of a cleaner, safer, better-managed world. Supranationalism drew on that support, encouraged it, and helped shape its intellectual content.

Yet for the third time since the end of World War II, tangible results were modest, as traditional nationalism resisted major change. The reasons for this lack of progress were complex and mutually reinforcing—divided expert opinion regarding the nature of global problems, the public's limited attention span, the inherently slow pace of functional gradualism, the vagueness and abstract idealism of ultimate objectives, and the under-estimation of enduring loyalties to the nation-state. By the 1980s, the movement would again be in retreat, suffering from intense hostility and cold indifference.

Unlike earlier crises, when global threats such as atomic weapons and Soviet expansionism seemed easy to identify, the problems of the 1970s were much harder to define. Arms limitation was a complicated, esoteric subject; world economic affairs attracted legions of experts offering contra-dictory analysis and advice; and environmental issues defied consensus regarding their precise nature and seriousness. Was the earth heating or cooling? Were the seas dangerously polluted or were they ideal garbage dumps for the unwanted by-products of industrial progress? Were multina-tional corporations threats to national sovereignty or weakly vulnerable to local regulation? Reformers were always aiming at moving targets, and the public was understandably confused.

An especially good example of this was the great ozone scare of the mid-seventies. At that time, several prestigious scientists suggested that rapidly increasing amounts of chlorofluorocarbons released by man into the upper atmosphere posed a threat to the vital ozone layer that protects human life from solar radiation. Frightened by that prospect, Americans reduced their purchases of aerosol sprays and inundated Congress with the greatest deluge of mail since the Vietnam War. In response, the national govern-ment restricted the "nonessential" use of chlorofluorocarbons (in spray cans, but not refrigerators), an action that calmed the public but left many scientists unsatisfied. A major difficulty in subsequent years, however, was the inability of scientific experts to agree on the likely extent of eventual ozone depletion. Atmospheric chemical reactions from natural and man-made causes are complex; direct causal relationships are hard to establish; and predictions are impossible to substantiate until conditions have slipped lethally beyond the point of no return. For a decade, scientists, industrial lobbyists, and government officials debated the implications of wildly vary-ing, inconclusive evidence while the public complacently assumed that the crisis had passed. Not until 1985 was it generally realized that there had been a substantial loss of ozone over Antarctica (6 to 10 percent in twenty years), a revelation that inspired renewed speculation about the probable consequences for climate, agricultural production, and incidents of skin cancer. Only then did the Environmental Protection Agency reconsider its cautious regulations and the international community agree to discuss global standards. Despairing over so much delay, California chemist Sher-wood Roland blamed an enervating combination of scientific inde-cisiveness, public ignorance, governmental timidity, and industrial obstruction.[90]

This sort of issue was difficult to handle politically because the necessity for action, often unpleasant action, was so hard to demonstrate. Involved here were not self-evident crises occurring before the public eye, but rather provisional, hypothetical disasters whose understanding required major acts of creative imagination. There were many prestigious observers, such as John Maddox, editor of *Nature*, who calmly insisted that environmental fears were exaggerated and that practical solutions to even the most serious problems were not beyond the capabilities of traditional political institutions. Pessimists, therefore, did not have an easy time as they demanded radical change based on highly speculative belief.[91]

Predictably, the American public became confused, impatient, and ultimately bored with problematic predictions of dire emergency. As in the past, fear that was unconfirmed by events had limited power to motivate politically. Day-to-day preoccupations intervened, and natural desires to hope for the best prevailed. Moreover, it was seldom clear how vague fears could be harnessed to meaningful political responses. How could the individual influence world economic institutions or the arms race, and how could protest movements save the environment? It was so difficult to focus general concern on activities modest enough to be achievable yet significant enough to help solve the problems. It was easy for larger purposes to get lost in the immediate attention devoted to Earth Days, spray cans, or the nuclear freeze.

Relatedly, there was a contradiction between emphasis on fear (the deathbed purchase of salvation) and hopes placed on functionalism's incremental or gradualist approach to global administration. Theoretically, nations would slowly extend their cooperative activities until truly effective supranational organizations would fall into place, but waiting for the necessary form to follow function could take decades—fifty to one hundred years, according to Richard Falk. Recent history encouraged those cautious expectations: UN agencies had evolved little since 1945, and the process of European economic and political integration had stalled in the 1960s. Yet how could such leisurely development be reconciled with a continuing sense of impending doom?[92]

Another motivational hazard was inherent in functionalist distrust of economic growth. After centuries during which people were aroused from resigned acceptance of their customary fate by promises of greater affluence, how could they now be told to embrace a cause that offered so little? How could wealthy nations be persuaded to accept lower levels of economic activity, and how could poorer states be reconciled to permanent inequality? Unless most of the world's citizens were either extremely frightened about the planet's survival or were suddenly converted to the romantic values of the 1960s American counterculture, such material sacrifice would be unlikely. Functionalist reformers could not easily mobilize their political legions by promising them less.[93]

Generally, these reformers, despite their pragmatic gradualism, were extremely idealistic. While pessimistic about the fate of the earth, they remained naively optimistic about human moral capabilities, about promoting change through appeals to reason and informed intellect, and about achieving a peaceful, cooperative harmony of interests. Herein lay another contradiction, for if the world was as competitive and destructively self-interested as reformers claimed, how could nations ever agree to common government? A Hobbesian interpretation of routine political behavior was being hitched to a Kantian appeal for moral improvement. Somehow, the world could become essentially free of major conflict, apolitically managed by denationalized, bureaucratic experts.[94]

This faith in experts was a traditional tenet of American liberal faith. Ever since the Progressive reform period of the early twentieth century, many Americans had believed that politically neutral, scientific professionals could disinterestedly study important social problems and administer appropriate solutions acceptable to a well-informed public. After decades of commissions, boards, blue-ribbon panels, and hired managers, experience cast doubt on the validity of those old assumptions. The decisions of experts were hardly "above politics," and to the extent that such administrators were insulated from the political process, they were often perceived as dangerously elitist. Yet despite such disappointments domestically and internationally, functional supranationalists retained hope in a "scientific" approach to global management. Progress depended on learning the facts, enlightening the public, and then allowing transnational experts freedom to do their job, and somehow the result would be public-spirited efficiency rather than soulless bureaucratic tyranny or highly politicized incompetence.[95]

Reacting to so much wishful vagueness, critics maintained that supranationalists were hopelessly unclear about both the nature of their good society and their means of achieving it. Where were their theories of social change and their coherent, fully elaborated descriptions of a viable supranationalist community? Richard Falk and his coworkers on the World Order Models Project advocated both decentralized, participatory democracy and "centralized guidance mechanisms," both ecological balance and Third World economic development, both world order and social justice. But were all those objectives compatible, and what would happen to traditional sources of conflict other than those derived from the nation-state system itself? Social justice would be difficult to define, let alone realize; economic development would injure the environment without necessarily promoting international harmony; and the imposition of order implies the perpetuation of some less than perfect status quo. To a great extent, critics were correct when they charged reformers with constructing a future with the politics left out.[96]

Finally, in addition to their tactical and ideological problems, functional supranationalists confronted a renewed defense of the nation-state at home and abroad. The American Far Right sustained its usual vigilance, warning of a "master conspiracy" in which American socialist "insiders" were plotting to establish world government, and more moderate conservatives, those who attained power with Ronald Reagan, were wary of any international or supranational commitments that would restrict the narrow pursuit of American national interests. The administration deemphasized environmental protection, refused to sign the Law of the Sea Treaty, avoided international economic cooperation, and reduced its financial support to the United Nations. Meanwhile, Third World nationalism showed no signs of weakening—indeed, those peoples perceived their national governments as instruments of protection against transnational or supranational forces controlled by the already rich and powerful. Recently liberated from Western colonialism, the developing nations were extremely reluctant to limit their sovereignty. Typically, Indian writer Rajni Kothari objected to "the hollow sounds of comfortable, angry men from the Northern Hemisphere, hopping from one continent to another in a bid to transform the whole world—the latest edition of the white man's burden." One-worlders, he concluded are "myth-makers utilizing modern mass media and communication and conference facilities for building elaborate defenses around basic structures of political and intellectual domination."[97]

Critics of supranationalism also claimed that national governments were not basically dysfunctional compared to some mythical golden past. Nation-states, they argued, had seldom been able to guarantee their citizens' security, and modern governments had seldom done a better job at facilitating economic prosperity or providing for the general welfare. Recent transnational activities were not new and did not necessarily, as in a zero-sum game, significantly undermine the authority of the nation-state. And perhaps this was for the best, critics suggested, lest visionary supranationalism distract national governments from doing what they could to ameliorate the world's common problems. The state system could make useful contributions to world order, environmental protection, and economic justice, contributions resting securely on negotiated self-interests.[98]

Thus, much like their supranationalist predecessors, functionalists met stout resistance from patriotic organizations, vested national interests, radical reformers, and pragmatic skeptics. Never able to distinguish themselves clearly from more moderate internationalists, functional one-worlders also failed, even in alliance with moderates, to acquire durable mass public support. The issues were so complex and proposed solutions so long-term that effective political action was virtually impossible, especially on behalf of ideas that challenged peoples' fundamental loyalties and customary habits of thought. Even the most promising international developments could become counterproductive, as increasing interdependence led vulnerable nation-states to reassert their authority and as efforts at cooperation generated anxiety and suspicion. Despite a host of serious global problems, the traditional state system resisted major change.

The functionalist movement, however, could point to several accomplishments. It had helped ring the alarm bells needed to awaken the public to a series of interrelated threats to the planet's collective welfare. Supranationalist reformers had then stimulated discussion about those dangers and suggested remedies that would gradually expand the limits of cooperative action. Functionalists addressed the general public, offered advice to governmental and corporate elites, and facilitated international responses such as United Nations conferences and the negotiation of a new law of the sea. The result of all those activities was a growing awareness that in so many ways humans shared an interdependence that demanded some sort of global management. If reformers often pressed beyond certain knowledge and exaggerated the extent of crisis, they nonetheless clarified the disastrous consequences of excessive ignorance, complacency, and national selfishness.

The nation-state was hardly obsolete, but it was decreasingly able to cope with the rapidly developing technologies that made the earth so small and fragile. Modern supranationalism offered a foggy vision of an idealized future, but at least it was asking useful questions about the present and suggesting ways of avoiding the likely penalties of political inertia. Amid the heavy prophesies of doom and the plaintive calls for a global counterculture, there was wisdom about the shared fate of peoples too much at the mercy of forces beyond effective national control.

Afterword

IX.

SEEKING UNITY IN A NATIONALISTIC WORLD

> We need to identify and clarify the limits of
> our planetary existence and plan to live
> within those limits. The task is urgent.
> There is a growing gap between the unity
> of the world of facts and the fragmentation
> of the world of authority and power.
>
> —Richard A. Falk, *This Endangered Planet*,
> 1971

Since the end of World War II, there have been three major waves of American supranationalism—the world government movement in the late 1940s, Atlantic unionism in the early 1950s, and global functionalism in the 1970s. All of those efforts were responses to a sense of crisis; all had similar intellectual characteristics; and all, after some political success, collapsed with dramatic rapidity. Repeatedly, supranationalists alerted Americans to serious dangers and mobilized public support behind measures intended to reform the international system, but, each time, popular concern quickly diminished while superficial political responses undermined demands for more fundamental change. Moreover, the very success of supranationalist movements ironically encouraged decline, as deceptively vague arguments had to be clarified, as a larger public skeptically weighed the potential costs of diminished sovereignty, and as nationalistic critics at home and abroad sought to defend the established order. While the nation-state may have become increasingly obsolescent, nationalism remained strong in a world unable to transcend traditional competition for power and material gain.

Educable reformers concluded that effective change would not be an inevitable product of potential, or imagined, crisis. In the 1940s Americans had been frightened by the prospects of atomic destruction, a possibility dramatically foreshadowed by Hiroshima. In the early fifties fears of war with the Soviet Union intensified, especially after the Korean invasion and Russia's acquisition of atomic weapons. In the seventies profound concerns about the fate of the earth emerged, particularly among environmentalists who believed that mankind was damaging the global ecosystem essential to life. Yet the bombs did not fall, violent Soviet-American conflict failed to ignite, and the environment was not pushed to its life-sustaining limits. Urgency yielded to complacency as people learned to compartmentalize their lives, to push dark anxieties to the backs of their minds, and to avoid debilitating worry about problems that seemed so abstract, indefinite, and intractable.

Since it was difficult to sustain a political movement so dependent on fear, supranationalists also counted heavily on reasoned argument. Professing to understand the fundamental determinants of world affairs, reformers advanced a general theory of technological determinism, assumed the natural competitiveness of men and nations, and logically concluded that only supranational institutions could make possible the enforced cooperation required for peace, the defense of Western civilization, or effective global management. Although inclined to exaggerate predetermined, systemic causes of conflict, supranationalists nonetheless convincingly demonstrated that nation-states were being overwhelmed by threats to their security and welfare.

Considerable emphasis was placed on technological change as the basic cause of national incompetence. New weapons of mass destruction and their advanced delivery systems left all countries vulnerable to devastating attack; fast transportation, instant communication, and computerized management facilitated the creation of a closely knit global economy; and rapid population growth and industrial development threatened the earth's natural environment. There was compelling evidence that the historical emergence of larger political units had been a response to new technology, and it seemed dangerous to permit future interdependence to outpace effective administration. World government advocates were concerned mostly about avoiding war, Atlantic unionists about the West's freedom and peaceful security, and functionalists about safe and efficient global management, but all could cogently argue that their objectives required the creation of political institutions able to protect man from his own inventiveness.

Given these technological imperatives, mankind's collective well-being would necessitate strong, enlightened responses from individuals and national governments. But according to most supranationalists, human beings were customarily selfish and power seeking, and nations, within the traditional state system, were condemned to competition unregulated by any higher authority and restrained only by delicate balances of power. The system had never assured lasting peace, and independent governments had proved ineffectual in promoting coordinated world economic policies, cooperative use of the high seas, or a significantly safer global environment. In their analysis of contemporary society, supranationalists were political realists who expected little immediate improvement in human behavior and little voluntary cooperation from governments trapped in a state of anarchy. Contrary to common belief, these reformers were not wide-eyed innocents who viewed society as being just a law or two away from New Harmony or Brook Farm. Although routinely guilty of idealizing their objectives, few expected to make works of art out of common clay.

Fundamental change could come only from restructured institutions and more communal philosophies of life.

Most advocates of world government were well-educated, solid citizens deeply rooted in establishment culture, who, in promoting global law and order, were not prepared to rely on individual moral conversion or international good will. Frightened by weapons that terminated America's secure isolation and worried about inescapable great power rivalry, one-worlders desperately sought a new, supranational order. This centralized authority could not promise justice or eliminate civil conflict, but the alternative of sovereign nations relentlessly maneuvering for maximum advantage in a heavily armed atomic world seemed a greater risk. Ideally, well-crafted federalism would allow safe passage between tyranny and chaos, thereby ensuring that, as in domestic society, political and economic rivalry would be disciplined by law and the predominant power of the state. Much would depend on wise and creative statesmanship.

As the cold war intensified, many world government supporters reluctantly conceded that their goal was slipping beyond immediate reach. Never an integral part of the mainstream peace movement, federalists could therefore adapt to their new environment, albeit with sadness and regret. Soviet-American conflict was hardly a surprise (the system assured it), and without supranationalist order, American security could be maintained only with increased national power. Federalists favored rearmament and President Harry Truman's intervention in Korea, and there was logic, not intellectual betrayal, in Thomas K. Finletter's willingness to become secretary of the air force and in Cord Meyer's decision to join the CIA.

Supranationalism now seemed most achievable in the West where Europeans were determined to attain greater integration and where close coordination of North Atlantic political and military policies was deemed necessary to contain Soviet expansionism at an acceptable cost. Borrowing from the prewar theories of Clarence Streit, Atlantic unionists sought a federation of all Western democracies, a common government intended to guarantee free trade, pooled human and material resources, and a single anti-Communist foreign policy. Consequently, its proponents argued, Western strength would be enhanced, prosperity sustained, and domestic institutions spared the heavy burdens of militarization. A democratic federation could be more easily negotiated than could a world state and would be less likely to endanger political liberty. Moreover, as additional nations became democratic, they would want to join a union enjoying rapid economic growth and unchallengeable international security, a desire that would facilitate gradual attainment of more universal government.

Atlantic union never materialized, but a functionalist approach to particular problems in Europe and the Western alliance became relevant in later years when the world faced serious issues of global management. Here again, the reasoning was seductive. With the nation-state still mired in inevitable competition at a time when cooperation seemed essential to human survival, functionalism was an evolutionary method of building supranational institutions that would address specific problems without generally threatening local autonomy. Slowly, there would develop a maturing sense of planetary citizenship, a growing body of transnational civil servants, and a relatively painless subordination of self-destructive national interests to the common good. Progress would be incremental but tangible, a steady development able to contain the many insidious threats to the welfare of human community.

These three supranationalist movements were different in some respects. World federalists were the best organized, the most popular politically, and the most ambitious in suggesting institutional change. Atlantic unionists were more ideologically conservative and the least committed to one world. Functionalists were the most politically diverse, ranging from IBM executives to radical proponents of global harmony based on economic justice and spiritual renewal. They were also the most intellectually obscure as they navigated the foggy boundaries between voluntary international cooperation and enforced supranational order. But the cases for each movement also had much in common in both content and presentation—they all offered well-reasoned arguments to demonstrate that, in a world transformed by technology indifferent to human survival, the nation-state was dangerously ineffectual.

Support for that proposition has been substantial during periods of perceived crisis. Receiving considerable publicity from several best-selling books and from the sympathetic curiosity of press and radio, the United World Federalists campaigned effectively enough to influence large proportions of both public and congressional opinion. Atlantic unionism was more elitist, but it too gained a significant congressional following while enjoying easy access to the executive branch. And, while functionalism was never a coherent political movement, its ideas earned intellectual respect both inside and outside of government. It became part of conventional wisdom in the 1970s to note the world's increasing interdependence and to favor new institutional methods of managing dangerous common problems.

There was some interest abroad in the supranationalist cause. World government gained prominent adherents among Western statesmen, and a meaningful international movement held together for several years. While Europeans were then preoccupied with their own regional integration, some leaders, eager for American economic assistance and anxious about Russian ambitions, appealed for Atlantic rather than merely Western European union. Later, Common Market members would hope that their functionalist pioneering could prove globally useful, although with European transnational reform efforts (such as environmentalism) awareness of planetary responsibilities coexisted uneasily with demands for political decentralization. Meanwhile, Third World governments overcame their normal hostility toward supranationalism in order to support a new law of the sea treaty that promised to prevent technologically advanced countries from monopolizing oceanic wealth.

However, by far the greatest enthusiasm for attempts to transcend the nation-state came from Americans, a paradoxical contribution from such a nationalistic people. Liberal idealism was important here, but so too was awareness of American national interests—a desire to escape the country's new postwar strategic vulnerability, to perpetuate world power relationships favorable to the United States, and to guarantee economic freedom of action in the face of increased competitiveness and scarcity. As the most powerful and wealthy of nations, the United States had the most to protect through the imposition of greater order. Relatedly, Americans were traditionally prepared to refashion the world according to their own values and institutional experience. After exporting liberty and Christianity in the nineteenth century and trying to make the world safe for democracy and private enterprise in the twentieth, it was consistently ethnocentric to suggest that American-style federalism could provide limited, but effective, global administration. Federalism, Western values, the 1960s counterculture, New Deal regulatory agencies, and giant corporations—all were considered appropriate models for the entire planet. Supranationalists never entirely shed their American nationalism, although they certainly looked well beyond the country's narrowest self-interest. Provincial opportunism and altruistic concern for the general welfare developed comfortably together.

But if supranationalism in the United States enjoyed a relatively favorable intellectual and political climate, why did the movement encounter so many obstacles to success? Public apathy was partially responsible, since levels of fear high enough to motivate political action cannot long endure unless reinforced by events. Traditional nationalism was a major factor, as Americans have always been reluctant to concede any of their accustomed freedom of action. Nearly as significant, however, have been weaknesses inherent in supranationalism itself—its vagueness, its peculiar idealism about ultimate objectives, and its desperate need for incremental progress.

Without exception, the three varieties of supranationalism since 1945 were extremely vague about both the nature of global institutions and the proper way of achieving them. Initially this was an advantage, since internal disagreements about ends and means could be concealed and potential public hostility over specific details avoided. But what was gained in organizational cohesion and immediate popularity was lost at the scholarly and governmental level when political proposals had to withstand close, critical scrutiny. Exactly what would a world government look like? How could it be attained? What sacrifices would be made in accepting its jurisdiction? Confronted with such serious inquiry, reformers faced a discouraging dilemma. If vague ideas were given specific content, risks and costs became obvious to unsuspecting supporters, but if tough questions were dodged, critics complained of irrelevant utopianism. Supranationalists preferred to move step-by-step toward a generalized objective, but astute fellow travelers wanted to know more about the proposed route and the quality of the destination.

Complexities of transition were almost never elaborated. Most proposals anticipated the coordinated action of many nations quite different in ideology, political systems, economic development, and military power. But how could such diverse units be persuaded to relinquish sovereignty for the common good (whatever that hazy concept meant), and why would leaders of national governments preside over their own diminished authority? Functionalists were especially elusive as they blurred distinctions between internationalism and supranationalism—somehow, the one was supposed to evolve into the other in such a gradual, effortless way that no one would notice. That vaguely described process, however, did not satisfy wary policymakers sensitive to any erosion of their power, nor academic critics, who, like the old world federalists, doubted that small steps would carry nations across the broad moat protecting traditional sovereignty. It was hardly sufficient to assume that powerful nationalistic sentiments could be overridden by some relatively simple combination of public anxiety and charismatic bureaucratic efficiency.

Such vagueness regarding purposes and methods included an idealism that was surprising given supranationalism's almost Hobbesian analyses of contemporary politics. World federalists were best able to avoid anticipating a golden future of peace and justice, for they narrowly concentrated on establishing higher levels of government to restrain the traditional ambitions of individuals and nations. No New Man was to be created in the process. Functionalists, however, often lapsed into visionary descriptions of people living less competitively with each other and in harmony with nature, guided by a "new consciousness" appropriate to a hazardous world of limited resources. Obligatory supranational institutions could thus coexist with considerable political decentralization because, in this "greening of the planet," human nature itself was to be modified.

Awkwardly, then, realistic analysis was harnessed to utopian descriptions of ultimate objectives. It was difficult for any supranationalist reformer to resist a little castle building in the air, to exaggerate hopes for the future in order to hold the faithful and convert the apathetic. Such visions, however, could be naive in their expectations of peace and harmony and in their neglect of potential trade-offs. What would be the consequences of granting predominant power to a centralized world state? How could functional management of global problems avoid strong bureaucratic authority and a corresponding loss of individual freedom? How could a new system devoted to law, order, and peaceful change address the grievances of peoples insisting upon a major redistribution of wealth and power? And how could man's conquest of nature ever be reconciled with the demands of undeveloped nations for economic equality? Such questions could not be indefinitely avoided.

Relatedly, the achievement of idealized objectives seemed so distant that supranationalists were constantly tempted to embrace more modest measures in order to appear progressive. Fear had to be combined with hope, and hope necessitated perceptible movement toward the desired result.

However, support for diluted internationalism could disillusion the true believers while permitting the general public to assume the adequacy of superficial accomplishment. Reformers continually had to decide whether to ally with moderates favoring less fundamental change or to attack them as enemies of genuine advance. In the end, compromise proved irresistible, as supranationalists sacrificed their identity on behalf of weak congressional resolutions, symbolic gestures of Western unity, or toothless UN declarations endorsing functional cooperation.

Again, functionalism provided the most extreme examples. Since it was unclear where internationalism stopped and supranationalism began, any instances of cooperation were welcomed. Environmental conference reports, fishing conventions, the demilitarization of Antarctica and outer space, great power economic collaboration, and the new Law of the Sea Treaty were all perceived as significant achievements, although, when the dust settled, the nation-state system remained basically unchanged. Years before, federalists had warned that functionalism was an appealing road to nowhere, that incremental progress would stall before witnessing much sacrifice of national authority. Governments could not be lulled into lasting complacency, nor would their peoples react kindly to a steady loss of self-determination. There could be no subtle, unnoticed theft of sovereignty under the cover of transitional darkness.

For many reasons, then, supranationalism was a fragile movement. Largely dependent on wrenching crisis, it needed to control fear with hope and provide a sense of progress without losing a sense of direction. It needed realism to undermine the past and idealism to promote a better future. And it needed to suggest achievable institutional changes that would balance self-interest and self-denial, order and justice, conservation and development, authority and democracy. These were heavy demands on a loosely organized movement whose moments of political opportunity were few and far between.

There is a tragic quality about these determined reformers. Accomplished at analyzing mankind's most serious problems, they revealed and publicized fundamental truths about international interdependence and the growing senility of the nation-state. In so doing, supranationalists helped awaken Americans to the perils of atomic weaponry, environmental degradation, unmanaged economic relations, and maritime anarchy. But while reformers could persuasively define problems, they were unable to promote their solutions or means of achieving them. This was a peculiar situation in which many sympathetic citizens accepted the premises of an argument while rejecting its subsequent conclusions. The movement did encourage international control of atomic energy, the unity of Western Europe in close association with the United States, and new approaches to global administration (including a new legal order for the oceans), but always reformers halted well short of their major goals.

There are three possible implications of that faltering political experience. It could be suggested that the problems facing mankind are not nearly so serious as reformers have claimed. This is a difficult question to address, since knowledge of those complex issues is imperfect and anticipated disasters are products more of imagination than of experience. But given what is known about the probable effects of nuclear war, the deterioration of the environment, and the chaos of competitive international economics, it is difficult to deny that these are vitally important matters that mankind cannot safely ignore. Simply muddling through, hoping that problems are being exaggerated, has been a risky course of action relying heavily on optimistic faith.

It could be argued, however, that mankind's common problems (however serious) can be handled within the existing nation-state system. Statesmen can try to negotiate issues of peace and prosperity; nations can seek cooperative regulation of large corporations, maritime commerce, and environmental pollution; and scientists can develop technologies intended to help save the life of the planet. These are powerful arguments reinforced by awareness that national governments offer important protections for their citizens that many would be reluctant to sacrifice. The traditional system has provided considerable security, defense of economic interests, and preservation of cultural diversity. Moreover, since the system is not easily changed, there are strong pressures on reformers to work within it. The best should not become an enemy of the good.

Yet even such cautious pragmatism has entailed acts of faith and acceptance of risk. Ignoring traditional defects in the nation-state system, pragmatists have sanguinely denied that past failures contain lessons for an even more threatening future. It seems likely that demands for common action will exceed capabilities and that governments will be unable to venture much beyond the systemic imperatives of national competition. Publics will expect no less, and statesmen will realize that unilateral self-denial rewards the unscrupulous. It has been difficult to save the whales, but that task is child's play compared to regulating industrialization sufficiently to save the environment. Like supranationalists, defenders of the nation-state rely on willpower generated by fear: somehow a sense of crisis will lead to an effective response. Perhaps so, but experience is hardly a source of inspiration, and anticipated crises are too hypothetical to inspire political heroism.

Finally, one could conclude that, although the problems are genuine and nation-states unable to cope, the world is hardly prepared to sacrifice national autonomy until absolutely necessary. As in the past, events will provide the best instruction. Disastrous crises will have to occur; nation-states will have to demonstrate dramatically their incompetence; and the most powerful governments will have to impose solutions. Only then will supranationalism enjoy significant success, although limited and probably costly in terms of the values national sovereignty has usually helped protect. Idealists may envision a general conversion to a harmonious new consciousness, but improved world management will likely come at the price of reduced pluralism and freedom. As humans come to live in a single global city, they will have to accept the type of regulated behavior presently common to urban life. Checks and balances can be constructed, but order, efficiency, and public safety will demand that personal and national liberty make concessions to centralized authority.

The contribution of supranationalism thus far has been essentially intellectual—a warning of future perils, a cogent analysis of the inherent weakness of nation-states, and the planning of a more workable society. Such planning has been abstract and nearly devoid of realistic strategies of achievement, defects that testify to nationalism's enduring influence. That influence suggests that, should it come, fundamental change will be the result of traumatic experience, and if supranationalists have offered an accurate description of normal political behavior, the new order will be less devoted to the good life than making the trains run on time. This is not an ennobling prospect, but it may be unavoidable for people forced to conclude that the nation's traditional pursuit of wealth and power no longer optimizes the achievement of secure independence and sound economic development.

Postwar supranationalism has been bewildered by the public's acceptance of reformist arguments and rejection of subsequent action. It has not been easy to be a prophet of doom and a proponent of centralized power in a country historically devoted to optimism, nationalism, and limited government, but it has been especially frustrating to see intellectual converts fail to act on the strength of their own convictions. When pressured by events, many thoughtful Americans have doubted the utility of the nation-state system, but they have also feared the consequences of proposed alternatives. Trapped between the dangers of inertia and the hazards of change, people have understandably preferred to think about other things, a reaction reinforced by awareness of so many obstacles to reform. Future experience will be much the same: an enduring political commitment to new systems of world order will precariously depend on some dramatic failure of the old.

NOTES

I. Learning to Fear the Bomb

1. *Newsweek*, Aug. 27, 1945, p. 29; *Life*, Aug. 27, 1945, pp. 21–27.
2. *Time*, Aug. 20, 1945, p. 19.
3. *Newsweek*, Dec. 17, 1945, p. 37.
4. John Hersey, *Hiroshima* (New York, 1946), pp. 32–33, 54–55; Joseph Luft and W. M. Wheeler, "Reaction to John Hersey's 'Hiroshima,' " *Journal of Social Psychology*, 1948, pp. 135–40; *New Republic*, March 10, 1947, pp. 41–42.
5. *Opinion News*, May 5, 1945, p. 1; *New York Herald-Tribune*, Feb. 20, 1947, p. 25.
6. The Gallup Poll, Feb. 2, 1943, March 11, 1945, and June 7, 1946, in *The Gallup Poll: Public Opinion 1935–1971* (New York, 1972), pp. 367, 492, 581–82.
7. See Roper's report of a 1945 poll indicating that only about 10 percent of the American public advocated an essentially isolationist foreign policy. *New York Herald-Tribune*, Nov. 21, 1946, p. 29. Also, the Gallup Poll found that only 15 percent were firmly convinced that the United Nations would prevent future wars. *Opinion News*, Aug. 7, 1945, p. 6.
8. For example, see Harold Urey, "I'm a Frightened Man," *Collier's*, Jan. 5, 1946, p. 19; *United States News*, Aug. 17, 1945, pp. 38–39; and *Time*, Aug. 20, 1945, p. 30.
9. Editorial, *Modern Industry*, Sept. 15, 1946.
10. *Opinion News*, June 11, 1946, p. 2.
11. Alice K. Smith, *A Peril and a Hope: The Scientists' Movement in America, 1945–47* (Chicago, 1965), pp. 102, 130–32; President Truman's "Radio Report on the Potsdam Conference," Aug. 6, 1945, in *Public Papers of the Presidents of the United States: Harry S. Truman, April 12 to December 31, 1945* (Washington, 1961), pp. 212–13.
12. Winthrop S. Hudson, "Must We Be Scared to Death?" *Christian Century*, Jan. 9, 1946, p. 47.
13. Urey, "I'm a Frightened Man," p. 18; Raymond Swing, *In the Name of Sanity* (New York, 1946), p. 89; Hudson, "Must We Be Scared to Death?" p. 47.
14. *Newsweek*, Oct. 29, 1945, p. 33; ibid., Nov. 26, 1945, p. 34; *Life*, Oct. 29, 1945, p. 36; *Saturday Evening Post*, July 13, 1946, reprinted in *Reader's Digest*, Sept. 1946, pp. 5–8; Urey, "I'm a Frightened Man," p. 19.
15. Smith, *Peril and a Hope*, chaps. 1–2.
16. Dr. Daniel Q. Posin to Albert Einstein, Oct. 21, 1945, in Otto Nathan and Heinz Norden, eds., *Einstein on Peace* (New York, 1960), p. 342; Einstein address to Nobel Anniversary Dinner, Dec. 10, 1945, ibid., p. 355; Louis Falstein, "The Men Who Made the A-Bomb," *New Republic*, Nov. 26, 1945, p. 708.
17. *New Yorker*, Dec. 15, 1945, p. 24.
18. See John A. Simpson, "The Scientists as Public Educators: A Two Year Summary," *Bulletin of the Atomic Scientists*, Sept. 1947, pp. 243–46; Smith, *Peril and a Hope*.
19. Simpson, "Scientists as Public Educators," p. 244.
20. See "A Statement of Purpose by the Emergency Committee of Atomic Scien-

tists," University of Chicago Library, Emergency Committee of the Atomic Scientists MSS, box XIII, folder 1.

21. Smith, *Peril and a Hope,* pp. 203–11, 287–91.

22. Dexter Masters and Katherine Way, eds., *One World or None: A Report to the Public on the Full Meaning of the Atomic Bomb* (New York, 1946).

23. See *Life,* March 17, 1947, pp. 75–81; Nathan Reingold, "MGM Meets the Atomic Bomb," *Wilson Quarterly,* Autumn 1984, pp. 155–63.

24. *New Yorker,* Nov. 16, 1946, p. 98.

25. *Look,* March 5, 1946, pp. 19–32. A similar, but much calmer, article appeared in *Life,* Oct. 29, 1945, pp. 45–48.

26. President Truman, "Special Message to Congress on Atomic Energy," Oct. 3, 1945, in *Public Papers of the Presidents,* p. 365; Smith, *Peril and a Hope,* pp. 271–75, 475–76.

27. Sylvia Eberhart, "How the American People Feel about the Atomic Bomb," *Bulletin of the Atomic Scientists,* June 1947, pp. 146–49, 168.

28. *New Yorker,* Nov. 16, 1946, p. 98; Leo Szilard to Harold Urey, June 9, 1947, Emergency Committee of Atomic Scientists MSS, box IV, folder 2.

II. Realism, Reason, and Resolution: The Case for World Government

1. Albert Einstein, "Einstein on the Atomic Bomb," *Atlantic Monthly,* Nov. 1945, pp. 43–45; *New York Times,* Oct. 10, 1945, p. 20; *Reader's Digest,* Dec. 1945, pp. 123–35; ibid., Jan. 1946, pp. 145–60; Emery Reves, *The Anatomy of Peace* (New York, 1945). Among the additional signers of Roberts's letter were Congressman J. William Fulbright, Senator Claude Pepper, Senator Elbert Thomas, Gardner Cowles, Jr., Dorothy Canfield Fisher, and Carl and Mark Van Doren.

2. *Current Biography,* July 1946, pp. 505–507.

3. Emery Reves, *A Democratic Manifesto* (New York, 1942).

4. Reves, *Anatomy of Peace,* chap. 1.

5. Ibid., chaps. 2–3, 5.

6. Ibid., chaps. 6–8.

7. Ibid., pp. 126–29.

8. Ibid., p. 125.

9. Ibid., chaps. 4, 9, 11–14.

10. Ibid., chaps. 10, 14.

11. Ibid., chaps. 8, 15.

12. Ibid., chap. 15.

13. Walter Lippmann, *U.S. Foreign Policy: Shield of the Republic* (Boston, 1943); Walter Lippmann, *U.S. War Aims* (Boston, 1944); Frederick Schuman, "Might and Right at San Francisco," *Nation,* April 28, 1945, pp. 479–81; Frederick Schuman, "Regionalism and Spheres of Influence," in Hans J. Morgenthau, ed., *Peace, Security and the United Nations* (Chicago, 1946), pp. 83–106; Hans J. Morgenthau, *Politics among Nations* (New York, 1948).

14. Cord Meyer, Jr., "A Faith to Live By—Institutions and Men," *Nation,* March 8, 1947, p. 270; Albert Einstein, CBS radio broadcast, May 28, 1946, in Otto Nathan and Heinz Norden, eds., *Einstein on Peace* (New York, 1960), p. 387; Norman Cousins, *Modern Man Is Obsolete* (New York, 1945), pp. 9–10.

15. Reves, *Anatomy of Peace,* p. 238; Vernon Nash, *The World Must Be Governed* (New York, 1949), p. 118.

16. Cord Meyer, Jr., "A Serviceman Looks at the Peace," *Atlantic Monthly,* Sept. 1945, p. 44.

17. Leo Szilard, "Shall We Face the Facts?" *Bulletin of the Atomic Scientists,* Oct. 1949, p. 273.

18. Cord Meyer, Jr., *Peace or Anarchy* (Boston, 1948), chaps. 4–5.

19. Reves, *Anatomy of Peace*, p. 238; Einstein to Robert Hutchins, Sept. 10, 1945, in Nathan and Norden, eds., *Einstein on Peace*, p. 337; Einstein radio interview with Raymond Swing, July 17, 1947, ibid., p. 418.

20. Wendell L. Willkie, *One World* (New York, 1943), pp. 1–2; Meyer, "Serviceman Looks at the Peace," p. 44.

21. Harris Wofford, Jr., *It's Up to Us: Federal World Government in Our Time* (New York, 1946), p. 69.

22. Einstein statement, May 1947, in Nathan and Norden, eds., *Einstein on Peace*, p. 407.

23. Reves, *Anatomy of Peace*, p. 195.

24. Cousins, *Modern Man Is Obsolete*, pp. 20–23; Reves, *Anatomy of Peace*, p. 195.

25. Susanne K. Langer, "Make Your Own World," *Fortune*, March 1945, pp. 156–60; Reves, *Anatomy of Peace*, p. 42; Einstein to Robert Oppenheimer, Sept. 29, 1945, in Nathan and Norden, eds., *Einstein on Peace*, p. 339; Meyer, "Serviceman Looks at the Peace," p. 44.

26. Cousins, *Modern Man Is Obsolete*, pp. 46–47; Albert Einstein, "Atomic War or Peace," *Atlantic Monthly*, Nov. 1945, p. 44.

27. Nash, *World Must Be Governed*, pp. 19–25, 30–31, 113–17, 133.

28. Ibid., pp. 20–22, 126–31.

29. Raymond Swing, *In the Name of Sanity* (New York, 1946), pp. 75–76, 108.

30. Nash, *World Must Be Governed*, p. 160.

31. Robert Hutchins, "The Good News of Damnation," *Human Events Pamphlets*, Feb. 1947, p. 5; NBC radio broadcast, "The Making of World Government," *University of Chicago Roundtable*, Nov. 10, 1946.

32. Meyer, *Peace or Anarchy*, chaps. 8–9.

33. Nash, *World Must Be Governed*, pp. xi, 7, 39, 51, 145–46; *A Constitution for the World* (Santa Barbara, 1965), pp. 26–27.

34. Reves, *Anatomy of Peace*, pp. 257-61.

35. For example, see Albert Einstein's memorandum to Harold Urey regarding the future of the Emergency Committee of Atomic Scientists, June 14, 1947, in Nathan and Norden, eds., *Einstein on Peace*, pp. 409–10.

36. Cousins, *Modern Man Is Obsolete*, pp. 27–29.

37. See Carl Van Doren, *The Great Rehearsal: The Story of the Making and Ratifying of the Constitution of the United States* (New York, 1948), pp. vii–x; and Lionel Curtis, *World Revolution in the Cause of Peace* (Oxford, Eng., 1949), pp. 37–42, 141.

38. Curtis, *World Revolution*, pp. 24–25. See also Nash, *World Must Be Governed*, pp. 100–104.

39. Cousins, *Modern Man Is Obsolete*, p. 12; Nash, *World Must Be Governed*, p. 186; Albert Guérard, *Education of a Humanist* (Cambridge, Mass., 1949), p. 7.

III. The Politics of Salvation

1. Crosswell Bowen, "Young Man in Quest of Peace," *PM*, March 21, 1948, p. M6; Merle Miller, "From a One-World Crusade to the 'Department of Dirty Tricks,' " *New York Times Magazine*, Jan. 7, 1973, p. 53.

2. Bowen, "Young Man," pp. M6–M7.

3. Ibid., p. M7; Miller, "From a One-World Crusade"; *New York Times*, March 30, 1967, p. 30; Cord Meyer, Jr., *Facing Reality: From World Federation to the CIA* (New York, 1980), pp. 2–4.

4. Bowen, "Young Man"; Cord Meyer, Jr., "On the Beaches—the Pacific," *Atlantic Monthly*, Oct. 1944, p. 44.

5. Cord Meyer, Jr., "Waves of Darkness," *Atlantic Monthly*, Jan. 1946, p. 76.

6. Ibid., p. 77.

7. Ibid., p. 80.

8. Ibid., p. 81.

9. Bowen, "Young Man," p. M8; Miller, "From a One-World Crusade," p. 54; Meyer, *Facing Reality,* p. 35.

10. Bowen, "Young Man"; Meyer, *Facing Reality,* pp. 36–39.

11. Cord Meyer, Jr., "A Serviceman Looks at the Peace," *Atlantic Monthly,* Sept. 1948, p. 48.

12. Bowen, "Young Man," p. M9; Meyer, *Facing Reality,* pp. 41–42.

13. Thomas Mahoney, "Grenville Clark," *World Government News,* Feb. 1949, pp. 15–20.

14. Eleanor Fowle, *Cranston: The Senator from California* (San Rafael, Calif., 1980), p. 78; "Grenville Clark—Statesman Incognito," *Fortune,* Feb. 1946, p. 110.

15. Ibid., pp. 186–88.

16. "Declaration of the Dublin Conference," *New York Times,* Oct. 17, 1945, p. 21.

17. Ibid.

18. "Grenville Clark," p. 112; Fowle, *Cranston,* pp. 81–82.

19. Meyer, *Facing Reality,* p. 42; Bowen, "Young Man"; Miller, "From a One-World Crusade," pp. 9, 63.

20. Bowen, "Young Man"; United World Federalists Executive Council Minutes, March 25, 1947, Lilly Library, Indiana University, United World Federalists MSS, drawer 43; Meyer, *Facing Reality,* pp. 43–44.

21. Miller, "From a One-World Crusade," p. 55; Cord Meyer, Jr., *Peace or Anarchy* (Boston, 1947).

22. Robert A. Divine, *Second Chance: The Triumph of Internationalism in America during World War II* (New York, 1967), pp. 166–67, 215, 231–32.

23. Ibid., pp. 249–50.

24. Ibid., pp. 302–303; Americans United Statement of Principles, Sept. 27, 1945, University of Chicago Library, Federation of American Scientists MSS, box IV, folder 9.

25. *World Government News,* March 1946; Ulric Bell to John L. Balderston, March 27, 1946, University of Chicago Library, Association of Oak Ridge Engineers and Scientists MSS, box VII, folder 7; *Newsweek,* Oct. 14, 1946, p. 45; Harrison Brown, "The World Government Movement in the United States," *Bulletin of the Atomic Scientists,* June 1947, pp. 156–57.

26. World Federalists, U.S.A., leaflet, University of Chicago Library, Robert Hutchins MSS, box 158, folder 4; *Newsweek,* Oct. 14, 1946, p. 45.

27. *World Government News,* Nov. 1945, July 1948; World Federalists, U.S.A., leaflet, Hutchins MSS, box 158, folder 4.

28. Vernon Nash, *The World Must Be Governed* (New York, 1949), p. 169.

29. Harris Wofford, Jr., *It's Up to Us: Federal World Government in Our Time* (New York, 1946), pp. 3–7, 17–21, 27, 31–32, 41, 45.

30. Ibid., pp. 83–87, 104, 116, 136–39.

31. *Newsweek,* Oct. 14, 1946, p. 45.

32. Ibid.; *Christian Science Monitor,* March 1, 1947, p. 6.

33. *Christian Science Monitor,* March 1, 1947, p. 6; Brown, "Young Man."

34. *World Government News,* Dec. 1946; Memorandum regarding the Chicago meeting, Nov. 28–29, 1946, Association of Oak Ridge Engineers and Scientists MSS, box VIII, folder 8.

35. Brown, "Young Man."

36. Memorandum from Harrison Brown to members of executive committee of Atomic Scientists of Chicago, n.d., University of Chicago Library, Emergency Committee of Atomic Scientists MSS, box IV, folder 2.

37. *Los Alamos Newsletter,* April 10, May 2, 1946, Federation of American Scientists MSS, box XVII, folder 7.

38. Chester I. Barnard, "Security through the Sacrifice of Sovereignty," *Bulletin*

of the Atomic Scientists, Oct. 1, 1946, p. 30; "The Third Year of the Atomic Age: What Should We Do Now?" *University of Chicago Roundtable*, Aug. 24, 1947, p. 9.

39. J. Robert Oppenheimer, "International Control of Atomic Energy," *Foreign Affairs*, Jan. 1948, pp. 251–52; Harold Urey, "Atomic Energy Control Is Impossible without World Government," *Bulletin of the Atomic Scientists*, Dec. 1948, p. 365; Cord Meyer to W. A. Higinbotham, April 30, 1947, Federation of American Scientists MSS, box XVII, folder 7.

40. Memorandum from Harrison Brown to members of executive committee of Atomic Scientists of Chicago, n.d., Emergency Committee of Atomic Scientists MSS, box IV, folder 2.

41. Memorandum regarding formation of Federation of American Scientists, Federation of American Scientists MSS, box LV, folder 1; Norton Gerber to AORES executive committee, Dec. 5, 1946, Association of Oak Ridge Engineers and Scientists MSS, box VIII, folder 8; Eugene Rabinowitch editorial, *Bulletin of the Atomic Scientists*, Dec. 1947.

42. World Government Committee, AORES, History of the Committee, May 16, 1946, Association of Oak Ridge Engineers and Scientists MSS, box VIII, folder 9.

43. Report of the World Government Committee, Sept. 16, 1946, ibid., box IX, folder 4.

44. World Government Committee, AORES, History of the Committee, May 16, 1946, ibid., box VIII, folder 9.

45. Leo Szilard to Harold Urey, June 9, 1947, Emergency Committee of Atomic Scientists MSS, box IV, folder 4.

46. Statement of the Lake Geneva Conference of Scientists, June 21, 1947, Federation of American Scientists MSS, box XIV, folder 1.

47. Ibid.; Alice Kimball Smith, *A Peril and a Hope: The Scientists' Movement in America, 1945–47* (Chicago, 1965), p. 33.

48. Memorandum from G. A. Borgese and Richard P. McKeon to Robert Hutchins, in *Common Cause*, July 1951, pp. 619–23.

49. Biographical material on Robert Hutchins, in Hutchins MSS, part I, box 15.

50. G. A. Borgese report, n.d. [1945], Hutchins MSS, part III, box 3; Robert Hutchins, *Human Events Pamphlets*, Dec. 1945, pp. 11–12.

51. G. A. Borgese to Robert Hutchins, Oct. 20, 1945, and Borgese report, n.d. [1945], Hutchins MSS, part III, box 3.

52. Brief History of the Committee," *Common Cause*, July 1947, pp. 13–14.

53. A reprinted version is available: *A Constitution for the World* (Santa Barbara, Calif., 1965). The committee's documents were microfilmed by the American Council on World Affairs and entitled *World Government Problems: A Compilation of the Documents of the Committee to Frame a World Constitution, 1945–1948*.

54. *Constitution for the World.*

55. Ibid.

56. Borgese report, n.d. [1945], Hutchins MSS, part III, box 3.

57. Culbertson book review in *Indiana Law Review*, Spring 1949, pp. 474–75.

58. Ely Culbertson, *Total Peace: What Makes Wars and How to Organize Peace* (Garden City, 1943), pp. 3–6. Also see his *The Strange Lives of One Man* (Chicago, 1940).

59. Culbertson, *Total Peace*, pp. 11–17; Ely Culbertson, "Minutes on Our Destiny," *Commonweal*, June 21, 1946, pp. 230–31.

60. Culbertson, "Minutes on Our Destiny," pp. 232–33.

61. *Citizens Committee for United Nations Reform Bulletin*, May 1947, pp. 2, 7.

62. O. K. Armstrong, "Grassroots Crusader," *Reader's Digest*, May 1946, pp. 45–46; *World Government News*, May, 1948, pp. 19–20.

63. "The Declaration of the Federation of the World," Federation of American Scientists MSS, box XXVI, folder 1.

64. Ibid.; Armstrong, "Grassroots Crusader."

65. Armstrong, "Grassroots Crusader."

66. Ibid.

67. *Common Cause,* Feb. 1948, p. 311; ibid., May 1948, p. 400; ibid., Nov. 1949, p. 188; *World Government News,* May 1948, p. 5; *Life,* June 21, 1948, pp. 49–56; George A. Bernstein, "World Government: Progress Report," *Nation,* June 5, 1948, pp. 628–30.

68. *World Government News,* May 1949, United World Federalist section; ibid., June 1949, p. 4; Joseph P. Lyford, "Vote for World Government," *New Republic,* Dec. 27, 1948, pp. 16–18; *Common Cause,* Nov. 1949, p. 188; Alan Cranston, "More on the California Plan," *Common Cause,* Oct. 1949, pp. 135–42.

69. United World Federalists MSS, drawers 5, 10, 13; *World Government News,* April 1945, pp. 15–16; ibid., Dec. 1949, p. 16.

70. National Opinion Research Corporation surveys, *Opinion News,* June 11, 1946, p. 2; ibid., Jan. 21, 1947, p. 1; ibid., Nov. 1, 1947, p. 8; ibid., Jan. 1, 1948, p. 12; ibid., Jan. 15, 1948, p. 3; Gallup Poll, *Opinion News,* Sept. 17, 1946, p. 4; ibid., Nov. 1, 1947, p. 6; Gallup Polls, April 19, 1948, and Oct. 10, 1949, in *The Gallup Poll: Public Opinion, 1935–1971* (New York, 1972), pp. 726, 857.

71. National Opinion Research Corporation survey, *Opinion News,* Nov. 27, 1945, p. 4; Gallup Polls, *Opinion News,* Sept. 17, 1946, p. 4; ibid., Nov. 1, 1947, p. 6.

72. National Opinion Research Corporation surveys, *Opinion News,* Jan. 21, 1947, p. 1; ibid., Nov. 1, 1947, p. 8.

73. Divine, *Second Chance,* pp. 91–92.

74. Ibid., pp. 94–96.

75. Ibid., pp. 141–53.

76. *Common Cause,* Feb. 1948, p. 311; *Newsweek,* May 17, 1948, p. 25.

77. *Newsweek,* May 17, 1948, pp. 25–26.

78. U.S. Congress, House, Committee on Foreign Affairs, *Structure of the United Nations and the Relations of the United States to the United Nations, Hearings,* May 4–14, 1948, 80th Cong., 2d sess., pp. 205–11.

79. Ibid., pp. 3–25, 40–55, 205–11, 226–34, 306–29, 373–82.

80. Ibid., pp. 44–45.

81. *World Government News,* Nov. 1945; Henry Wallace, "Toward World Federalism," *New Republic,* Feb. 23, 1948, p. 10; Kirk Porter and Donald Johnson, eds., *National Party Platforms* (Urbana, 1970), p. 439.

82. *World Government News,* Feb. 1948, p. 3; ibid., June 1948, pp. 16–18; Porter and Johnson, eds., *National Party Platforms,* p. 453.

83. Porter and Johnson, eds., *National Party Platforms,* p. 431; "Remarks upon Receiving an Honorary Degree from the University of Kansas City," June 28, 1945, in *Public Papers of the Presidents of the United States: Harry S. Truman, April 12–December 31, 1945* (Washington, 1961), p. 151; "Message to the Congress on the State of the Union," Jan. 21, 1946, in *Public Papers of the Presidents of the United States: Harry S. Truman, 1946* (Washington, 1962), p. 39; *World Government News,* May 1951, p. 12; Alfred Tennyson, "Locksley Hall," in *The Poems and Plays of Alfred Lord Tennyson* (New York, 1938), p. 173.

84. *World Government News,* Oct. 1948, p. 14; ibid., Nov. 1948, p. 17; ibid., Dec. 1948, p. 4.

85. Ibid., Feb. 1946.

86. Ibid., April 1946; *Common Cause,* Oct. 1947, pp. 151–53; ibid., Sept. 1953, p. 112; Memorandum re National Association of Manufacturers, United World Federalists MSS, drawer 86.

87. Chester Bowles, "World Government—Yes, But," *Harper's,* March 1949, pp. 21–27; National Advisory Board, UWF Statement of Beliefs, Purposes, and Policies, Oct. 29, 1949, University of Chicago Library, Elisabeth Mann Borgese MSS, box 21; Claire Lee Chenault, *Way of a Fighter* (New York, 1949), pp. xxi–xxii; Douglas

MacArthur, address to Allied Council for Japan, April 5, 1946, in V. E. Whan, Jr., ed., *A Soldier Speaks: Public Papers and Speeches of General of the Army Douglas MacArthur* (New York, 1965), pp. 168–70.

88. *Chicago Daily Tribune,* Aug. 6, 1946; Fowle, *Cranston,* p. 85.

89. *World Government News,* May 1948, p. 4; ibid., Jan. 1950, UWF section; UWF Executive Council Minutes, March 26–27, 1949, United World Federalists MSS, drawer 36; *Common Cause,* Jan. 1949, pp. 239–40.

90. "Proposals for Now Revising the United Nations into a Federal World Government," *Congressional Digest,* Aug.–Sept. 1948, p. 193; *Nation,* June 12, 1948, pp. 660–62; "The World Government Crusade," *Christian Century,* Jan. 28, 1948, pp. 102–104.

91. Great Britain, Parliament, *Parliamentary Debates* (House of Commons), 5th ser., vol. 413 (1 Aug.–24 Aug. 1945), p. 81.

92. Ibid., vol. 416 (19 Nov.–7 Dec. 1945), p. 786.

93. Wambly Bald, "World Government His Dream," *New York Post,* Oct. 10, 1947, p. 57; *Christian Century,* Oct. 8, 1947, p. 1196.

94. *Nation,* June 12, 1948, pp. 660–62; Emergency Committee of Atomic Scientists MSS, box XIV, folder 13; Norton Gerber to Fyke Farmer, Dec. 18, 1946, Association of Oak Ridge Engineers and Scientists MSS, box VIII, folder 10; *Nashville Tennessean,* April 11, 1949; *Common Cause,* Nov. 1947, pp. 161–64.

95. *New York Times,* June 10, 1949, p. 3; *Nation,* June 12, 1948, pp. 660–62; *Common Cause,* July 1949, p. 480.

96. *Time,* Jan. 10, 1949, pp. 19–20; World Student Federalist *Newsletter,* Dec.–Jan. 1949, Emergency Committee of Atomic Scientists MSS, box XV, folder 1.

97. World Student Federalist *Newsletter,* Dec.–Jan. 1949; *World Government News,* Nov. 1948, p. 3; ibid., Jan. 1949, pp. 6–8.

98. Garry Davis to Elisabeth Mann Borgese, University of Chicago Library, Committee to Frame a World Constitution MSS, box X, folder 8.

99. United World Federalist Branch and Chapter Letter, Sept. 24, 1948, Emergency Committee of Atomic Scientists MSS, box XV, folder 2; Stewart Ogilvy to Mrs. Estabrook, United World Federalist MSS, drawer 68.

100. *Common Cause,* Nov. 1949, p. 189; *World Government News,* July 1949, pp. 3–4.

101. *Common Cause,* Feb. 1950, pp. 346–52.

102. U.S. Congress, House, Committee on Foreign Affairs, *To Seek the Development of the United Nations into a World Federation, Hearings,* Oct. 12–13, 1949, 81st Cong., 1st sess., pp. 212, 272–73.

103. Warren Austin to Cord Meyer, Sept. 20, 1949, United World Federalist MSS, drawer 5; UWF Executive Council minutes, Oct. 27, 1949, ibid., drawer 36.

104. U.S. Congress, Senate, Committee on Foreign Relations, *Revision of the United Nations Charter, Hearings,* Feb. 2–20, 1950, 81st Cong., 2d sess., pp. 379–403, 414–34.

105. Meyer, *Facing Reality,* pp. 56–57; *New York Times,* March 30, 1967, p. 30; Miller, "From a One-World Crusade," p. 55.

106. Meyer, *Facing Reality,* pp. 55–59.

107. Ibid., pp. 60–63.

108. Ibid., pp. 63–65.

IV. Collapse

1. Hobart Pendleton, "Another Look at World Federalism," *American Mercury,* June 1952, p. 58; *New York Times,* June 10, 1949, p. 3; Merle Miller, "From a One-World Crusade to the 'Department of Dirty Tricks,' " *New York Times Magazine,* Jan. 7, 1973, p. 63.

2. UWF Executive Council minutes, March 26–27, 1949, June 4–5, 1949, Oct.

27, 1949, Lilly Library, Indiana University, United World Federalists MSS, drawer 36; report of Cord Meyer, UWF President, January 1–March 31, 1949, University of Chicago Library, Emergency Committee of Atomic Scientists MSS, box XV, folder 2.

3. UWF Executive Council minutes, September 8–9, 1951, United World Federalists MSS, drawer 5; *World Government News*, May 1950, p. 20; Cranston address to Washington General Assembly, Oct. 13, 1950, United World Federalists MSS, drawer 35; Cranston report, 1952, Chicago Historical Society, United World Federalists, Chicago Branch, MSS, box 31.

4. Harrison Brown to Albert Einstein, Jan. 15, 1948, Emergency Committee of Atomic Scientists MSS, box III, folder 6; Otto Nathan and Heinz Norden, eds., *Einstein on Peace* (New York, 1960), pp. 504–505; Eugene Rabinowitch to Clifford Grobstein, June 5, 1951, University of Chicago Library, Federation of American Scientists MSS, box XII, folder 7.

5. Elisabeth Mann Borgese to Alan Cranston, Feb. 12, 1950, United World Federalists MSS, drawer 17, Lord Boyd Orr file; report of J. K. Killby to Executive Committee of the World Movement, Sept. 5, 1950, University of Chicago Library, Elisabeth Mann Borgese MSS, box XII, folder 1; letter from Treasurer, World Student Federalists, ibid., box IV, folder 1; Elisabeth Borgese to Mary Lloyd, Nov. 22, 1950, ibid., box IV, folder 3; Ruth Allanbrook to Elisabeth Borgese, July 5, 1949, ibid., box II, folder 5; UNESCO Secretariat to Elisabeth Borgese, April 2, 1951, ibid., box III, folder 6; *New York Herald-Tribune*, Sept. 3, 1949; *Christian Science Monitor*, Sept. 8, 1949, p. 1.

6. *World Government News*, May 1949, pp. 3–4; ibid., July 1949, p. 5; ibid., March 1950, p. 7; ibid., May 1950, p. 3; ibid., June 1950, p. 16; ibid., Aug. 1950, p. 12; ibid., Dec. 1950, p. 5; ibid., Jan. 1951, p. 14; ibid., March 1951, pp. 5–6; ibid., June 1951, pp. 12–13.

7. Ibid., April 1950, p. 5; ibid., Sept. 1950, p. 12; ibid., Nov. 1950, pp. 17–18; ibid., Dec. 1950, pp. 3–4; ibid., March 1951, p. 4; Pendleton, "Another Look," p. 59.

8. U.S. Congress, House, Committee on Foreign Affairs, *To Seek Development of the United Nations into a World Federation, Hearings*, 81st Cong., 1st sess., Oct. 12–13, 1949, pp. 204–205.

9. *Bulletin of the Atomic Scientists*, Feb. 1949, p. 37.

10. Bertrand Russell, "The Atomic Bomb and the Prevention of War," *Bulletin of the Atomic Scientists*, Oct. 1946, pp. 19–20.

11. James Burnham, *The Struggle for the World* (New York, 1947), pp. 35–52, 89, 149, 162, 187–98; *Life*, March 31, 1947, pp. 59–62.

12. *Newsweek*, May 17, 1948, pp. 30–32; *Life*, July 5, 1948, pp. 34–44; ibid., Aug. 16, 1948, pp. 90, 103–04; Harry S. Truman, *Memoirs: Years of Trial and Hope* (Garden City, 1956), p. 383.

13. William O. Douglas address, UWF General Assembly, Oct. 14, 1950, United World Federalists MSS, drawer 26; UWF statement of purposes, Oct. 1950, ibid., drawer 30.

14. Russell, "Atomic Bomb," p. 21; Harold Urey, "Atomic Energy and World Peace," *Bulletin of the Atomic Scientists*, Nov. 1, 1946, p. 4; Albert Einstein, "Atomic War or Peace," *Atlantic Monthly*, Nov. 1945, p. 32.

15. "The Cliché Expert Testifies on the Atom," *New Yorker*, Nov. 17, 1945, pp. 27–29.

16. Joseph P. Lyford, "Vote for World Government," *New Republic*, Dec. 27, 1948, pp. 16–18.

17. U.S. Congress, House, Committee on Foreign Affairs, *Structure of the United Nations and the Relations of the United States to the United Nations, Hearings*, 80th Cong., 2d sess., May 4–14, 1948, pp. 2–7; Committee on Foreign Affairs, *To Seek Development of the United Nations into a World Federation, Hearings*, pp. 3–10, 203, 273.

18. U.S. Congress, Senate, Subcommittee of the Committee on Foreign Rela-

tions, *Revision of the United Nations Charter, Hearings*, 81st Cong., 2d sess., February 2–20, 1950, pp. 379–80, 408.

19. Ibid., pp. 427–30.

20. Leo Szilard memorandum to Franklin Roosevelt, March 25, 1945, and Leo Szilard memorandum to the Emergency Committee of Atomic Scientists, Dec. 1946, Emergency Committee of the Atomic Scientists MSS, box IV, folder 2.

21. "Questions Raised on Specific Problems Relating to World Federation and Possible Answers of a Tentative Nature," United World Federalists MSS, drawer 30; *Modern Industry*, April 15, 1946, editorial.

22. Committee on Foreign Affairs, *To Seek Development of the United Nations into a World Federation, Hearings*, pp. 160–61; *Modern Industry*, April 15, 1946, editorial.

23. Robert Hutchins press release, July 16, 1948, University of Chicago Library, Robert Hutchins MSS, part III, box 3, General, 1948.

24. Harold Lasswell, "Technical Possibilities for the Achievement of a World State," University of Chicago Library, Atomic Scientists of Chicago MSS, box I, folder 13.

25. Carl Van Doren, *The Great Rehearsal: The Story of the Making and Ratifying of the Constitution of the United States* (New York, 1948).

26. Reinhold Niebuhr, "The Myth of World Government," *Nation*, March 16, 1946, p. 312; Reinhold Niebuhr, "The Illusion of World Government," *Bulletin of the Atomic Scientists*, Oct. 1949, pp. 289–90; Crane Brinton, *From Many One: The Process of Political Integration; The Problem of World Government* (Cambridge, Mass., 1948), pp. 8–10, 85, 104; Walter Lippmann, "World Government: Is it a Practical Goal?" *American Scholar*, Summer 1948, pp. 350–51.

27. *Common Cause*, March 1949, pp. 318–19; Gertrude S. Hooker, "More on Blackett's Bombshell," ibid., May 1949, pp. 367–69; G. A. Borgese, "Third Year," ibid., Aug. 1949, pp. 6–7; Harold Urey to J. T. Balderston, Oct. 7, 1946, University of Chicago Library, Association of Oak Ridge Engineers and Scientists MSS, box IX, folder 2.

28. UWF statement of purposes, Oct. 15, 1950, United World Federalists MSS, drawer 30, Washington Assembly file; Cranston to UWF membership, Oct. 2, 1950, ibid., drawer 5, Project V.I.P. file.

29. UWF statement of purposes, Oct. 15, 1950, ibid., drawer 30, Washington Assembly file.

30. Cranston memorandum to UWF branches and chapters, Jan. 5, 1951, ibid., drawer 5.

31. UWF sample advertisement, 1952, ibid., drawer 41.

32. Cranston report to UWF Executive Council, April 21–22, 1951, ibid., drawer 5; Executive Council's Resolution on the Stockholm Peace Appeal, August 26–27, 1950, ibid., drawer 27.

33. UWF memorandum regarding the Culbertson Plan, ibid., drawer 19.

34. Committee on Foreign Affairs, *Structure of the United Nations and Relations of the United States to the United Nations, Hearings*, pp. 373, 377, 381.

35. Ibid., pp. 387–90; Committee on Foreign Affairs, *To Seek Development of the United Nations into a World Federation, Hearings*, p. 117; Subcommittee on Foreign Relations, *Revisions of the United Nations Charter, Hearings*, p. 223.

36. *San Francisco Examiner*, Feb. 7, 1950, editorial page; ibid., Nov. 16, 1950, editorial page.

37. *Chicago Daily Tribune*, Aug. 6, 1946, p. 1; ibid., Nov. 15, 1949, editorial.

38. Stanley K. Bigman, "The 'New Internationalism' under Attack," *Public Opinion Quarterly*, Summer 1950, pp. 238–43, 249; *Economic Council Letter*, June 1, 1949, p. 4.

39. Bigman, " 'New Internationalism,' " p. 239; *World Government News*, Oct. 1949, pp. 17–19; ibid., March 1950, pp. 19–21; Joseph P. Kamp, *We Must Abolish the*

United States: The Hidden Facts Behind the Crusade for World Government (New York, 1950), p. 12.

40. Ernie Adamson, Counsel, Committee on Un-American Activities, Preliminary Report, House Committee on Un-American Activities, June 26, 1946, University of Chicago Library, Association of Oak Ridge Engineers and Scientists MSS, box X, folder 3; report from Committee on Un-American Activities for Congressman Roy O. Woodruff, United World Federalists, Chicago Branch MSS, box 4; *New York Times*, June 7, 1950, p. 23; *Newsweek*, Feb. 2, 1953, p. 10.

41. UWF advertisement, "We're in the Middle . . . and Proud of It," 1950, Hutchins MSS, box 146, folder 11; UWF statement of purposes, Oct. 15, 1950, United World Federalists MSS, drawer 30, Washington Assembly file.

42. *World Government News*, June 1950, p. 11; minutes of UWF Second Annual Assembly, Minneapolis, Nov. 11–14, 1948, and statement of Sovereignty Preservation Council, Sept. 30, 1950, United World Federalists MSS, drawers 5, 35; *Common Cause*, Dec. 1950, p. 280.

43. *Newsweek*, Sept. 20, 1948, pp. 32–34.

44. Ibid.; Elisabeth Borgese to Robert Hutchins, Sept. 8, 1949, Hutchins MSS, box 158, folder 4.

45. *Chicago Daily Tribune*, March 25, 1948, p. 24.

46. Ibid., Aug. 6, 1946, pp. 1, 4.

47. *Labor Action*, June 6, 1949; *Daily Worker*, March 19, 1950.

48. Text of Radio Moscow broadcast, Sept. 13, 1948, Hutchins MSS, part I, box 15; Sergei Vavilov, et al., "Dr. Einstein's Mistaken Notions," in Nathan and Norden, eds., *Einstein on Peace*, pp. 443–49.

49. "Analysis of UWF Policy Positions," 1949, United World Fedralists MSS, drawer 30; "1950: World Movement at the Divide," *Common Cause*, Dec. 1950, pp. 227–29.

50. Minutes of UWF Executive Committee, Oct. 12, 1950, United World Federalists MSS, drawer 27; Donald Harrington to Elisabeth Borgese, March 27, May 2, 1951, and to Henri Koch, Sept. 8, 1950, Borgese MSS, box IV, folder 1.

51. Francis H. Russell, "Toward a Stronger World Organization," *Department of State Bulletin*, Aug. 7, 1950, pp. 220–24.

52. Reinhold Niebuhr, "The Illusion of World Government," *Bulletin of the Atomic Scientists*, Oct. 1949, pp. 289–92.

53. Warren Austin, "A Warning on World Government," *Harper's*, May 1949, pp. 95–96; Clark Eichelberger to members of the American Association for the United Nations, May 9, 1946, Association of Oak Ridge Engineers and Scientists MSS, box IX, folder 6.

54. Alan Cranston to UWF Executive Council, Dec. 1950, United World Federalist MSS, drawer 5.

55. Merle Miller, "From a One-World Crusade to the 'Department of Dirty Tricks,'" *New York Times Magazine*, Jan. 7, 1973, p. 63.

56. Vernon Nash to Reverend G. Grant, Feb. 7, 1963, United World Federalists, Chicago Branch, MSS, box 15.

57. Major historical accounts of the world federalists include: Ernest S. Lent, "The Development of United World Federalist Thought and Policy," *International Organization*, Nov. 1955, pp. 486–501; Bernard Hennessy, "A Case Study of Intra-Pressure Group Conflicts: The United World Federalists," *Journal of Politics*, Feb. 1954, pp. 76–95; Jon A. Yoder, "The United World Federalists: Liberals for Law and Order," in Chalres Chatfield, ed., *Peace Movements in America* (New York, 1973), pp. 95–115; Lawrence S. Wittner, *Rebels against War: The American Peace Movement, 1941–1960* (New York, 1969), chaps 5–7.

58. Frederick L. Schuman, *The Commonwealth of Man: An Inquiry into Power, Politics, and World Government* (New York, 1952), pp. 489–93.

V. Losing the Cold War: The Need for a Union of the Free

1. Harry S. Truman, announcement of first atomic explosion in the U.S.S.R., Sept. 23, 1949, in *Public Papers of the President: Harry S. Truman, 1949* (Washington, 1964), p. 485.

2. "NCS-68: A Report to the National Security Council by the Executive Secretary on United States Objectives and Programs for National Security," April 14, 1950, *Naval War College Review,* May–June 1975, pp. 64–65.

3. Gallup Poll, Dec. 2, 1949, in *The Gallup Poll: Public Opinion, 1935–1971* (New York, 1972), pp. 869–70; *Time,* Oct. 3, 1949, p. 8; ibid., Nov. 28, 1949, p. 32; ibid., Feb. 20, 1950, p. 9; ibid., March 13, 1950, p. 35.

4. *Time,* Oct. 2, 1950, p. 12; ibid., April 9, 1951, p. 16.

5. Ibid., Oct. 2, 1950, pp. 12–14; ibid., Oct. 8, 1951, p. 101.

6. Ibid., Dec. 25, 1950, p. 52; ibid., May 14, 1951, p. 77; ibid., Oct. 1, 1951, pp. 98–100; *Saturday Review of Literature,* Oct. 6, 1951, p. 35.

7. Gallup Polls, Aug. 19, 1950, Nov. 29, 1950, February 2, 1951, in *Gallup Poll,* pp. 933, 949, 963.

8. "NSC-68," pp. 54, 56–57; Trevor Barnes, "The Secret Cold War: The C.I.A. and American Foreign Policy in Europe, 1946–1956," *Historical Journal,* March 1982, p. 653.

9. *Time,* March 13, 1950, p. 15; ibid., Oct. 16, 1950, p. 14; ibid., Jan. 22, 1951, p. 13.

10. *Collier's,* Oct. 27, 1951; *Time,* Oct. 29, 1951, p. 55.

11. *Time,* Sept. 18, 1950, p. 18.

12. Ibid., July 31, 1950, p. 13; ibid., Sept. 4, 1950, p. 11; *New York Times,* April 22, 1951, p. 11; Gallup Poll, May 21, 1950, in *Gallup Poll,* pp. 911–12.

13. Dean Acheson, *Present at the Creation: My Years at the State Department* (New York, 1969), pp. 378–79; *Time,* June 26, 1950, p. 52.

14. *Fortune,* April 1949, pp. 77–78.

15. *Current Biography,* 1950, p. 552; *Time,* March 27, 1950, p. 13.

16. *Time,* March 27, 1950, p. 13; Clarence Streit, *Union Now: The Proposal for Inter-Democracy Federal Union* (New York, 1940), pp. 231–32.

17. Streit, *Union Now,* pp. 233–34.

18. *Current Biography,* 1950, p. 553.

19. Streit, *Union Now,* pp. 243–46.

20. *Time,* March 27, 1950, p. 13.

21. *Current Biography,* 1950, p. 553.

22. *Time,* March 27, 1950, p. 14.

23. *Newsweek,* Sept. 30, 1946, p. 62; *Time,* Nov. 22, 1943, p. 3.

24. *Newsweek,* Sept. 30, 1946, p. 62.

25. Clarence Streit, *Union Now: A Proposal for an Atlantic Federal Union of the Free* (New York, 1949), pp. 268–76.

26. Ibid., pp. 11–12, 19, 31–32.

27. *Freedom and Union,* Nov. 1946, p. 2; ibid., June 1947, pp. 1–3; ibid., Sept. 1948, pp. 12–15.

28. Streit, *Union Now* (1949), pp. 19, 54–56, 101–103.

29. Ibid., pp. 15–16.

30. Ibid., pp. 8–10, 65–69.

31. Ibid., pp. 13–16, 95–100.

32. Clarence Streit, "Federal Union's Division of Power," in Clarence Streit, Owen Roberts, and John Schmidt, *The New Federalist* (New York, 1950), pp. 21–25.

33. Streit, *Union Now* (1949), pp. 142–49; Clarence Streit and John Schmidt, "The Essentials in a Federal Legislature," in Streit, Roberts, and Schmidt, *New Federalist,* pp. 50–58.

34. Clarence Streit, "Essentials in a Federal Executive," in Streit, Roberts, and Schmidt, *New Federalist*, pp. 62–66.

35. Owen Roberts, "The Essentials in a Federal Judiciary," in ibid., pp. 66–74.

36. Streit, *Union Now* (1949), pp. 13–14, 124–26; Livingston Hartley, "Why Atlantic Union?" *Freedom and Union*, Feb. 1950, pp. 7–8; Elmo Roper, "A Way to One Free World," *Freedom and Union*, May 1948, p. 8.

37. Streit, *Union Now* (1949), pp. 182–87.

38. Ibid., p. 251; Harold Urey, "The Paramount Problem of 1949," *Bulletin of the Atomic Scientists*, Oct. 1949, p. 285; William L. Clayton testimony before House Foreign Affairs Committee, Jan. 23, 1950, Rice University Library, William L. Clayton MSS, box 22; U.S. Congress, Senate, Subcommittee of Committee on Foreign Relations, *Revision of the United Nations Charter, Hearings*, Feb. 2–20, 1950, 81st Cong., 2d sess., p. 232.

39. See Istvan Szent-Miklosy, *The Atlantic Union Movement: Its Significance in World Politics* (New York, 1965), chap. 2; John Foster Dulles, "Faith in Individual Man," *Freedom and Union*, Feb. 1950, pp. 27–32; Streit, *Union Now* (1949), pp. 311–12; *Freedom and Union*, Oct. 1946, p. 3.

40. Streit, *Union Now* (1949), pp. 271–73.

41. Ibid., p. 262; Arnold Toynbee, "The Next Step in History," *Look*, Nov. 18, 1952, pp. 31–32.

42. U.S. Congress, Senate, Senator Estes Kefauver speaking on behalf of Atlantic Union, March 13, 1950, *Congressional Record*, 81st Cong., 2d sess., XCVI, 3205–08, 1950; *Freedom and Union*, Oct. 1947, p. 1; ibid., Sept. 1948, pp. 1–3; Owen Roberts, "The World Needs a Cop on the Corner," *Saturday Evening Post*, March 24, 1951, pp. 29, 122.

43. *Freedom and Union*, March 1947, pp. 1–4; ibid., July 1947, pp. 2–3; ibid., Jan. 1948, pp. 9–11; ibid., Feb. 1949, p. 4; Streit, *Union Now* (1949), pp. 281–82.

44. *Freedom and Union*, Feb. 1950, p. 9; ibid., Nov. 1950, p. 4; ibid., Jan. 1951, pp. 4–5.

45. Ibid., July–Aug. 1951, pp. 2–4; ibid., Oct. 1951, p. 16.

46. Streit, Roberts, and Schmidt, *New Federalist*, pp. xv–xvii; Streit, *Union Now* (1949), pp. 29, 297; *Freedom and Union*, June 1947, pp. 1–3.

47. Streit, *Union Now* (1949), pp. 212–25.

48. Ibid., pp. 62–67; *Freedom and Union*, March 1949, pp. 26–27.

49. *Freedom and Union*, April 1948, pp. 30–31; Streit, *Union Now* (1949), pp. xi (introduction by Senator Estes Kefauver), 269–70.

50. *Freedom and Union*, Jan. 1947, p. 14; ibid., April 1947, p. 12; ibid., April 1948, pp. 30–31.

51. United World Federalists, Executive Council minutes, July 16, 1949, Lilly Library, Indiana University, United World Federalists MSS, drawer 36.

VI. The Rise and Fall of the Atlantic Union Committee

1. *Current Biography*, 1941, p. 714; *New York Times*, May 18, 1955, p. 31.

2. *Current Biography*, 1941, pp. 715–16.

3. Ibid.

4. Ibid.; *Freedom and Union*, April 1949, pp. 6–7; William L. Clayton to Averell Harriman, Feb. 6, 1947, Rice University Library, William L. Clayton MSS, box 17.

5. *New York Times*, Feb. 9, 1966, p. 39.

6. *Current Biography*, 1944, p. 95.

7. Ibid., pp. 95–96.

8. Ibid., pp. 96–97.

9. Ibid., pp. 96–98; *Fortune*, November 1945, p. 139.

10. Oveta Culp Hobby to William L. Clayton, Dec. 31, 1947, Clayton to Oveta

Culp Hobby, Jan. 2, 1948, Clayton to Cord Meyer, March 12, 1948, Clayton memo-randum, March 5, 1947, Clayton to Cass Canfield, Nov. 17, 1948, Clayton to Jesse Andrews, Nov. 18, 1948, Clayton MSS, boxes 17–20.

11. *Current Biography*, 1944, p. 99; *New York Times*, Feb. 9, 1966, p. 39.

12. *Current Biography*, 1941, p. 654.

13. Ibid., pp. 654–55.

14. Ibid.; *New York Times*, Jan. 23, 1952, p. 20.

15. Ibid.; *Current Biography*, 1941, p. 655.

16. *Freedom and Union*, April 1949, p. 6; Library of Congress, Atlantic Union Committee MSS, box 2 (General, 1949).

17. Atlantic Union Committee pamphlet, [1949?], Lilly Library, Indiana University, United World Federalists MSS, drawer 9.

18. Walden Moore to Robert P. Patterson, March 10, 1949, Library of Congress, Robert P. Patterson MSS, box 29 (AUC); AUC Board of Governors Biographies, Atlantic Union Committee MSS, box 3; Robert A. Divine, *Second Chance: The Triumph of Internationalism in America during World War II* (New York, 1967), p. 99; *Current Biography*, 1945, pp. 13–15.

19. *New York Times*, March 16, 1949, p. 14; *Freedom and Union*, April 1949, p. 7.

20. Ibid.; Report on meeting with Secretary of State, Feb. 19, 1953, Atlantic Union Committee MSS, box 2 (General, 1953–58).

21. *New York Times*, June 24, 1949, p. 2; AUC memorandum, 1949, and Board of Governors meeting, June 1, 1949, Atlantic Union Committee MSS, box 2 (General, 1949) and box 49 (Minutes of Executive Committee, 1950).

22. Charles L. Fontenay, *Estes Kefauver: A Biography* (Knoxville, 1980), chaps. 6, 8, pp. 328–29.

23. Atlantic Union Committee pamphlet, [1949?] United World Federalists MSS, drawer 9; *New York Times*, July 27, 1949, p. 1.

24. U.S. Congress, Senate, Senator Estes Kefauver speaking on the Atlantic Pact and Atlantic Union, July 11, 1949, *Congressional Record*, 81st Cong., 1st sess., XCV, 9211–14.

25. *New York Times*, July 28, 1949, p. 3.

26. David P. Calleo, *Europe's Future: The Grand Alternatives* (New York, 1967), pp. 38–41; Ronald Steel, *The End of Alliance: America and the Future of Europe* (New York, 1964), pp. 21–24.

27. Calleo, *Europe's Future*.

28. Ibid., pp. 138–39; Max Beloff, *The United States and the Unity of Europe* (New York, 1963), pp. 24–43, 61–62, 108–11; Robert Osgood, *NATO: The Entangling Alliance* (Chicago, 1962), chap. 2.

29. Calleo, *Europe's Future*, pp. 31, 83; Kenneth W. Thompson, *American Diplomacy and Emergent Patterns* (New York, 1962), p. 261; Gallup Polls, April 1948, Oct. 1950, in George H. Gallup, ed., *The Gallup International Public Opinion Polls, France, 1939, 1944–1975* (New York, 1976), pp. 111, 144.

30. *Time*, Aug. 22, 1949, p. 18; ibid., Aug. 29, 1949, p. 18.

31. Ibid., Nov. 14, 1949, p. 22; ibid., Dec. 5, 1949, p. 16; ibid., Dec. 12, 1949, p. 22; ibid., Dec. 3, 1951, pp. 27–28; Beloff, *United States and the Unity of Europe*, p. 101.

32. *New York Times*, March 31, 1950, p. 13; ibid., April 20, 1950, p. 28.

33. Norman A. Graebner, ed., *Ideas and Diplomacy: Readings in the Intellectual Tradition of American Foreign Policy* (New York, 1964), p. 723; *Time*, July 16, 1951, p. 25.

34. Walter Lippmann, *U.S. War Aims* (Boston, 1944), pp. 73–77.

35. *New York Times*, Oct. 30, 1949, p. 3; ibid., May 8, 1951, p. 25; ibid., June 15, 1951, p. 6; ibid., Sept. 19, 1951, p. 1; *Freedom and Union*, July–Aug. 1950, p. 27; ibid., Feb. 1951, p. 9; Annual Report of the Executive Director, AUC, Sept. 15, 1951, United World Federalists MSS, drawer 86.

36. *Time*, May 29, 1950, p. 16; *Freedom and Union*, May 1949, p. 19; ibid., May 1952, pp. 27–28; *New York Times*, Sept. 23, 1951, sec. IV, p. 3; ibid., Sept. 24, 1951, p. 26.

37. William L. Clayton to Charles R. Hook, Nov. 28, 1949, and Clayton speech, May 17, 1950, Clayton MSS, box 22; *Freedom and Union*, April 1948, pp. 2–3; ibid., June, 1950, p. 3; Draft Joint Statement on a United Europe by Atlantic Union Committee and American Committee for a United Europe, n.d., Atlantic Union Committee MSS, box 1.

38. Atlantic Union Committee Pamphlet, [1949?], United World Federalists MSS, drawer 9; *New York Times*, Sept. 19, 1951, p. 1.

39. Annual Report of the Executive Director, AUC, Sept. 15, 1951, United World Federalists MSS, drawer 86; *Freedom and Union*, May 1949, pp. 10–13; ibid., Sept. 1949, pp. 11–13; ibid., Oct. 1949, pp. 19–20; ibid., May 1950, pp. 12–13.

40. *Freedom and Union*, May 1949, p. 12; ibid., March 1950, p. 13.

41. Ibid., July–Aug. 1950, p. 21.

42. *Fortune*, April 1949, pp. 77–78; *Life*, April 9, 1951, p. 36; *Time*, March 27, 1950, pp. 12–15.

43. Annual Report of the Executive Director, AUC, September 15, 1951, United World Federalists MSS, drawer 86; Owen Roberts, "The World Needs a Cop on the Corner," *Saturday Evening Post*, March 24, 1951, pp. 29, 120–24; Lester Pearson, "The Beginning of a World Community," *Kiwanis Magazine*, July 1951, pp. 6, 38, 40; *Commonweal*, April 28, 1950, p. 61; *Freedom and Union*, July–Aug. 1950, p. 21; ibid., Jan. 1951, pp. 14–15.

44. Gallup Poll, March 13, March 22, May 1, Aug. 19, Nov. 29, 1950, Feb. 2, May 25, June 25, 1951, in *The Gallup Poll: Public Opinion, 1935–1971* (New York, 1972), pp. 895, 897, 906, 933, 949, 963, 984, 992.

45. *World Government News*, Nov. 1950, pp. 10–11; *Public Opinion Quarterly*, Fall 1950, p. 599.

46. *Public Opinion Quarterly*, Fall 1950, p. 599; ibid., Summer 1951, p. 390.

47. Minutes of AUC Executive Committee, Jan. 20, 1952, University of Michigan Library, Stella Osborn MSS, box 2.

48. *Freedom and Union*, Dec. 1949, p. 20; ibid., Feb. 1950, p. 18; ibid., March 1950, p. 18; Atlantic Union Committee pamphlet, [1949?], United World Federalists MSS, drawer 9.

49. *New York Times*, Aug. 7, 1950, p. 13; ibid., Oct. 20, 1950, p. 5; ibid., Feb. 12, 1951, p. 9.

50. U.S. Congress, House, Committee on Foreign Affairs, *To Seek Development of the United Nations into a World Federation, Hearings*, 81st Cong., 1st sess., 1949, pp. 29–30, 144–49.

51. U.S. Congress, Senate, Subcommittee of the Committee on Foreign Relations, *Revision of the United Nations Charter, Hearings*, 81st Cong., 2nd sess., 1950, pp. 228–30.

52. Ibid., pp. 232–311.

53. Ibid., pp. 402–03, 436–46.

54. U.S. Congress, Senate, Senator Kafauver speaking for the Atlantic Union resolution, March 13, 1950, *Congressional Record*, 81st Cong., 2d sess., XCVI, 3205–208.

55. Ibid.

56. Minutes of AUC Board of Governors, May 18, 1951, and Edwin Martin, Director of Office of European Regional Affairs, to M/Sgt. Donald O. Shirley, Dec. 14, 1951, Atlantic Union Committee MSS, boxes 1, 49; Minutes of Atlantic Citizens Congress, Nov. 14, 1952, University of Pittsburgh Library, Adolph Schmidt MSS, drawer 5.

57. John Foster Dulles to Clarence Streit, Jan. 23, Oct. 24, 1939, Nov. 14, 1940, Princeton University Library, John Foster Dulles MSS, box 2; Report on meeting

with Secretary of State, Feb. 19, 1953, Atlantic Union Committee MSS, box 2; Elmo Roper to William L. Clayton, Feb. 1, 1955, and Justin Blackwelder to William L. Clayton, Sept. 4, 1958, Clayton MSS, boxes 26, 28.

58. *New York Times*, Jan. 21, 1950, p. 3; William D. Hassett, secretary to President Truman, to Owen Roberts, Nov. 3, 1951, Harry S. Truman Library, Harry S. Truman MSS, official file; Charles L. Fontenay, *Estes Kefauver: A Biography* (Knoxville, 1980), p. 124; President Truman's address at dinner of Civil Defense Conference, May 7, 1951, in *Public Papers of the Presidents: Harry S. Truman, January 1, 1952–January 20, 1953* (Washington, 1966), p. 1123.

59. William L. Clayton to Ellen Garwood, November 19, 1949, Clayton MSS, box 22; Annual Report of the Executive Director, AUC, Sept. 15, 1951, United World Federalists MSS, drawer 86.

60. Minutes of AUC Board of Directors, March 13, Sept. 20, 1951; Minutes of AUC Executive Committee, Jan. 15, May 3, July 17, 1951, Atlantic Union Committee MSS, box 49, Osborn MSS, box 2; Elmo Roper, "American Attitudes toward World Organization," *Public Opinion Quarterly*, Winter 1953–54, p. 408.

61. Clarence Streit to Christian Herter, March 13, 1962, Schmidt MSS, drawer 3.

62. Minutes of AUC Executive Committee, Dec. 12, 1950, March 22, 1951, Atlantic Union Committee MSS, box 49.

63. *Time*, March 2, 1951, p. 20; ibid., April 4, 1951, p. 14; ibid., April 9, 1951, p. 11.

64. Report of R. J. Bishop to AUC Board of Governors, July 23, 1951, Atlantic Union Committee MSS, box 49; Annual Report of the AUC Executive Director, Sept. 15, 1951, United World Federalists MSS, drawer 86.

65. *New York Times*, Aug. 8, 1949, p. 2.

66. *Saturday Evening Post*, Dec. 29, 1951, p. 8; *Chicago Tribune*, April 25, 1950, p. 18; Hugh Moore correspondence, Atlantic Union Committee MSS, box 13 (General Correspondence, 1951).

67. *Detroit Free Press*, July 24, 1949.

68. Joseph P. Kamp, *We Must Abolish the United States: The Hidden Facts behind the Crusade for World Government* (New York, 1950), chap. 11; John T. Flynn, "Mr. Dulles and 'Hands Across the Sea,' " *American Mercury*, Oct. 1953, pp. 26–29.

69. Edgar Bissanz to Walden Moore, April 18, 1950, Atlantic Union Committee MSS, box 11, Stella Osborn to J. Edgar Hoover, Sept. 16, 1950, Stella Osborn to *Washington Post* (unpublished), Sept. 8, 1950, and Clare Hoffman to Stella Osborn, March 19, 1951, Osborn MSS, box 2.

70. *Freedom and Union*, Nov. 1952, pp. 9–10.

71. Ibid., July 1947, pp. 2–3; ibid., Jan. 1948, pp. 2–3; ibid., Feb. 1950, pp. 7–9; ibid., May 1951, pp. 5–7.

72. Ibid., March 1951, p. 14.

73. William L. Clayton to Michael Straight, April 30, 1949, Clayton MSS, box 21.

74. Stella Osborn to Estes Kefauver, Aug. 5, 1950, Osborn MSS, box 1.

75. Harris Wofford, "Straight Is the Gate: Considering Alternative Routes to One World," *Common Cause*, June 1948, p. 426.

76. William L. Clayton to Noel P. Hunt, July 6, 1950, Clayton MSS, box 23; Clarence Streit, Owen Roberts, and John Schmidt, *The New Federalist* (New York, 1946), p. 47.

77. United World Federalist resolution on Federal Union, March 27, 1949, University of Chicago Library, Emergency Committee of Atomic Scientists MSS, box 15, folder 2; Philip Morrison and Robert R. Wilson, "Half a World . . . and None: Partial World Government Criticized," *Bulletin of the Atomic Scientists*, July 1947, p. 181.

78. Ibid.

79. Clarence Streit, *Union Now* (New York, 1949), p. xi; *Freedom and Union*, April 1948, pp. 30–31.

80. William L. Clayton to Cord Meyer, April 8, 1948, Clayton MSS, box 19.

81. Livingston Hartley to Colonel Matthews, Dec. 14, 1960, Schmidt MSS, drawer 2 (AUC—1961); Justin Blackwelder letter, March 28, 1960, Atlantic Union Committee MSS, box 16.

82. Adolph Schmidt to Mrs. Raymond T. Elligett, 1961, and Clarence Streit memorandum, [1964?], Schmidt MSS, drawer 3 (Schmidt, May–Sept. 1961, and Clarence Streit, 1961–64).

83. Clarence Streit to Adolph Schmidt, Sept. 27, 1961, Stella Osborn memorandum regarding International Movement for Atlantic Union, 1958, AUC Executive Committee minutes, January 16, 1958, and June 18, 1958, ibid., drawer 1 (Executive Committee minutes), drawer 2 (Executive Committee minutes), drawer 2 (International Movement for Atlantic Union), drawer 3 (Clarence Streit); Justin Balckwelder letter, Sept. 16, 1960, Atlantic Union Committee MSS, box 16; *New York Times*, May 19, 1955, p. 11; ibid., Oct. 8, 1955, p. 10.

84. Justin Blackwelder to John P. Apperson, Oct. 25, 1960, Blackwelder to William B. Johnstone, July 7, 1960, Blackwelder to T. C. P. Martin, June 13, 1960, Blackwelder to Nelson Rockefeller, July 3, 1960, Atlantic Union Committee MSS, boxes 16, 17.

85. Justin Blackwelder to Bernard Cogan, April 4, 1960, Blackwelder to Robert J. Bishop, Aug. 16, 1960, Blackwelder to Hugh Moore, March 29, April 6, 1960, ibid.

86. U.S. Congress, House, *Report of the Activities of the United States Citizens Commission on NATO*, H. Doc. 433, 87th Cong., 2d sess., 1962, pp. 1–4, 9–10.

87. Walden Moore, "Atlanticus at the Bridge," Jan. 21, 1962, Osborn MSS, box 24.

VII. The Imperatives of Interdependence

1. *Newsweek*, April 3, 1967, p. 46; ibid., April 10, 1967, pp. 48–51; *Life*, April 14, 1967, pp. 26–34; Richard A. Falk, *This Endangered Planet: Prospects and Proposals for Human Survival* (New York, 1971), p. 284.

2. Robert and Leona Train Rienow, "Last Chance for the Nation's Waterways," *Saturday Review*, May 22, 1965, p. 36; Barry Commoner, *The Closing Circle: Nature, Man, and Technology* (New York, 1971), chaps. 5–6; *Time*, Feb. 2, 1970, p. 46.

3. John J. Putman, "Quicksilver and Slow Death," *National Geographic*, Oct. 1972, pp. 514–16, 521–23; *Time*, Dec. 21, 1970, p. 36.

4. *Time*, Sept. 28, 1970, p. 73; ibid., Dec. 28, 1970, p. 48; ibid., Nov. 8, 1971, p. 44; Environmental Action, *Earth Day: The Beginning* (New York, 1970), p. 2; Thor Heyerdahl, "The Voyage of the Ra II," *National Geographic*, Jan. 1971, p. 55.

5. *Time*, Feb. 2, 1970, pp. 43–45; ibid., April 13, 1970, p. 55; *Saturday Review*, May 22, 1965, p. 31; Stella Margold, "Needed: World-Wide Environmental Solutions," *American City*, March 1971, p. 74.

6. Commoner, *Closing Circle*, pp. 29–31, 227.

7. Paul Ehrlich and Richard L. Harriman, *How to Be a Survivor: A Plan to Save Spaceship Earth* (New York, 1971), pp. 2–6.

8. Lester R. Brown, *World without Borders* (New York, 1973), chaps. 3–5; Falk, *This Endangered Planet*, pp. 132–59.

9. Brown, *World without Borders*, chap. 10; Lester R. Brown, *The Global Economic Prospect: New Sources of Economic Stress*, Worldwatch Institute Paper #20, May, 1978; Joseph S. Nye, Jr., "Independence and Interdependence," *Foreign Policy*, Spring 1976, pp. 132–33, 155–61; Stanley Hoffmann, *Primacy or World Order: American Foreign Policy since the Cold War* (New York, 1978), chap. 3; Robert Heilbroner, *An Inquiry into the Human Prospect* (New York, 1974), chap. 5.

10. Raymond Vernon, "Economic Sovereignty at Bay," *Foreign Affairs*, Oct. 1968, pp. 117–19; Lester R. Brown, *The Interdependence of Nations*, Foreign Policy Associa-

tion Headline Series #212, Oct. 1972, pp. 3–6; Walt W. Rostow, "The Value of the Limits to Growth," *Wilson Quarterly,* Autumn 1976, p. 53.

11. Commoner, *Closing Circle,* pp. 50–52.

12. Ibid., pp. 53–56.

13. Falk, *This Endangered Planet,* pp. 9, 126–28.

14. Commoner, *Closing Circle,* p. 21.

15. Dennis L. Meadows et al., *The Limits to Growth: A Report for the Club of Rome's Project on the Predicament of Man* (New York, 1972), pp. 9–11.

16. Ibid., pp. 11, 20–24.

17. Ibid., chap. 2.

18. Ibid., chaps. 3–4.

19. Sam Cole, "The Global Futures Debate, 1965–1976," in Richard A. Falk et al., eds., *Toward a Just World Order* (Boulder, 1982), p. 507.

20. Heilbroner, *Inquiry into the Human Prospect,* chap. 5; C. P. Snow, *The State of Siege* (New York, 1969), pp. 3, 14, 31; Eugene Rabinowitch, "Living Dangerously in the Age of Science," *Bulletin of the Atomic Scientists,* Jan. 1972, p. 5; Richard M. Nixon, Message to Congress Transmitting the First Annual Report of the Council on Environmental Quality, Aug. 10, 1970, in Richard M. Nixon, *A New Road for America* (Garden City, 1972), p. 161; Meadows et al., *Limits to Growth,* p. 17.

21. Hazel Erskine, "The Polls: Pollution and Its Costs," *Public Opinion Quarterly,* Spring 1972, pp. 120, 125, 130; Thomas E. Fusso, "The Polls: The Energy Crisis in Perspective," *Public Opinion Quarterly,* Spring 1978, p. 129; John G. Stoessinger, *Henry Kissinger: The Anguish of Power* (New York, 1976), pp. 7–9; Henry Brandon, *The Retreat of American Power* (New York, 1973), pp. 41–45; Jimmy Carter, *Keeping Faith: Memoirs of a President* (New York, 1982), pp. 115, 120–21.

22. For references to "spaceship earth," see R. Buckminster Fuller, *Operating Manual for Spaceship Earth* (Carbondale, Ill., 1969); and Ehrlich and Harriman, *How to Be a Survivor,* chap. 7.

23. Walter A. Rosenbaum, *The Politics of Environmental Concern* (New York, 1973), pp. 53–57.

24. Ibid., pp. 57–68.

25. Lord Ritchie-Calder, "Mortgaging the Old Homestead," *Foreign Affairs,* Jan. 1970, p. 207.

26. *Current Biography,* 1970, pp. 91–94; *Time,* Feb. 2, 1970, p. 44.

27. Commoner, *Closing Circle,* chaps. 1–2, p. 295.

28. *Current Biography,* 1951, pp. 100–102; Stewart L. Udall, "The Legacy of Rachel Carson," *Saturday Review,* May 16, 1964, pp. 23, 59.

29. Rachel Carson, *Silent Spring* (Greenwich, Conn., 1962), pp. 18, 28–31.

30. For Mead and White quotations, see Carson, *Silent Spring,* p. 12 and back cover; Falk, *This Endangered Planet,* pp. 27, 266–67.

31. Lewis Mumford, *The Pentagon of Power* (New York, 1970), pp. 52–57.

32. Heilbroner, *Inquiry into the Human Prospect,* p. 142.

33. Ehrlich and Harriman, *How to Be a Survivor,* chap. 7; Dennis Meadows et al., *Limits to Growth,* p. 195; Heilbroner, *Inquiry into the Human Prospect,* pp. 143–44; Barry Commoner, *Closing Circle,* p. 292.

34. George F. Kennan, "To Prevent a World Wasteland: A Proposal," *Foreign Affairs,* April 1970, p. 403; Barbara Ward, *Spaceship Earth* (New York, 1966), p. 17.

35. Kennan, "To Prevent a World Wasteland," pp. 404–13.

36. Brown, *World without Borders,* dedication, chap. 15.

37. Falk, *This Endangered Planet,* chap. 1, pp. 244–45.

38. Ibid., pp. 6, 38, 107, 128.

39. Ibid., pp. 65–67.

40. Garrett Hardin, "The Tragedy of the Commons," *Science,* Dec. 13, 1968, pp. 1244–45.

41. Ibid., pp. 1245–47.

42. Falk, *This Endangered Planet*, pp. 14–15, 35, 53.
43. Ibid., pp. 35, 55, 91, 276–78.
44. Ibid., chap. 7.
45. Ibid., pp. 364–65.
46. Ibid., pp. 5–15.
47. Ibid., pp. 263–65, 362.
48. Ibid., pp. 431–37; Richard Falk, "Beyond Internationalism," *Foreign Policy,* Fall 1976, p. 87.
49. Falk, *This Endangered Planet*, chap. 10; Charles Pentland, *International Theory and European Integration* (London, 1973), p. 69.

VIII. Progress and Second Thoughts

1. *Time,* May 4, 1970, p. 18; *New Republic,* March 7, 1970, pp. 8–9; *New Yorker,* May 2, 1970, p. 29.
2. *Time,* May 4, 1970, p. 18; *Science,* May 8, 1970, p. 657.
3. *Time,* Jan. 26, 1970, p. 49; ibid., April 27, 1970, p. 42; Environmental Action, *Earth Day: The Beginning* (New York, 1970), p. xv.
4. *Science,* May 8, 1970, p. 657.
5. Richard A. Falk, *This Endangered Planet: Prospects and Proposals for Human Survival* (New York, 1971), pp. 484–85; Walter A. Rosenbaum, *The Politics of Environmental Concern* (New York, 1973), pp. 76–79.
6. Rosenbaum, *Politics of Environmental Concern,* pp. 13, 71–75; *Time,* Oct. 5, 1970, p. 57; ibid., June 5, 1972, p. 68; ibid., Dec. 25, 1972, p. 13.
7. Rosenbaum, *Politics of Environmental Concern,* pp. 8, 116–25; *Time,* Feb. 23, 1970, pp. 39–40; ibid., April 13, 1970, pp. 54–55; ibid., Nov. 13, 1970, p. 25; ibid., Feb. 22, 1971, pp. 23, 43; ibid., Oct. 16, 1972, p. 44; ibid., Oct. 30, 1972, p. 62.
8. George Kennan, "To Prevent a World Wasteland: A Proposal," *Foreign Affairs,* April 1970, pp. 401–402; Abel Wolman, "Pollution as an International Issue," *Foreign Affairs,* Oct. 1968, pp. 164–67; Charles C. Humpstone, "Pollution: Precedent and Prospect," *Foreign Affairs,* Jan. 1972, p. 328.
9. *Fortune,* Jan. 1971, p. 70; Paul R. Ehrlich and Richard L. Harriman, *How to Be a Survivor: A Plan to Save Spaceship Earth* (New York, 1971), pp. 115–16; Lester R. Brown, *World without Borders* (New York, 1973), chap. 15; Richard Gardner, "The Hard Road to World Order," *Foreign Affairs,* April 1974, p. 558; Kennan, "To Prevent a World Wasteland," p. 412.
10. C. M. Stanley, President's Report, 1965 World Federalists Assembly, San Francisco, Lilly Library, Indiana University, United World Federalists MSS, drawer 81; *Saturday Review,* March 7, 1970, p. 47.
11. Falk, *This Endangered Planet*, pp. 267–69; Brown, *World without Borders*, p. 354; Ehrlich and Harriman, *How to Be a Survivor,* chap. 6; Gardner, "Hard Road to World Order," p. 557.
12. For a good theoretical discussion of functionalism and neofunctionalism, see Charles Pentland, *International Theory and European Integration* (London, 1973), chaps. 3–4.
13. *Time,* March 23, 1970, p. 72; *American Forests,* June 1970, pp. 32–33; *American City,* March 1971, p. 74; *New Yorker,* May 23, 1970, pp. 93–105.
14. Maurice Strong, "One Year after Stockholm," *Foreign Affairs,* July 1973, pp. 690–92; Barry Commoner, "Motherhood in Stockholm," *Harper's,* June 1972, pp. 49–50; Richard Gardner, "U.N. as Policeman," *Saturday Review,* Aug. 7, 1971, p. 47.
15. Strong, "One Year after Stockholm," p. 693; Commoner, "Motherhood in Stockholm."
16. Gardner, "U.N. as Policeman."

17. Ibid., p. 49; Commoner, "Motherhood in Stockholm," p. 49.

18. Strong, "One Year after Stockholm," pp. 691–92; Commoner, "Motherhood in Stockholm," p. 50; *Time*, May 22, 1972, p. 55.

19. Commoner, "Motherhood in Stockholm," pp. 51–53.

20. Ibid., pp. 53–54.

21. Ibid., p. 54; *Time*, June 19, 1972, p. 69.

22. Strong, "One Year after Stockholm," pp. 693–95; "World Environment Newsletter," *World*, Aug. 14, 1973, p. 25; Gardner, "U.N. as Policeman," p. 47.

23. "The Ecology Craze," *New Republic*, March 7, 1970, p. 8.

24. Ibid.; *Time*, March 23, 1970, p. 72; Rosenbaum, *Politics of Environmental Concern*, pp. 73–74.

25. Max Ways, "How to Think about the Environment," *Fortune*, Feb. 1970, pp. 98–101, 159–66; Peter F. Drucker, "Saving the Crusade," *Harper's*, Jan. 1972, pp. 66–71.

26. *Time*, May 4, 1970, p. 18; Melvin J. Grayson and Thomas R. Shepard, Jr., *The Disaster Lobby* (Chicago, 1973), pp. 5–6.

27. John Maddox, *The Doomsday Syndrome* (New York, 1972), pp. 30–31.

28. Ibid., pp. 6–7, 36, 48–49, 76–79, 121, 257; Drucker, "Saving the Crusade," p. 66.

29. Maddox, *Doomsday Syndrome*, pp. 25–28, 32, 283–87.

30. Jeremy Main, "Conservationists at the Barricades," *Fortune*, Feb. 1970, pp. 144–50.

31. *Time*, Feb. 22, 1971, p. 23; *Newsweek*, Feb. 3, 1975, p. 55.

32. Betty Radcliffe and Luther Gerlack, "The Ecology Movement after Ten Years," *Natural History*, Jan. 1981, pp. 12–18; *Newsweek*, May 5, 1980, pp. 80–82; *Time*, May 5, 1980, p. 36.

33. George W. Ball, *The Past Has Another Pattern* (New York, 1982), chap. 1; *Current Biography*, 1962, pp. 23–25.

34. Ball, *Past Has Another Pattern*, chaps. 2–4.

35. Ibid., chaps. 6–7.

36. Ibid., pp. 104–106.

37. Remarks by George W. Ball at the Annual Dinner of the British National Committee of the International Chamber of Commerce, London, England, Oct. 18, 1967, Chicago Historical Society, United World Federalists, Chicago Branch, MSS, box 3.

38. Ibid.

39. Ibid.; Report of the Blue Ribbon Commission on the Role and Priorities of World Federalists, USA, Jan. 23, 1972, ibid., box 33; Holly Sklar, ed., *Trilateralism: The Trilateral Commission and Elite Planning for World Management* (Boston, 1980), p. 100.

40. Richard J. Barnet and Ronald E. Müller, *Global Reach: The Power of the Multinational Corporations* (New York, 1974), pp. 13–14, 56.

41. Ibid., pp. 14, 20, 55.

42. Ibid., pp. 18–19, 55.

43. Ibid., pp. 45–47.

44. Geoffrey Shields, "The Multinationals," *World Issues*, Dec. 1977/Jan. 1978, p. 3; Raymond Vernon, "Economic Sovereignty at Bay," *Foreign Affairs*, Oct. 1968, pp. 111–13.

45. Raymond Vernon, *Sovereignty at Bay: The Multinational Spread of U.S. Enterprises* (New York, 1971), chap. 7; Ronald Segal, "Everywhere at Home, Home Nowhere," *Center Magazine*, May/June 1973, pp. 8–14; Joseph S. Nye, Jr., "Multinational Corporations in World Politics," *Foreign Affairs*, Oct. 1974, pp. 156–61.

46. Vernon, *Sovereignty at Bay*, pp. 249, 284.

47. Ibid., pp. 262–65; Barnet and Müller, *Global Reach*, pp. 16, 56.

48. Nye, "Multinational Corporations in World Politics," pp. 166–67; Raymond Vernon, "Storm over the Multinationals: Problems and Prospects," *Foreign Affairs*, Jan. 1977, p. 261.

49. Vernon, "Storm over the Multinationals," pp. 247–52.

50. Barnet and Müller, *Global Reach*, p. 364.

51. Ibid., pp. 385–86; Nye, "Multinational Corporations," pp. 153–54; Robert W. Cox, "Labor and the Multinationals," *Foreign Affairs*, Jan. 1976, pp. 359–65; Vernon, "Storm Over the Multinationals," p. 261.

52. Zbigniew Brzezinski, *Between Two Ages: America's Role in the Technocratic Era* (New York: 1970), pp. 3–8; Daniel Bell, "The Future World Disorder: The Structural Context of Crisis," *Foreign Policy*, Summer 1977, pp. 131–32.

53. Brzezinski, *Between Two Ages*, pp. 58–62.

54. Ibid., pp. 293–304.

55. Ibid., pp. 308–309.

56. See Richard H. Ullman, "Trilateralism: 'Partnership' for What?" *Foreign Affairs*, Oct. 1976, pp. 3–4; "The Trilateral Energy Study: A Discussion with Franklin Tugwell," *World Issues*, Feb.–March 1979, p. 3; Holly Sklar, "Trilateralism: Managing Dependence and Democracy—An Overview," in Sklar, ed., *Trilateralism*, pp. 5–8.

57. Sklar, "Trilateralism: Managing Dependence and Democracy"; Holly Sklar, "Founding the Trilateral Commission: Chronology, 1970–1977"; and Holly Sklar and Ros Everdell, "Who's Who on the Trilateral Commission"; in Sklar, ed., *Trilateralism*, pp. 1–3, 76–82, 90–131; Ullman, "Trilateralism," pp. 4–5.

58. Sklar, "Trilateralism: Managing Dependence and Democracy," pp. 21–24; Ullman, "Trilateralism," p. 12.

59. Sklar, "Trilateralism: Managing Dependence and Democracy," pp. 20–27, 43, 52.

60. Robert L. Paarlberg, "Domesticating Global Management," *Foreign Affairs*, April 1976, pp. 563–71; Jahangir Amuzegar, "A Requiem for the North–South Conference," *Foreign Affairs*, Oct. 1977, pp. 136–42; Ullman, "Trilateralism," pp. 6–8; Joseph Kraft, "Regan and Reagan," *Vancouver Sun*, July 22, 1985, p. A-4.

61. Robert S. Walters, "International Organizations and the Multinational Corporation," *Annals of the American Academy of Political and Social Science*, Sept. 1972, pp. 127–38.

62. For a recent study reaffirming the illusions of national economic sovereignty, see British economist Michael Stewart's *Controlling the Economic Future* (Brighton, Sussex, 1983).

63. John Temple Swing, "Who Will Own the Oceans?" *Foreign Affairs*, April 1976, pp. 527–28.

64. Ibid., pp. 528–31; Louis Henkin, "Politics and the Changing Law of the Sea," *Political Science Quarterly*, March 1974, pp. 49–51.

65. Elisabeth Mann Borgese, "A Center Report: The Republic of the Deep Seas," *Center Magazine*, May 1968, pp. 18–20; Arvid Pardo, "Who Will Control the Seabed?" *Foreign Affairs*, Oct. 1968, p. 133.

66. Seyom Brown and Larry L. Fabian, "Diplomats at Sea," *Foreign Affairs*, Jan. 1974, p. 301; Borgese, "Center Report," p. 27; Elizabeth Young, "To Guard the Sea," *Foreign Affairs*, Oct. 1971, p. 138; E. W. Seabrook Hull, "The Political Ocean," *Foreign Affairs*, April 1967, p. 502; Swing, "Who Will Own the Oceans?" p. 546.

67. Pardo, "Who Will Control the Seabed?" pp. 123, 134–35; Henkin, "Politics and the Changing Law of the Sea," pp. 53–54.

68. James K. Sebenius, *Negotiating the Law of the Sea* (Cambridge, Mass., 1984), pp. 11, 80; William Wertenbaker, "The Law of the Sea," *New Yorker*, Aug. 1, 1983, p. 47; Henkin, "Politics and the Changing Law of the Sea," pp. 64–65; Brown and Fabian, "Diplomats at Sea," p. 318; Pardo, "Who Will Control the Seabed?" p. 134; Richard G. Darman, "The Law of the Sea: Rethinking U.S. Interests," *Foreign Affairs*,

Jan. 1978, p. 381; Elliott Richardson, "Power, Mobility, and the Law of the Sea," *Foreign Affairs*, Spring 1980, p. 919.

69. Ervin Laszlo et al., *Goals for Mankind: A Report to the Club of Rome on the New Horizons of Global Community* (New York, 1977), p. 216; Richard A. Falk, *A Study of Future Worlds* (New York, 1975), p. 335; Brown, *World without Borders*, pp. 306–07.

70. World Federalists, USA, "Policy Statement," June 23, 1969, (in my possession); *World*, June 5, 1973, p. 37; "The World Is Her Field: An Interview with Elisabeth Mann Borgese," *World Issues*, Dec. 1978–Jan. 1979, pp. 17, 21.

71. Wertenbaker, "Law of the Sea," *New Yorker*, Aug. 1, 1983, pp. 51–53, 56–63; ibid., Aug. 8, 1983, p. 57.

72. Wertenbaker, "Law of the Sea," *New Yorker*, Aug. 8, 1983, p. 57; Darman, "Law of the Sea," p. 395.

73. Wertenbaker, "Law of the Sea," *New Yorker*, Aug. 8, 1983, pp. 68, 70, 73–80; James L. Malone, "Who Needs the Sea Treaty?" *Foreign Policy*, Spring 1984, pp. 45–47.

74. Sebenius, *Negotiating the Law of the Sea*, pp. 82–84; Jack N. Barkenbus, "How to Make Peace on the Seabed," *Foreign Policy*, Winter 1976–77, pp. 212–14; Malone, "Who Needs the Sea Treaty?" pp. 60–63; Ann L. Hollick, "Managing the Oceans," *Wilson Quarterly*, Summer 1984, pp. 85–86.

75. Darman, "Law of the Sea," pp. 390–91.

76. See Leon Wieseltier, *Nuclear War, Nuclear Peace* (New York, 1983), pp. 10–12.

77. Carl Sagan, "To Preserve a World Graced by Life," *Bulletin of the Atomic Scientists*, Jan. 1983, pp. 2–3; Carl Sagan, "Nuclear War and Climatic Catastrophe," *Foreign Affairs*, Winter 1983–84, pp. 257–92; *Time*, Nov. 14, 1983, p. 43; R. P. Turco et al., "Nuclear Winter: Global Consequences of Multiple Nuclear Explosions," *Science*, Dec. 23, 1983, pp. 1282–92; Ellen Goodman, "Reminiscences of a Scared Dinosaur Groupie," *Victoria Times-Colonist*, Jan. 3, 1984, p. A-5.

78. Jonathan Schell, "The Fate of the Earth," *New Yorker*, Feb. 1, 1982, pp. 47–48.

79. Ibid., pp. 55–61, 85–90, 113.

80. Schell, "Fate of the Earth," ibid., Feb. 8, 1982, pp. 59–60, 84–86.

81. Ibid., pp. 55, 78; Schell, "Fate of the Earth," ibid., Feb. 15, 1982, p. 51.

82. Jonathan Schell, "The Abolitions: A Deliberate Policy," ibid., Jan. 9, 1984, pp. 49–62, 72–77.

83. Ibid., pp. 43–44.

84. Ibid., pp. 88–92.

85. Falk, *This Endangered Planet*, pp. 257–62.

86. Ibid., pp. 267–69.

87. Ibid., pp. 274–79, 296.

88. Ibid., p. 297.

89. See W. Warren Wagar, "Toward the City of Man," *Center Magazine*, Sept. 1968, pp. 33–41; Louis René Beres and Harry R. Targ, *Constructing Alternative World Futures* (Cambridge, Mass., 1977), pp. 133–38.

90. Paul Brodeur, "Annals of Chemistry: In the Face of Doubt," *New Yorker*, June 9, 1986, pp. 70–87.

91. A. J. Miller, "Doomsday Politics: Prospects for International Cooperation," *International Journal*, 1972–73, p. 122; Ian Clark, "World Order Reform and Utopian Thought: A Contemporary Watershed?," *Review of Politics*, Jan. 1979, pp. 112–15.

92. Miller, "Doomsday Politics," pp. 126–30; Tom J. Farer, "The Greening of the Globe: A Preliminary Appraisal of the World Order Models Project," *International Organization*, Winter 1977, p. 133.

93. Farer, "Greening of the Globe," pp. 139–40.

94. Clark, "World Order Reform," pp. 97–100, 108–12, 115–16.

95. Miller, "Doomsday Politics," p. 127.

96. Farer, "Greening of the Globe," pp. 130, 134–39; Robert W. Cox, "On Think-

ing about Future World Order," *World Politics*, Jan. 1976, pp. 192–95.

97. *Newsweek*, March 15, 1982, p. 17; Hedley Bull, *The Anarchical Society: A Study of Order in World Politics* (London, 1977), p. 304.

98. See Bull, *Anarchical Society*, chaps. 11–12; Farer, "Greening of the Globe," pp. 144–47.

BIBLIOGRAPHY

Manuscript Collections

Ann Arbor, Michigan. University of Michigan. Stella Osborn Papers.
Bloomington, Indiana. Indiana University. United World Federalists MSS.
Chicago, Illinois. Chicago Historical Society. United World Federalists, Chicago
    Branch MSS.
Chicago, Illinois. University of Chicago.
    Association of Oak Ridge Engineers and Scientists MSS.
    Atomic Scientists of Chicago MSS.
    Bulletin of the Atomic Scientists MSS.
    Committee to Frame a World Constitution MSS.
    Elisabeth Mann Borgese Papers.
    Emergency Committee of Atomic Scientists MSS.
    Federation of American Scientists MSS.
    Robert Hutchins Papers.
Houston, Texas. Rice University. William L. Clayton Papers.
Pittsburgh, Pennsylvania. University of Pittsburgh. Adolph Schmidt Papers.
Princeton, New Jersey. Princeton University. John Foster Dulles Papers.
Washington, D.C. Library of Congress.
    Atlantic Union Committee MSS.
    Owen Roberts Papers.
    Robert P. Patterson Papers.

Documents

Committee to Frame a World Constitution. *A Constitution for the World.* Santa
    Barbara, California: Center for the Study of Democratic Institutions, 1965.
Committee to Frame a World Constitution. *World Government Problems: A Compila-
    tion of the Documents of the Committee to Frame a World Constitution, 1945–1948.*
    American Council on World Affairs microfilm.
Gallup, George H., ed. *The Gallup International Public Opinion Polls, France, 1939,
    1944–1975.* New York: Random House, 1976.
————, ed. *The Gallup Poll: Public Opinion, 1935–1971.* 2 vols. New York: Random
    House, 1972.
Graebner, Norman A., ed. *Ideas and Diplomacy: Readings in the Intellectual Tradition of
    American Foreign Policy.* New York: Oxford University Press, 1964.
Great Britain. Parliament. *Parliamentary Debates,* Commons, 5th series, vols. 413, 416
    (1945).
"NSC-68." *Naval War College Review* (May June 1975), pp. 51–108.
Porter, Kirk, and Johnson, Donald, eds. *National Party Platforms.* Urbana: University
    of Illinois Press, 1970.

231

Public Papers of the Presidents: Harry S. Truman, April 12 to December 31, 1945. Washington, D.C.: U.S. Government Printing Office, 1961.

Public Papers of the Presidents: Harry S. Truman, 1949. Washington D.C.: U.S. Government Printing Office, 1964.

Public Papers of the Presidents: Harry S. Truman, January 1, 1952 to January 20, 1953. Washington, D.C.: U.S. Government Printing Office, 1966.

U. S. Congress. House. *Report of the Activities of the United States Citizens Commission on NATO.* H. Doc. 433, 87th Cong., 2d sess., 1962.

U.S. Congress. House. Committee on Foreign Affairs. *Structure of the United Nations and the Relations of the United States to the United Nations. Hearings,* 80th Cong., 2d sess., 1948.

U.S. Congress. House. Committee on Foreign Affairs. *To Seek Development of the United Nations into a World Federation. Hearings,* 81st Cong., 1st sess., 1949.

U.S. Congress. Senate. Committee on Foreign Relations. *Revision of the United States Charter. Hearings before a Subcommittee of the Senate Committee on Foreign Relations,* 81st Cong., 2d sess., 1950.

Whan, V. E., Jr., ed. *A Soldier Speaks: Public Papers and Speeches of General of the Army Douglas MacArthur.* New York: Frederick A. Praeger, 1965.

Books

Acheson, Dean. *Present at the Creation: My Years at the State Department.* New York: W. W. Norton, 1969.

Ball, George W. *The Discipline of Power: Essentials of Modern World Structure.* London: Bodley Head, 1968.

————. *The Past Has Another Pattern.* New York: W. W. Norton, 1982.

Barnet, Richard J., and Müller, Ronald E. *Global Reach: Power of the Multinational Corporations.* New York: Simon and Schuster, 1974.

Beloff, Max. *The United States and the Unity of Europe.* New York: Vintage Books, 1963.

Beres, L. R., and Targ, H. R. *Constructing Alternative World Futures.* Cambridge, Mass.: Schenkman, 1977.

Borgese, Elisabeth Mann, ed. *Pacem in Maribus.* New York: Dodd, Mead, 1972.

Boyer, Paul. *By the Bomb's Early Light: American Thought and Culture at the Dawn of the Atomic Age.* New York: Pantheon Books, 1985.

Brandon, Henry. *The Retreat of American Power.* New York: Dell, 1973.

Brinton, Crane. *From Many One: The Process of Political Integration; The Problem of World Government.* Cambridge, Mass.: Harvard University Press, 1948.

Brown, Lester R. *World without Borders.* New York: Vintage Books, 1973.

Brown, Seyom. *New Forces in World Politics.* Washington, D.C.: Brookings Institution, 1974.

Brucan, Silviu. *The Dissolution of Power: A Sociology of International Relations and Politics.* New York: Alfred A. Knopf, 1971.

Brzezinski, Zbigniew. *Between Two Ages: America's Role in the Technocratic Era.* New York: Viking Press, 1970.

Bull, Hedley. *The Anarchical Society: A Study of Order in World Politics.* London: Macmillan, 1977.

Burnham, James. *The Struggle for the World.* New York: J. Day, 1947.

Buzan, Barry. *Seabed Politics.* New York: Praeger, 1976.

Calleo, David P. *Europe's Future: The Grand Alternatives.* New York: W. W. Norton, 1967.

Carson, Rachel. *Silent Spring.* Greenwich, Conn.: Fawcett, 1962.

Carter, Jimmy. *Keeping Faith: Memoirs of a President.* New York: Bantam Books, 1982.

Chase, Stuart. *The Most Probable World.* New York: Harper & Row, 1968.

Chenault, Claire Lee. *Way of a Fighter.* New York: G. P. Putnam's Sons, 1949.

Cole, Sam. "The Global Futures Debate, 1965–1976." In *Toward a Just World Order.* Edited by Richard A. Falk. Boulder, Colorado: Westview Press, 1982.

Commoner, Barry. *The Closing Circle: Nature, Man, and Technology.* New York: Alfred A. Knopf, 1971.

Cousins, Norman. *Modern Man is Obsolete.* New York: Viking Press, 1945.

Culbertson, Ely. *The Strange Lives of One Man.* Chicago: John C. Winston, 1940.

———. *Total Peace: What Makes Wars and How to Organize Peace.* Garden City, N.Y.: Doubleday, Doran, 1943.

Curtis, Lionel. *World Revolution in the Cause of Peace.* Oxford: Basil Blackwell, 1949.

DeBenedetti, Charles. *The Peace Reform in American History.* Bloomington: Indiana University Press, 1980.

Divine, Robert A. *Second Chance: The Triumph of Internationalism in America during World War II.* New York: Atheneum, 1967.

Douglas, William O. *Towards a Global Federalism.* New York: University of London Press, 1968.

Ehrlich, Paul, and Harriman, Richard L. *How to Be a Survivor: A Plan to Save Spaceship Earth.* New York: Ballantine Books, 1971.

Environmental Action. *Earth Day: The Beginning.* New York: Bantam Books, 1970.

Falk, Richard A., and Kim, Samuel S. *An Approach to World Order Studies and the World System.* New York: Institute for World Order, 1982.

Falk, Richard A. *This Endangered Planet: Prospects and Proposals for Human Survival.* New York: Random House, 1971.

———. *A Study of Future Worlds.* New York: Free Press, 1975.

Fontenay, Charles L. *Estes Kefauver: A Biography.* Knoxville: University of Tennessee Press, 1980.

Fowle, Eleanor. *Cranston: The Senator from California.* San Rafael, California: Presidio Press, 1980.

Fuller, R. Buckminster. *Operating Manual for Spaceship Earth.* Carbondale: Southern Illinois University Press, 1969.

Grayson, Melvin J., and Shepard, Thomas R., Jr. *The Disaster Lobby.* Chicago: Follet, 1973.

Guérard, Albert. *Education of a Humanist.* Cambridge, Mass.: Harvard University Press, 1949.

Heilbroner, Robert. *An Inquiry into the Human Prospect.* New York: W. W. Norton, 1974.

Hersey, John. *Hiroshima.* New York: Alfred A. Knopf, 1946.

Hoffmann, Stanley. *Primary or World Order: American Foreign Policy since the Cold War.* New York: McGraw-Hill, 1978.

Kamp, Joseph P. *We Must Abolish the United States: The Hidden Facts behind the Crusade for World Government.* New York: Constitutional Educational League, 1950.

Kennan, George. *The Nuclear Delusion: Soviet-American Relations in the Atomic Age.* New York: Pantheon Books, 1982.

Laszlo, Ervin, et al. *Goals for Mankind: A Report to the Club of Rome on the New Horizons of Global Community.* New York: E. P. Dutton, 1977.

Lippmann, Walter. *U.S. Foreign Policy: Shield of the Republic.* Boston: Little, Brown, 1943.

———. *U.S. War Aims.* Boston: Little, Brown, 1944.

———. *Western Unity and the Common Market.* Boston: Little, Brown, 1962.

Maddox, John. *The Doomsday Syndrome.* New York: McGraw-Hill, 1972.

Masters, Dexter, and Way, Katherine, eds. *One World or None: A Report to the Public on the Full Meaning of the Atomic Bomb.* New York: McGraw-Hill, 1946.

Meadows, Dennis L., et al. *The Limits to Growth: A Report for the Club of Rome's Project on the Predicament of Man.* New York: Universe Books, 1972.

Meyer, Cord. *Facing Reality: From World Federalism to the C.I.A.* New York: Harper & Row, 1980.

Meyer, Cord, Jr. *Peace or Anarchy.* Boston: Little, Brown, 1947.

Morgenthau, Hans J. *Politics among Nations.* New York: Alfred A. Knopf, 1948.

Mumford, Lewis. *The Pentagon of Power.* New York: Harcourt, Brace, Jovanovich, 1970.

Nash, Vernon. *The World Must Be Governed.* New York: Harper & Brothers, 1949.

Nathan, Otto, and Norden, Heinz, eds. *Einstein on Peace.* New York: Simon and Schuster, 1960.

Nixon, Richard M. *A New Road for America.* Garden City, N.Y.: Doubleday, 1972.

Osgood, Robert. *NATO: The Entangling Alliance.* Chicago: University of Chicago Press, 1962.

Pentland, Charles. *International Theory and European Integration.* London: Faber and Faber, 1973.

Reves, Emery. *The Anatomy of Peace.* New York: Harper & Brothers, 1945.

――――. *A Democratic Manifesto.* New York: Random House, 1942.

Roberts, Owen; Schmidt, John; and Streit, Clarence. *The New Federalist.* New York: Harper & Brothers, 1950.

Rosenbaum, Walter A. *The Politics of Environmental Concern.* New York: Praeger, 1973.

Schuman, Frederick L. *The Commonwealth of Man: An Inquiry into Power, Politics, and World Government.* New York: Alfred A. Knopf, 1952.

――――. "Regionalism and Spheres of Influence." In *Peace, Security, and the United Nations.* Edited by Hans J. Morgenthau. Chicago: University of Chicago Press, 1946.

Sebenius, James K. *Negotiating the Law of the Sea.* Cambridge, Mass.: Harvard University Press, 1984.

Sklar, Holly, ed. *Trilateralism: The Trilateral Commission and Elite Planning for World Management.* Boston: South End Press, 1980.

Smith, Alice K. *A Peril and a Hope: The Scientists' Movement in America, 1945–47.* Chicago: University of Chicago Press, 1965.

Snow, C. P. *The State of Seige.* New York: Charles Scribner's Sons, 1969.

Sprout, Harold, and Sprout, Margaret. *Toward a Politics of the Planet Earth.* New York: Van Norstrand Reinhold, 1971.

Steel, Ronald. *The End of Alliance: America and the Future of Europe.* New York: Dell, 1964.

Stewart, Michael. *Controlling the Economic Future.* Brighton, Sussex: Wheatsheaf Books, 1983.

Stoessinger, John G. *Henry Kissinger: The Anguish of Power.* New York: W. W. Norton, 1976.

Streit, Clarence. *Union Now: A Proposal for an Atlantic Federal Union of the Free.* New York: Harper & Brothers, 1949.

――――. *Union Now: The Proposal for Inter-Democracy Federal Union.* New York: Harper & Brothers, 1940.

Swing, Raymond. *In the Name of Sanity.* New York: Harper & Brothers, 1946.

Szent-Miklosy, Istvan. *The Atlantic Union Movement: Its Significance in World Politics.* New York: Fountainhead Publishers, 1965.

Teller, Edward. *The Reluctant Revolutionary.* Columbia: University of Missouri Press, 1964.

Thompson, Kenneth W. *American Diplomacy and Emergent Patterns.* New York: New York University Press, 1962.

Truman, Harry S. *Memoirs: Years of Trial and Hope.* Garden City, N.Y.: Doubleday, 1956.

Van Doren, Carl. *The Great Rehearsal: The Story of the Making and Ratifying of the Constitution of the United States.* New York: Viking Press, 1948.

Vernon, Raymond. *Sovereignty at Bay: The Multinational Spread of U.S. Enterprises.* New York: Basic Books, 1971.

Von Laue, Theodore H. *The Global City: Freedom, Power, and Necessity in the Age of Revolutions.* New York: J. B. Lippincott, 1969.

Ward, Barbara. *Spaceship Earth.* New York: Columbia University Press, 1966.

Wieseltier, Leon. *Nuclear War, Nuclear Peace.* New York: Holt, Rinehart, and Winston, 1983.

Willkie, Wendell L. *One World.* New York: Simon and Schuster, 1943.

Wittner, Lawrence S. *Rebels against War: The American Peace Movement, 1941–1960.* New York: Columbia University Press, 1969.

Wofford, Harris, Jr. *It's Up to Us: Federal World Government in Our Time.* New York: Harcourt, Brace, and Company, 1946.

Yoder, Jon A. "The United World Federalists: Liberals for Law and Order." In *Peace Movements in America.* Edited by Charles Chatfield. New York: Schocken Books, 1973.

Articles

Amuzegar, Jahangir. "A Requiem for the North-South Conference." *Foreign Affairs,* 56 (Oct. 1977), pp. 136–59.

Armstrong, O. K. "Grassroots Crusader." *Reader's Digest,* May 1946, pp. 45–49.

Austin, Warren. "A Warning on World Government." *Harper's,* May 1949, pp. 93–97.

Bald, Wambly. "World Government His Dream." *New York Post,* Oct. 10, 1947, p. 57.

Barkenbus, Jack N. "How to Make Peace on the Seabed." *Foreign Policy,* no. 25 (Winter 1976–77), pp. 211–29.

Barnard, Chester I. "Security through the Sacrifice of Sovereignty." *Bulletin of the Atomic Scientists,* Oct. 1, 1946, pp. 30–31.

Barnes, Trevor. "The Secret Cold War: The C.I.A. and American Foreign Policy in Europe, 1946–1956." *Historical Journal,* 25 (March 1982), pp. 649–70.

Bell, Daniel. "The Future World Disorder: The Structural Context of Crisis." *Foreign Policy,* no. 27 (Summer 1977), pp. 109–35.

Bernstein, George A. "World Government: Progress Report." *Nation,* June 5, 1948, pp. 628–30.

Bigman, Stanley K. "The New Internationalism under Attack." *Public Opinion Quarterly,* 14 (Summer 1950), pp. 235–61.

Borgese, Elisabeth Mann. "A Center Report: The Republic of the Deep Seas." *Center Magazine,* 1 (May 1968), pp. 18–27.

Borgese, G. A. "Third Year." *Common Cause,* Aug. 1949, pp. 1–7.

Bowen, Crosswell. "Young Man in Quest of Peace." *PM,* March 21, 1948, p. M6.

Bowles, Chester. "World Government—Yes, But." *Harper's,* March 1949, pp. 21–27.

Brodeur, Paul. "Annals of Chemistry: In the Face of Doubt." *New Yorker,* June 9, 1986, pp. 70–87.

Brown, Harrison. "The World Government Movement in the United States." *Bulletin of the Atomic Scientists,* June 1947, pp. 156–57, 166.

Brown, Lester R. "The Global Economic Prospect: New Sources of Economic Stress." *Worldwatch Institute Paper #20,* May 1978.

———. "The Interdependence of Nations." *Foreign Policy Association Headliner Series #212,* Oct. 1972.

Brown, Seyom, and Fabian, Larry L. "Diplomats at Sea." *Foreign Affairs,* 52 (Jan. 1974), pp. 301–21.

Clark, Ian. "World Order Reform and Utopian Thought: A Contemporary Watershed?" *Review of Politics*, 41 (Jan. 1979), pp. 96–120.

"The Cliché Expert Testifies on the Atom." *New Yorker*, Nov. 17, 1945, pp. 27–29.

Commoner, Barry. "Motherhood in Stockholm." *Harper's*, June 1972, pp. 49–54.

Cousins, Norman. "Editorial." *Saturday Review*, March 7, 1970, p. 47.

———. "World Federalism Today." PBS Television Program, *Firing Line*, August 12, 1973.

Cox, Robert W. "Labor and the Multinationals." *Foreign Affairs*, 54 (Jan. 1976), pp. 344–65.

———. "On Thinking about Future World Order." *World Politics*, 28 (Jan. 1976), pp. 175–96.

Cranston, Alan. "More on the California Plan." *Common Cause*, Oct. 1949, pp. 135–42.

Culbertson, Ely. "Minutes on Our Destiny," *Commonweal*, June 21, 1946, pp. 230–34.

Darman, Richard G. "The Law of the Sea: Rethinking U.S. Interests." *Foreign Affairs*, 56 (Jan. 1978), pp. 373–95.

Drucker, Peter F. "Saving the Crusade." *Harper's*, Jan. 1972, pp. 66–71.

Dulles, John Foster. "Faith in Individual Man." *Freedom and Union*, Feb. 1950, pp. 27–32.

Eberhart, Sylvia. "How the American People Feel about the Atomic Bomb." *Bulletin of the Atomic Scientists*, June 1947, pp. 146–49, 168.

Einstein, Albert. "Atomic War or Peace." *Atlantic Monthly*, Nov. 1947, pp. 29–32.

Erskine, Hazel. "The Polls: Pollution and Its Costs." *Public Opinion Quarterly*, 36 (Spring 1972), pp. 120–35.

Falk, Raymond. "Beyond Internationalism." *Foreign Policy*, no. 24 (Fall 1976), pp. 65–113.

Falstein, Louis. "The Men Who Made the A-Bomb." *New Republic*, Nov. 26, 1945, pp. 707–709.

Farer, Tom, Jr. "The Greening of the Globe: A Preliminary Appraisal of the World Order Models Project." *International Organization*, 31 (Winter 1977), pp. 129–47.

Flynn, John T. "Mr. Dulles and 'Hands Across the Sea.'" *American Mercury*, Oct. 1953, pp. 25–30.

Fusso, Thomas E. "The Polls: The Energy Crisis in Perspective." *Public Opinion Quarterly*, 42 (Spring 1978), pp. 127–36.

Gardner, Richard. "The Hard Road to World Order." *Foreign Affairs*, 52 (April 1974), pp. 556–76.

———. "U.N. as Policeman." *Saturday Review*, Aug. 7, 1971, pp. 47–50.

Goodman, Ellen. "Reminiscences of a Scared Dinosaur Groupie." *Victoria Times-Colonist*, Jan. 3, 1984, p. A-5.

"Grenville Clark—Statesman Incognito." *Fortune*, Feb. 1946, pp. 110–15, 186–92.

Hardin, Garrett. "The Tragedy of the Commons." *Science*, Dec. 13, 1968, pp. 1244–47.

Hartley, Livingston. "Why Atlantic Union?" *Freedom and Union*, Feb. 1950, pp. 6–10.

Henkin, Louis. "Politics and the Changing Law of the Sea." *Political Science Quarterly*, 89 (March 1974), pp. 46–67.

Hennessy, Bernard. "A Case Study of Intra-Pressure Group Conflicts: The United World Federalists." *Journal of Politics*, 16 (Feb. 1954), pp. 76–95.

Heyerdahl, Thor. "The Voyage of the Ra II." *National Geographic*, Jan. 1971, pp. 44–71.

Hollick, Ann L. "Managing the Oceans." *Wilson Quarterly*, 8 (Summer 1984), pp. 70–86.

Hooker, Gertrude S. "More on Blackett's Bombshell." *Common Cause*, May 1949, pp. 367–69.

Hudson, Winthrop S. "Must We Be Scared to Death?" *Christian Century,* Jan. 9, 1946, pp. 46–48.

Hull, E. W. Seabrook. "The Political Ocean." *Foreign Affairs,* 45 (April 1967), pp. 492–502.

Humpstone, Charles C. "Pollution: Precedent and Prospect." *Foreign Affairs,* 50 (Jan. 1972), pp. 325–38.

Hutchins, Robert. "The Atomic Bomb versus Civilization." *Human Events Pamphlets,* Dec. 1945.

———. "The Good News of Damnation." *Human Events Pamphlets,* Feb. 1947.

Kennan, George F. "To Prevent a World Wasteland: A Proposal." *Foreign Affairs,* 48 (April 1970), pp. 401–13.

Kraft, Joseph. "Regan and Reagan." *Vancouver Sun,* July 22, 1985, p. A-4.

Langer, Susanne K. "Make Your Own World." *Fortune,* March 1945, pp. 156–60, 192–94.

Lent, Ernest S. "The Development of United World Federalist Thought and Policy." *International Organization,* 9 (Nov. 1955), pp. 486–501.

Lippmann, Walter. "World Government: Is It a Practical Goal?" *American Scholar,* Summer 1948, pp. 350–51.

Luft, Joseph, and Wheeler, W. M. "Reaction to John Hersey's 'Hiroshima.' " *Journal of Social Psychology,* 28 (1948), pp. 135–40.

Lyford, Joseph P. "Vote for World Government." *New Republic,* December 27, 1948, pp. 16–18.

Mahoney, Thomas. "Grenville Clark." *World Government News,* Feb. 1949, pp. 15–20.

Main, Jeremy. "Conservation at the Barricades." *Fortune,* Feb. 1970, pp. 144–47, 150–51.

"The Making of World Government." NBC Radio Broadcast, *University of Chicago Roundtable,* Nov. 10, 1946.

Malone, James L. "Who Needs the Sea Treaty?" *Foreign Policy,* 54 (Spring 1984), pp. 44–63.

Margold, Stella. "Needed: World-Wide Environmental Solutions." *American City,* March 1971, pp. 74–76.

Meyer, Cord, Jr. "A Faith to Live By: Institutions and Men." *Nation,* March 8, 1947, pp. 269–71.

———. "On the Beaches: The Pacific." *Atlantic Monthly,* Oct. 1944, pp. 42–46.

———. "A Serviceman Looks at the Peace." *Atlantic Monthly,* Sept. 1945, pp. 43–48.

———. "Waves of Darkness." *Atlantic Monthly,* Jan. 1946, pp. 74–81.

Miller, A. J. "Doomsday Politics: Prospects for International Cooperation." *International Journal,* 28 (1972–73), pp. 121–33.

Miller, Merle. "From a One-World Crusade to the 'Department of Dirty Tricks.' " *New York Times Magazine,* Jan. 7, 1973, pp. 9, 53–55, 63, 70.

Morrison, Philip, and Wilson, Robert R. "Half a World . . . and None: Partial World Government Criticized." *Bulletin of the Atomic Scientists,* July 1947, pp. 181–82.

Niebuhr, Reinhold. "The Illusion of World Government." *Bulletin of the Atomic Scientists,* Oct. 1949, pp. 289–92.

———. "The Myth of World Government." *Nation,* March 16, 1946, pp. 312–14.

Nye, Joseph S., Jr. "Independence and Interdependence." *Foreign Policy,* no. 22 (Spring 1976), pp. 129–61.

———. "Multinational Corporations in World Politics." *Foreign Affairs,* 53 (Oct. 1974), pp. 153–75.

Oppenheimer, J. Robert. "International Control of Atomic Energy." *Foreign Affairs,* 26 (Jan. 1948), pp. 239–52.

Paarlberg, Robert L. "Domesticating Global Management." *Foreign Affairs,* 54 (April 1976), pp. 563–76.

Pardo, Arvid. "Who Will Control the Seabed?" *Foreign Affairs,* 47 (Oct. 1968), pp.

123–37.

Pearson, Lester. "The Beginning of a World Community." *Kiwanis Magazine,* July 1951, pp. 6, 38–39.

Pendleton, Hobart. "Another Look at World Federalism." *American Mercury,* June 1952, pp. 56–64.

"Proposals for Now Revising the United Nations into a Federal World Government." *Congressional Digest,* Aug.–Sept. 1948, pp. 193–224.

Putman, John J. "Quicksilver and Slow Death." *National Geographic,* Oct. 1972, pp. 507–527.

Rabinowitch, Eugene. "Living Dangerously in the Age of Science." *Bulletin of the Atomic Scientists,* Jan. 1972, pp. 5–8.

Radcliffe, Betty, and Gerlack, Luther. "The Ecology Movement after Ten Years." *Natural History,* Jan. 1981, pp. 12–18.

Reingold, Nathan. "MGM Meets the Atomic Bomb." *Wilson Quarterly,* 8 (Autumn 1984), pp. 154–63.

Richardson, Elliott. "Power, Mobility, and the Law of the Sea." *Foreign Affairs,* 58 (Spring 1980), pp. 902–19.

Rienow, Robert, and Rienow, Leona Train. "Last Chance for the Nation's Waterways." *Saturday Review,* May 22, 1965, pp. 35–36, 96.

Ritchie-Calder, Lord. "Mortgaging the Old Homestead." *Foreign Affairs,* 48 (Jan. 1970), pp. 207–20.

Roberts, Owen. "The World Needs a Cop on the Corner." *Saturday Evening Post,* March 24, 1951, pp. 120–24.

Roper, Elmo. "American Attitudes toward World Organization." *Public Opinion Quarterly,* 17 (Winter 1953–54), pp. 405–42.

———. "A Way to One Free World." *Freedom and Union,* May 1948, pp. 8–9.

Rostow, Walt W. "The Value of the Limits to Growth." *Wilson Quarterly,* 1 (Autumn 1976), pp. 51–54.

Russell, Bertrand. "The Atomic Bomb and the Prevention of War." *Bulletin of the Atomic Scientists,* Oct. 1946, pp. 19–21.

Russell, Francis H. "Toward a Stronger World Organization." *Department of State Bulletin,* Aug. 7, 1950, pp. 220–24.

Sagan, Carl. "Nuclear War and Climatic Catastrophe." *Foreign Affairs,* 62 (Winter 1983–84), pp. 257–92.

———. "To Preserve a World Graced by Life." *Bulletin of the Atomic Scientists,* Jan. 1983, pp. 2–3.

Schell, Jonathan. "The Abolitions: A Deliberate Policy." *New Yorker,* Jan. 9, 1984, pp. 43–94.

———. "The Fate of the Earth." *New Yorker,* Feb. 1, 1982, pp. 47–113; ibid., Feb. 8, 1982, pp. 48–109; ibid., Feb. 15, 1982, pp. 45–107.

Schuman, Frederick. "Might and Right at San Francisco." *Nation,* April 28, 1945, pp. 479–81.

Segal, Ronald. "Everywhere at Home, Home Nowhere." *Center Magazine,* May–June 1973, pp. 8–14.

Shields, Geoffrey. "The Multinationals." *World Issues,* Dec. 1977–Jan. 1978, pp. 3–6.

Simpson, John A. "The Scientists as Public Educators: A Two Year Summary." *Bulletin of the Atomic Scientists,* Sept. 1947, pp. 243–46.

Strong, Maurice. "One Year after Stockholm." *Foreign Affairs,* 51 (July 1973), pp. 690–707.

Swing, John Temple. "Who Will Own the Oceans?" *Foreign Affairs,* 54 (April 1976), pp. 527–46.

Szilard, Leo. "Shall We Face the Facts?" *Bulletin of the Atomic Scientists,* Oct. 1949, pp. 269–73.

"The Third Year of the Atomic Age: What Should We Do Now?" NBC Radio Broadcast, *University of Chicago Roundtable,* Aug. 24, 1947.

Towell, William E. "Environmental Concern Is Global." *American Forests,* June 1970, pp. 32–33, 48.

Toynbee, Arnold. "The Next Step is History." *Look,* Nov. 18, 1952, pp. 31–33.

"The Trilateral Energy Study: A Discussion with Franklin Tugwell." *World Issues,* Feb.–March 1979, pp. 3–12.

Turco, R. P., et al. "Nuclear Winter: Global Consequences of Multiple Nuclear Explosions." *Science,* Dec. 23, 1983, pp. 1283–92.

Udall, Stewart L. "The Legacy of Rachel Carson." *Saturday Review,* May 16, 1964, pp. 23, 59.

Ullman, Richard H. "Trilateralism: 'Partnership' for What?" *Foreign Affairs,* 55 (Oct. 1976), pp. 1–19.

Urey, Harold. "Atomic Energy Control is Impossible without World Government." *Bulletin of the Atomic Scientists,* Dec. 1948, pp. 365–67.

———. "Atomic Energy and World Peace." *Bulletin of the Atomic Scientists,* Nov. 1, 1946, pp. 2–4.

———. "I'm a Frightened Man." *Collier's,* Jan. 5, 1946, pp. 18–19, 50–51.

———. "The Paramount Problem of 1949." *Bulletin of Atomic Scientists,* Oct. 1949, pp. 283–88.

Vernon, Raymond. "Economic Sovereignty at Bay." *Foreign Affairs,* 47 (Oct. 1968), pp. 110–22.

———. "Storm over the Multinationals: Problems and Prospects." *Foreign Affairs,* 55 (Jan. 1977), pp. 243–62.

Wagar, W. Warren. "Toward the City of Man." *Center Magazine,* Sept. 1968, pp. 33–41.

Wallace, Henry. "Toward World Federalism." *New Republic,* Feb. 23, 1948, p. 10.

Walters, Robert S. "International Organizations and the Multinational Corporation." *Annals of the American Academy of Political and Social Science,* 403 (Sept. 1972), pp. 127–38.

Ways, Max. "How to Think about the Environment." *Fortune,* Feb. 1970, pp. 98–101, 159–66.

Wertenbaker, William. "The Law of the Sea." *New Yorker,* Aug. 1, 1983, pp. 38–65; ibid., Aug. 8, 1983, pp. 56–83.

Wofford, Harris. "Straight Is the Gate: Considering Alternative Routes to One World." *Common Cause,* June 1948, pp. 425–28.

Wolman, Abel. "Pollution as an International Issue." *Foreign Affairs,* 47 (Oct. 1968), pp. 164–75.

"The World Government Crusade." *Christian Century,* Jan. 28, 1948, pp. 102–104.

"The World Is Her Field: An Interview with Elisabeth Mann Borgese." *World Issues,* Dec. 1978–Jan. 1979, pp. 17–26.

Young, Elizabeth. "To Guard the Sea." *Foreign Affairs,* 50 (Oct. 1971), pp. 136–47.

Other Magazines and Newspapers

Chicago Daily Tribune
Christian Century
Christian Science Monitor
Citizens Committee for United Nations
  Reform Bulletin
Collier's
Common Cause
Commonweal
Current Biography
Daily Worker
Detroit Free Press

Economic Council Letter
Freedom and Union
Labor Action
Life
Look
Los Alamos Newsletter
Modern Industry
Nashville Tennessean
Newsweek
New York Herald-Tribune
New York Times

Opinion News   *United States News*
Reader's Digest   *Washington Post*
San Francisco Examiner   *World*
Saturday Evening Post   *World Government News*
Time

INDEX

Acheson, Dean, 119
Americans United, 35
The Anatomy of Peace (Reves), 15; argument of, 16–18
Atlantic Union Committee (AUC): accomplishments of, 130; decline of, 120–21; federalist criticism of, 123–24; formation of, 106; lack of public support for, 114; leadership of, 115–16; and State Department, 117–18
Atlantic Unionist movement, 85–132; accomplishments of, 130; Atlantic Union Committee of, 106, 114–21; AUC leadership in, 115–16; Clarence Streit's role in, 89–98; decline of, 120–21; endorsement of NATO by, 106–108; Estes Kefauver's role in, 107, 112, 119, 123, 127; fear of Russians in, 85–87; federalist criticism of, 123–124; John Foster Dulles in, 98, 119, 128; Joseph McCarthy and, 89, 128; lack of public support for, 114; leadership of, 105; Marshall Plan of, 109, 110; in NATO, 111–12; Owen J. Roberts of, 101–102; Robert Patterson of, 104–105; William Clayton of, 102–104. *See also* Atlantic Union Committee; Cold War
Atomic bomb: anxiety and complacency over, 6; congressional concern over, 11; dropped on Japan, 3, 7; effects described by J. Robert Oppenheimer, 6; fear of, 3–13, 62; fear over Russia's development of, 85–87; Germany close to invention of, 7; as great equalizer, 5; guilt over, 7; Japanese close to invention of, 7; *Look* magazine article on, 10, 11, mixed public reaction to, 12; monopolizing "secrets" of, 6; *The New Yorker* description of, 4; scientific description of, 3; scientists on effects of, 7; scientists' opposition to dropping, 8; scientists' warnings about, 10

Ball, George W.: Atlantic community of, 167; life of, 166; on multi-national corporations, 169; on world government, 168
Barnet, Richard: on multi-national businesses, 170; on world managers, 169
Baruch plan: and atomic war, 39; presented to United Nations, 11; public support of, 48; tailored for Americans, 67

Bell, Daniel, 173
Between Two Ages: America's Role in the Technocratic Era (Brzezinski), 173
Borgese, G. A.: optimism of, 180; on world constitution, 42, 43
Brinton, Crane, 69
Brown, Lester, 148
Brzezinski, Zbigniew: on chaos and fragmentation, 173; and global cooperation, 174; proposed Trilateral Commission, 175; on transnational technocrats, 176
Burnham, James, 63

Carson, Rachel, 146
Chicago Committee to Frame a World Constitution, 41–44
Churchill, Winston, 53; "iron curtain" speech of, 110
The City of Man (Wager), 188
Clark, Grenville: and American constitutional principles, 69; and Dublin conference, 32; for minimal centralization, 65
Clay, Lucius, 86
Clayton, William: and Atlantic Union Committee, 104; on democratic union, 106; life of, 102–103; for National Atlantic Treaty, 107; on Soviets, 85
Cohn, Albert, 10
Cold War, 85–132; Clarence Streit in, 89–98; fear of Russians in, 85–87; Joseph McCarthy in, 89; Kennedy years of, 139
Commoner, Barry: on environmental crisis, 139, 147; life of, 145; on peace, 162; on reorganization of economics, 161
Cousins, Norman: against nationalism, 23; realism of, 14, 19; on world government, 27, 28
Cranston, Alan: on moral purpose, 71; suppressed criticism of Soviets, 73; testified before House Foreign Affairs Committee, 68; as United World Federalist, 47
Culbertson, Ely: life of, 44; on supranational system of security, 45

Darman, Richard, 181
Davis, Garry: life of, 54; on peace, 55
A Democratic Manifesto (Reves), 16

241

WESLEY T. WOOLEY teaches American political and diplomatic history at the University of Victoria, in British Columbia, Canada. A doctoral gradu-ate of the University of Chicago, where he worked with Hans Morgenthau and William McNeill, Professor Wooley is a published specialist in the areas of cold war diplomatic thought and modern American supranationalism.